Subject Index to Books for Primary Grades

SUBJECT INDEX
TO BOOKS
FOR
PRIMARY GRADES

SECOND EDITION

COMPILED BY MARY K. EAKIN
AND ELEANOR MERRITT

American Library Association
CHICAGO 1961

PREFACE

The second edition of the *Subject Index to Books for Primary Grades*[1]—like the first, which has long been considered a standard reference tool—is designed primarily for use by teachers and by librarians working with teachers in finding materials suited to classroom needs. During the years that have elapsed since the publication of the first edition, many changes in educational practices and theories have been incorporated into trade and textbooks published for use with children in the primary grades. Recognition of these changes is to be found in the present volume through the introduction of new subject headings and, in some instances, of new terminology for fairly traditional subject content. The listings include new trade titles and textbooks published since the first edition as well as new editions of textbooks and trade books.

This new edition of the *Subject Index* reflects the increasing number of trade books being published that are suitable for independent use by primary children. Many of these are in story form, but it is apparent that there is a growing quantity of informational books written in the straightforward, factually accurate style so appealing to modern children. These books are particularly evident in the areas of science and the social studies.

Grade levels are given for all materials. For textbooks, the publishers' gradings have been retained, and the abbreviations used for indicating grading are those commonly used for textbooks. They are:

PP	Preprimer
SPP	Senior Preprimer
P	Primer
1, 2, 3	First, Second, Third Readers
1–1	First Grade, First Semester
1–2	First Grade, Second Semester
2–1	Second Grade, First Semester
2–2	Second Grade, Second Semester
3–1	Third Grade, First Semester

[1] *Subject Index to Books for Primary Grades,* comp. by Eloise Rue (Chicago: American Library Association, 1943).

3–2	Third Grade, Second Semester
Alt.	Alternate
Comp.	Companion
Par.	Parallel
Read.	Readiness
Sup.	Supplementary
T	Teacher

For trade books, in the List of Books Indexed the grades indicated represent the range of grades in which the books might be used, whether for independent reading or as material to be read aloud. Trade book symbols in the Subject Index indicate both the level at which children might use the books independently and the level at which they would be read aloud by the teacher or librarian. Thus a story marked RA (K–3); In (2) is one that would be suitable for reading aloud to kindergarten through the third grade, and one that could be read independently by children who are reading at a second grade level. Books marked RA, with no grade levels indicated, are suited to reading aloud at all grade levels but are too difficult to be used independently at any of the primary grade levels. Many science books fall within this category, since it is easier to write science material that is suited to a child's listening vocabulary than it is to write material suited to his reading vocabulary.

The subject headings in the Subject Index, for the most part, follow the forms suggested in standard library tools. In a few instances they have been adapted to the new educational terminology as evidenced in typical courses of study and curriculum guides for the elementary grades.

Page numbers have been given in the Subject Index, even when the book itself does not have numbered pages. For such books the count of pages begins with the first page on which there is text or an illustration. Where no page numbers are given, the entire book contains materials on the subject but it is too diffuse to warrant specific page references.

Because this list is selective and is intended as a guide to the content of the books rather than as a purchasing guide, starring for first purchase has been omitted. The asterisks used in the Subject Index indicate, instead, materials that are of a fictionalized nature. Items not starred are essentially factual in their presentation of information.

Poetry and folk tales, as subject headings, have been omitted since these materials are adequately treated in such indexes as:

American Library Association. *Subject Index to Poetry for Children and Young People,* comp. by Violet Sell [and others]. Chicago: American Library Association, 1957.

Brewton, John E., and Brewton, Sara W., comps. *Index to Children's Poetry: A Title, Subject, Author, and First Line Index to Poetry in Collections for Children and Youth.* New York: Wilson, 1942 (First Supplement, New York: Wilson, 1954).

Eastman, Mary Huse. *Index to Fairy Tales, Myths, and Legends.* 2nd ed., rev.

and enl. Boston: Faxon, 1926 (Supplements, Boston: Faxon, 1937 and 1952).
The editors wish to express their appreciation to the librarians and curriculum specialists who helped in the work by checking the original list of titles from which the present selection of books indexed was made. They are:

Miss Althea Beery, Supervisor of Elementary Education, Cincinnati Public Schools, Cincinnati, Ohio

Miss Ruth Ersted, State Supervisor of School Libraries, St. Paul, Minnesota

Miss Virginia Haviland, Readers Adviser for Children, Boston Public Library, Boston, Massachusetts

Miss Sara Jaffarian, Director of Libraries, Greensboro Public Schools, Greensboro, North Carolina

Miss Gladys L. Lees, Director of School Libraries, Professional and Curriculum Library, Tacoma, Washington

Miss Jean A. Merrill, Director, Work with Children, Kansas City Public Library, Kansas City, Missouri

Miss Margaret Moss, Director of School Libraries, Madison Public Schools, Madison, Wisconsin

Miss Frances E. Neale, St. Cloud State College, St. Cloud, Minnesota

Miss Chandos Reid, Assistant to the Superintendent, Waterford Township Schools, Pontiac, Michigan

Miss Mabel F. Rice, Professor of Education and Director, Broadoaks School, Whittier College, Whittier, California

Mrs. Florence M. Sanborn, Regional Children's Librarian, West Los Angeles Regional Library, Los Angeles, California

Miss Thusnelda Schmidt, Librarian, Colfax Elementary School, Pittsburgh, Pennsylvania

Mary K. Eakin
Eleanor Merritt

Cedar Falls, Iowa

LIST OF BOOKS
INDEXED

ADAMS, GEORGE A. ABC Picture Book; illus. with color photographs. Platt & Munk, 1947. $1.50. 56p. (K–1)

ADRIAN, MARY. Fiddler Crab. Holiday, 1953. $2. 40p. (2–4)

—— Gray Squirrel; illus. by Walter Ferguson. Holiday, 1955. $2.50. 46p. (3–5)

ADSHEAD, GLADYS L. Brownies—It's Christmas; with pictures by Velma Ilsley. Walck, 1955. $2.50. 72p. (K–1)

AGLE, NAN HAYDEN, and WILSON, ELLEN JANET. Three Boys and a Helicopter; illus. by Marian Honigman. Scribner, 1958. $2.50. 128p. (1–5)

—— Three Boys and a Lighthouse; illus. by Marian Honigman. Scribner, 1951. $2.50. 100p. (3–5)

—— Three Boys and a Mine; illus. by Marian Honigman. Scribner, 1954. $2.50. 122p. (2–4)

—— Three Boys and a Tugboat; illus. by Marian Honigman. Scribner, 1953. $2.50. 121p. (3–5)

ALAIN. The Magic Stones: The Story of the Arch. Whittlesey, 1957. $2.50. 32p. (2–6)

ALDEN, RAYMOND MACDONALD. The Christmas Tree Forest; illus. by Rafaello Busoni. Bobbs-Merrill, 1958. $2.25. 32p. (2–5)

ALLEE, VEVA ELWELL. Sugar Beets to Beet Sugar; photographer: Robert Fogata. Melmont, 1956. $2.50. 23p. (3–4)

ALLISON, LEWIS. Fishing for Tuna; illus. by Robert Bartram. Melmont, 1957. $2.50. 35p. (2–4)

ANDERSON, CLARENCE WILLIAM. Billy and Blaze. Macmillan, 1936. $2. 56p. (2–4)

—— Blaze and the Forest Fire. Macmillan, 1938. $2.50. 55p. (2–4)

—— Blaze and the Gypsies. Macmillan, 1937. $2.50. 56p. (2–4)

—— Blaze Finds the Trail. Macmillan, 1950. $2.75. 48p. (2–4)

ANGLUND, JOAN WALSH. The Brave Cowboy. Harcourt, 1959. $1.95. 38p. (K–1)

1

ASBJØRNSEN, PETER CHRISTEN, and MOE, JØRGEN ENGEBRETSEN. The Three Billy Goats Gruff; pictures by Marcia Brown. Harcourt, 1957. $3. 32p. (K–1)

ASSOCIATION FOR CHILDHOOD EDUCATION INTERNATIONAL. Told under the Blue Umbrella: New Stories for New Children; illus. by Marguerite Davis. Macmillan, 1933. $2.75. 161p. (K–3)

—— Told under the Green Umbrella: Old Stories for New Children; pictures by Grace Gilkison. Macmillan, 1930. $3. 188p. (K–3)

—— Told under the Magic Umbrella: Modern Fanciful Stories for Young Children; illus. by Elizabeth Orton Jones. Macmillan, 1939. $3. 248p. (K–3)

AULAIRE, INGRI MORTENSON D', and AULAIRE, EDGAR PARIN D'. Abraham Lincoln. Doubleday, 1957. $3. 64p. (2–4)

—— Don't Count Your Chicks. Doubleday, 1943. $3. 40p. (1–4)

—— George Washington. Doubleday, 1936. $2.75. 55p. (2–4)

—— Ola. Doubleday, 1932. $3. 55p. (K–2)

AVERILL, ESTHER HOLDEN. Jenny's Adopted Brothers. Harper, 1952. $1.50. 32p. (2–4)

—— Jenny's Birthday Book. Harper, 1954. $2.50. 30p. (K–1)

—— Jenny's Moonlight Adventure. Harper, 1949. $1.75. 31p. (1–3)

—— The School for Cats. Harper, 1947. $1.50. 31p. (1–3)

AYER, JACQUELINE. Nu Dang and His Kite. Harcourt, 1959. $2.75. 32p. (1–3)

BAKER, ARTHUR O., and others. Junior Scientist Series. Rand McNally, 1955.
  Grade 2: Around the Corner. $2.20. (2)
  Grade 3: In Your Neighborhood. $2.40. (3)

BAKER, AUGUSTA B., ed. The Talking Tree: Fairy Tales from Fifteen Lands; illus. by Johannes Troyer. Lippincott, 1955. $3. 255p. (2–5)

BAKER, MARY ELIZABETH. Tammy Camps Out; illus. by Beth Krush. Houghton, 1958. $2.50. 56p. (1–4)

BALLARD, LOIS. The True Book of Reptiles; pictures by Irma Wilde. Childrens Pr., 1957. $2. 46p. (1–3)

BANNERMAN, HELEN. Story of Little Black Sambo. Lippincott, 1923. $1.25. 56p. (K–1)

BARE, ARNOLD EDWIN. Maui's Summer. Houghton, 1952. $2.50. 44p. (2–4)

BARNARD, J. DARRELL, and others. The Macmillan Science-Life Series. Unified Program in Science, Health, and Safety. Macmillan, 1959.
  Book 1: $2.18. (1)
  Book 2: $2.33. (2)
  Book 3: $2.55. (3)

BARNUM, JAY HYDE. The Little Old Truck. Morrow, 1953. $2.50. 48p. (1–3)

BARR, JENE. Ben's Busy Service Station; illus. by Chauncey Maltman. Whitman, 1956. $1.25. 32p. (1–2)

───── Fast Trains! Busy Trains! illus. by Chauncey Maltman. Whitman, 1956. $1.25. 32p. (1–2)

───── Mike, the Milkman; illus. by Chauncey Maltman. Whitman, 1953. $1.25. 32p. (1–2)

───── Policeman Paul; illus. by Chauncey Maltman. Whitman, 1952. $1.25. 32p. (2–3)

───── Texas Pete, Little Cowboy; pictures by Chauncey Maltman. Whitman, 1950. $1.25. 30p. (2–3)

BASIC SOCIAL STUDIES SERIES. Thomas J. Durell, director. Row, Peterson, 1958.
  Book 2: Basic Social Studies, by Thelma Kier Reese, $2.32. (2)
  Book 3: Basic Social Studies, by Dorothea Wein Partch. $2.72. (3)

BATE, NORMAN. Who Built the Bridge? Scribner, 1954. $2.75. 45p. (K–2)

BAUER, W. W., and others. Curriculum Foundation Series. Basic Health and Safety Program. Scott, Foresman, 1957.
  Primer: Just Like Me. $1.36. (P)
  Grade 1: Being Six. $1.60. (1)
  Grade 2: Seven or So. $1.76. (2)
  Grade 3: From Eight to Nine. $1.88. (3)

BEATTIE, JANET. In Came Horace; pictures and calligraphy by Anne Marie Jauss. Lippincott, 1954. $2.25. 32p. (K–2)

BEATTY, HETTY BURLINGAME. Droopy. Houghton, 1954. $2.50. 26p. (K–2)

───── Little Wild Horse. Houghton, 1949. $3.25. 31p. (K–1)

───── Saint Francis and the Wolf. Houghton, 1953. $2.50. 29p. (K–3)

BEAUCHAMP, WILBUR L., and others. Curriculum Foundation Series. Basic Studies in Science. Scott, Foresman, 1956.
  Book A: Look and Learn. $1.88. (1)
  Book B: All around Us. $2.08. (2)
  Book C: How Do We Know? $2.20. (3)

BEIM, JERROLD. Andy and the School Bus; illus. by Leonard Shortall. Morrow, 1947. $2.50. 46p. (K–2)

───── Country Fireman; illus. by Leonard Shortall. Morrow, 1948. $2.50. 46p. (K–2)

───── Country Garage; pictures by Louis Darling. Morrow, 1952. $2.50. 48p. (2–4)

───── Country School; pictures by Louis Darling. Morrow, 1955. $2.50. 48p. (1–3)

───── Country Train; illus. by Leonard Shortall. Morrow, 1950. $2.50. 46p. (2–4)

───── Shoeshine Boy; pictures by Louis Darling. Morrow, 1954. $2.50. 48p. (2–4)

—— The Smallest Boy in the Class; illus. by Meg Wohlberg. Morrow, 1949. $2.50. 47p. (K–3)

—— Tim and the Tool Chest; illus. by Tracy Sugarman. Morrow, 1951. $2.50. 46p. (2–4)

—— Twelve o'Clock Whistle. Morrow, 1946. $2.50. 61p. (K–2)

BEIM, LORRAINE LEVEY, and BEIM, JERROLD. Burro That Had a Name; pictures by Howard Simon. Harcourt, 1939. $2.75. 63p. (K–2)

—— Little Igloo; pictures by Howard Simon. Harcourt, 1941. $3. 72p. (2–4)

—— Lucky Pierre; pictures by Howard Simon. Harcourt, 1940. $2.75. 61p. (2–4)

—— Sasha and the Samovar; pictures by Rafaello Busoni. Harcourt, 1944. $2.50. 68p. (2–4)

—— Two Is a Team; pictures by Ernest Crichlow. Harcourt, 1945. $2.50. 61p. (K–3)

BELL, THELMA HARRINGTON. Pawnee; with drawings by Corydon Bell. Viking, 1950. $2.50. 60p. (2–4)

BEMELMANS, LUDWIG. Hansi. Viking, 1934. $3. 64p. (1–3)

—— Madeline. Simon & Schuster, 1939. $3.50. 48p. (K–2)

—— Madeline's Rescue. Viking, 1953. $3.50. 56p. (K–3)

BENDICK, JEANNE. All around You; foreword by Glenn O. Blough. Whittlesey, 1951. $3. 48p. (2–4)

BERKLEY, ETHEL S. The Size of It: A First Book about Sizes; illus. by Kathleen Elgin. W. R. Scott, 1950. $1. 23p. (1–3)

BESKOW, ELSA MAARTMAN. Pelle's New Suit; tr. by Marion Letcher Woodburn. Harper, 1929. $2. 32p. Also Hale (Cadmus Books). (K–2)

BETTINA. Cocolo Comes to America. Harper, 1949. $2.75. 32p. (2–4)

—— Pantaloni. Harper, 1957. $2.50. 32p. (K–2)

—— Piccolo. Harper, 1954. $1.25. 64p. (K–2)

BETTS, EMMETT A., and WELCH, CAROLYN M. The Language Arts Series. The ABC Betts Basic Readers. 2nd ed. American Book, 1958.
 The ABC On Our Way. 76c. (1st PP)
 The ABC Time To Play. 80c. (2nd PP)
 The ABC All in a Day. 84c. (3rd PP)
 The ABC Up the Street and Down. $1.80. (P)
 The ABC Around Green Hills. $1.96. (1)
 The ABC Down Singing River. $2.40. (2–1)
 The ABC Over a City Bridge. $2.40. (2–2)
 The ABC Beyond Treasure Valley. $2.42. (3–1)
 The ABC Along Friendly Roads. $2.72. (3–2)

BIANCO, MARGERY WILLIAMS. The Little Wooden Doll; with pictures by Pamela Bianco. Macmillan, 1925. $1.50. 65p. (2–4)

——— The Velveteen Rabbit: or How Toys Become Real; with illus. by William Nicholson. Doubleday, 1926. $2.25. 33p. (2–4)

BIRNBAUM, ABE. Green Eyes. Capitol, 1953. $2.95. 40p. (K–1)

BISHOP, CLAIRE HUCHET. Five Chinese Brothers; illus. by Kurt Wiese. Coward-McCann, 1938. $2.50. 50p. Also Hale (Cadmus Books). (K–2)

——— Man Who Lost His Head; illus. by Robert McCloskey. Viking, 1942. $2. 53p. (K–2)

BLACK, IRMA SIMONTON. Dusty and His Friends; pictures by Barbara Latham. Holiday, 1950. $2. 56p. (2–4)

BLENDED SOCIAL STUDIES SERIES. Rand McNally, 1957. Hugley, Laura Mengert, and McGuigan, Jane. Around the Home. $3.20. (3)

BLOUGH, GLENN O. Basic Science Education Series, Primary. Row, Peterson. 48c each, paper.
  Animals and Their Young. 1951. (3)
  Animals round the Year. 1955. (3)
  Animals That Live Together. 1950. (3)
  An Aquarium. 1957. (3)
  Birds in the Big Woods. 1950. (3)
  Birds in Your Backyard, by Bertha Morris Parker. 1949. (2)
  Doing Work. 1948. (3)
  Fall Is Here, by Bertha Morris Parker. 1950. (1)
  How the Sun Helps Us. 1950. (3)
  Insect Parade. 1957. (3)
  Leaves, by Bertha Morris Parker. 1949. (2)
  Pet Show. 1956. (3)
  Plants round the Year. 1943. (3)
  Six-legged Neighbors, by Bertha Morris Parker. 1956. (2)
  Spring Is Here, by Bertha Morris Parker. 1950. (1)
  Summer Is Here, by Bertha Morris Parker. 1950. (1)
  Toys, by Bertha Morris Parker. 1949. (2)
  Useful Plants and Animals. 1955. (3)
  Water Appears and Disappears. 1953. (3)
  Winter Is Here, by Bertha Morris Parker. 1950. (1)

——— Who Lives in This House? pictures by Jeanne Bendick. Whittlesey, 1957. $2.50. 48p. (2–4)

BOND, AUSTIN D., and others. Developmental Science Series. Lyons & Carnahan, 1958.
  Primer: Getting Ready. $1.80. (P)
  Grade 1: Looking at Science. $1.80. (1)
  Grade 2: Thinking about Science. $2.20. (2)
  Grade 3: Knowing about Science. $2.40. (3)

BOND, GUY L., and others. Developmental Reading Series. Lyons & Carnahan.
  Three of Us. 1955. 56c. (Basic PP1)

Play with Us. 1955. 56c. (Basic PP2)
Fun with Us. 1955. 56c. (Basic PP3)
Ride with Us. 1955. 56c. (Basic PP4)
See Us Come. 1958. 56c. (Comp. PP1)
See Us Play. 1958. 56c. (Comp. PP2)
See Us Have Fun. 1958. 56c. (Comp. PP3)
See Us Ride. 1958. 56c. (Comp. PP4)
Many Surprises. 1954. $1.56. (P)
Happy Times. 1954. $1.68. (1)
Down Our Way. 1954. $1.88. (2–1)
Just for Fun. 1954. $1.76. (2–2)
Stories from Everywhere. 1954. $2.08. (3–1)
Once upon a Storytime. 1954. $1.92. (3–2)

BONTEMPS, ARNA WENDELL, and CONROY, JACK. The Fast Sooner Hound; illus. by Virginia Lee Burton. Houghton, 1942. $3. 28p. (2–4)

BOREMAN, JEAN. Mooloo, the Calf. Melmont, 1957. $2.50. 21p. (1–2)

BOUTWELL, EDNA. Red Rooster; illus. by Bernard Garbutt. Dutton, 1950. $2.75. 44p. (K–2)

BRACKEN, DOROTHY KENDALL. Rodeo; illus. by Elizabeth Rice. Steck, 1949. $3. 30p. (2–5)

BRADBURY, BIANCA. Muggins; with pictures by Diana Thorne. Houghton, 1944. $1.50. 20p. (3)

────── and NICHOLS, MARIE C. One Kitten Too Many. Houghton, 1952. $1.50. 32p. (2–4)

BRADLEY, DUANE. Cappy and the Jet Engine; pictures by Alice Cosgrove. Lippincott, 1957. $2.95. 141p. (2–4)

BRANLEY, FRANKLYN MANSFIELD. A Book of Satellites for You; illus. by Leonard Kessler. Crowell, 1959. $3. 48p. (1–3)

────── and VAUGHAN, ELEANOR K. Mickey's Magnet; drawings by Crockett Johnson. Crowell, 1956. $2.50. 48p. (K–2)

────── Timmy and the Tin-Can Telephone; illus. by Paul Galdone. Crowell, 1959. $2.50. 42p. (K–2)

BRANN, ESTHER. Patrick Was His Name. Macmillan, 1938. $1.75. 49p. (K–2)

BRENNER, ANITA. A Hero by Mistake; illus. by Jean Charlot. W. R. Scott, 1953. $2.50. 43p. (1–3)

BRIGHT, ROBERT. Georgie. Doubleday, 1944. $2. 42p. (1–3)

BROCK, EMMA LILLIAN. Mr. Wren's House. Knopf, 1944. $1.75. 63p. (2–4)

────── One Little Indian Boy. Knopf, 1950. $2.50. 44p. (K–2)

────── To Market! To Market! Knopf, 1930. $2.50. 41p. (K–2)

────── Umbrella Man. Knopf, 1945. $2. 48p. (2–4)

────── and others. Spooks and Spirits and Shadowy Shapes; illus. by Robert Doremus. Dutton, 1949. $2.50. 167p. (2–4)

BROMHALL, WINIFRED. Belinda's New Shoes. Knopf, 1945. $2.50. 31p. (K–3)

BRONSON, WILFRID SWANCOURT. Coyotes. Harcourt, 1946. $2.50. 63p. (2–5)

——— Turtles. Harcourt, 1945. $2.50. 63p. (K–3)

BROWN, JEANETTE PERKINS. Ronnie's Wish; drawings by Jean Martinez. Friendship Pr., 1954. $1.25. 32p. (K–1)

——— Surprise for Robin; drawings by Dorothy Papy. Friendship Pr., 1956. $1.25. 32p. (K–1)

BROWN, MARCIA JOAN. The Little Carousel. Scribner, 1946. $2.50. 32p. (K–2)

——— Stone Soup. Scribner, 1947. $2.50. 48p. (K–3)

BROWN, MARGARET WISE. Big Red Barn; illus. by Rosella Hartman. W. R. Scott, 1956. $2.25. 33p. (K–1)

——— The Color Kittens; illus. by Alice and Martin Provensen. Simon & Schuster, 1958. $1. 32p. (K–3)

——— Country Noisy Book; with illus. by Leonard Weisgard. Harper, 1940. $2.25. 44p. (K–1)

——— Home for a Bunny; pictures by Garth Williams. Simon & Schuster, 1956. $1.50. 28p. (1–2)

——— Indoor Noisy Book; pictures by Leonard Weisgard. Harper, 1942. $2.25. 44p. (K–1)

——— Little Chicken; pictures by Leonard Weisgard. Harper, 1943. $2. 39p. (K–1)

——— The Little Fir Tree; illus. by Barbara Cooney. Crowell, 1954. $2.75. 34p. (K–3)

——— Little Fisherman; illus. by Dahlov Ipcar. W. R. Scott, 1945. $2.50. 34p. (K–1)

——— Seashore Noisy Book; pictures by Leonard Weisgard. Harper, 1941. $2.25. 42p. (K–1)

——— Seven Stories about a Cat Named Sneakers; illus. by Jean Charlot. W. R. Scott, 1955. $2.50. 144p. (K–3)

——— The Sleepy Little Lion; photographs by Ylla. Harper, 1947. $2.50. 31p. (K–2)

——— Willie's Adventures; illus. by Crockett Johnson. W. R. Scott, 1954. $2. 68p. (1–3)

——— and GERGELY, TIBOR. Wheel on the Chimney. Lippincott, 1954. $3. 31p. (K–3)

BROWN, PALMER. Cheerful. Harper, 1957. $1.50. 58p. (K–1)

BROWN, PAUL. Sparkie and Puff Ball. Scribner, 1954. $2.75. 32p. (2–4)

BROWNELL, CLIFFORD LEE, and others. ABC Health Series. American Book, 1959.
All Day, Every Day. $1.92. (1)
Blue Skies. $2.08. (2)
Come Rain, Come Shine. $2.24. (3)

BRUNHOFF, JEAN DE. Babar and Father Christmas; tr. from the French by Merle Haas. Random, 1949. $1.50. 38p. (K–1)

BRYAN, CATHERINE, and MADDEN, MABRA. Pito's House: A Mexican Folk Tale. Macmillan, 1943. $2.75. 40p. (K–1)

BRYAN, DOROTHY, and BRYAN, MARGUERITE. Johnny Penguin. Doubleday, 1931. $2. 32p. (1–3)

BUCHHEIMER, NAOMI. Let's Go to a Candy Factory; illus. by Kathleen Voute. Putnam, 1958. $1.95. 44p. (2–3)

———— Let's Go to a Post Office; illus. by Ruth Van Sciver. Putnam, 1957. $1.95. 48p. (2–4)

BUCKLEY, HELEN E. Grandfather and I; illus. by Paul Galdone. Lothrop, 1959. $2.75. 25p. (K–3)

BUFF, MARY MARSH, and BUFF, CONRAD. Dash and Dart. Viking, 1942. $3. 73p. (K–3)

———— Elf Owl. Viking, 1958. $2.75. 72p. (2–4)

BULLA, CLYDE ROBERT. The Donkey Cart; drawings by Lois Lenski. Crowell, 1946. $2.75. 89p. (1–3)

———— Down the Mississippi; illus. by Peter Burchard. Crowell, 1954. $2.75. 113p. (2–4)

———— John Billington, Friend of Squanto; illus. by Peter Burchard. Crowell, 1956. $2.75. 88p. (2–4)

———— Old Charlie; illus. by Paul Galdone. Crowell, 1957. $2.75. 80p. (2–4)

———— The Poppy Seeds; illus. by Jean Charlot. Crowell, 1955. $3. 37p. (K–2)

———— Squanto, Friend of the White Men; illus. by Peter Burchard. Crowell, 1954. $2.75. 106p. (2–4)

———— The Sword in the Tree; illus. by Paul Galdone. Crowell, 1956. $2.75. 113p. (1–6)

BURCHARD, PETER. The *Carol Moran*. Macmillan, 1958. $3. 40p. (1–3)

BURKHARDT, RICHARD W., and McGUINNESS, ANN G. Home Environment Series. Benefic, 1955.
  Preprimer: Our Way. $1.28. (PP)
  Primer: Our Family. $1.48. (P)
  Grade 1: Our Home and School. $1.68. (1)
  Grade 2: Our Neighborhood. $2. (2)
  Grade 3: Our Community. $2.40. (3)

BURTON, VIRGINIA LEE. Calico, the Wonder Horse. Houghton, 1950. $3. 58p. (K–2)

———— Choo Choo: The Story of a Little Train Who Ran Away. New ed. Houghton, 1941. $3.50. 48p. (K–2)

———— Katy and the Big Snow. Houghton, 1943. $3. 32p. (K–2)

———— The Little House. Houghton, 1942. $3. 40p. (K–2)

—————— Maybelle, the Cable Car. Houghton, 1952. $2.75. 42p. (K–2)

—————— Mike Mulligan and His Steam Shovel. Houghton, 1939. $3. 48p. (K–2)

BURTON, WILLIAM H., and others. Reading for Living Series. Bobbs-Merrill, 1950.
  Don and Peggy. 56c. (PP1)
  Come and See. 60c. (PP2)
  Here We Play. 64c. (PP3)
  Days of Fun. $1.60. (P)
  Our Happy Ways. $1.72. (1)
  Meet Our Friends. $1.84. (2)
  Our Good Neighbors. $2.12. (3)

CARLSON, BERNICE WELLS. The Junior Party Book; illus. by Magdalena Tolson.
  Rev. ed. Abingdon, 1948. $2. 160p. (K–7)

CARPENTER, FRANCES. Our Little Neighbors at Work and Play: Here, There, Then,
  and Now. American Book, 1951. $2.96. (3)

CARRICK, VALERY. Picture Tales from the Russian; tr. by Nevill Forbes. Lippincott, 1913. $2. 119p. (2–4)

CARROLL, RUTH ROBINSON. Where's the Bunny? Walck, 1950. $2. 28p. (K–1)

—————— and CARROLL, LATROBE. Scuffles. Walck, 1943. $2.50. 47p. (2–4)

CAUDILL, REBECCA. Schoolhouse in the Woods; pictures by Decie Merwin. Winston, 1949. $2.95. 120p. (1–3)

CAVANAH, FRANCES. Our Country's Story; illus. by Janice Holland. Rand McNally,
  1945. $2.95. 71p. (1–3)

CHALMERS, AUDREY. Hundreds and Hundreds of Pancakes. Viking, 1942. $1.75.
  38p. (1–3)

—————— I Had a Penny. Viking, 1944. $1.25. 44p. (K–1)

CHARLES, ROBERT HENRY. Roundabout Turn; with drawings by L. Leslie Brooke.
  Warne, 1930. $2. 48p. (K–2)

CHARTERS, WERRETT WALLACE, and others. Your Health and Growth Series. Rev.
  ed. Macmillan, 1955.
  Grade 3: Health Secrets. $2.12. (3)

CHARUSHIN, EVENGII IVANOVICH. Baby Bears; tr. from the Russian by Marguerita
  Rudolph; illus. by George Korff. Macmillan, 1944. $2.25. 40p. (2–3)

CHILD STUDY ASSOCIATION OF AMERICA. Holiday Storybook; illus. by Phoebe
  Erickson. Crowell, 1952. $3.75. 373p. (2–4)

—————— Read Me Another Story; illus. by Barbara Cooney. Crowell, 1949. $2.50.
  161p. (K–2)

—————— Read-to-Me Storybook; illus. by Lois Lenski. Crowell, 1947. $2.50. 146p.
  (K–1)

CHRYSTIE, FRANCES NICHOLSON. First Book of Jokes and Funny Things; pictures
  by Ida Scheib. Watts, 1951. $1.95. 42p. (1–3)

—— Riddle Me This; pictures by Elizabeth B. Ripley. Walck, 1940. $1.50. 55p. (1–3)

CLARK, ANN NOLAN. In My Mother's House; illus. by Velino Herrera. Viking, 1941. $3. 56p. (2–4)

—— Little Indian Basket Maker; illus. by Harrison Begay. Melmont, 1957. $2.50. 31p. (1–3)

—— Little Indian Pottery Maker; illus. by Don Perceval. Melmont, 1955. $2.50. 32p. (1–3)

CLARK, MARGERY. Poppy Seed Cakes; illus. by Maud and Miska Petersham. Doubleday, 1924. $2.75. 124p. (2–4)

CLYMER, ELEANOR LOWENTON. A Yard for John; with pictures by Mildred Boyle. Dodd, 1957. $2.50. 94p. (1–3)

COBLENTZ, CATHERINE C. Martin and Abraham Lincoln: based on a true incident; pictures by Trientja. Childrens Pr., 1947. $2.50. 24p. (2–5)

COHN, NORMA. Little People in a Big Country; pictures by children of Soviet Russia. Walck, 1945. $2.50. 31p. (1–5)

COLLIN, HEDVIG. Wind Island. Viking, 1945. $3. 96p. (2–5)

COLONIUS, LILLIAN, and SCHROEDER, GLENN W. At the Airport. Melmont, 1953. $2.50. 24p. (2–4)

—— At the Library. Melmont, 1954. $2.50. 24p. (2–4)

—— At the Post Office. Melmont, 1953. $2.50. 32p. (2–4)

COOK, BERNADINE. Curious Little Kitten; pictures by Remy Charlip. W. R. Scott, 1956. $2.25. 46p. (K–3)

—— Looking for Susie; with illus. by Judith Shahn. W. R. Scott, 1959. $2.50. 48p. (1–3)

COOKE, EMOGENE. Fun-Time Window Garden. Childrens Pr., 1957. $2.50. 32p. (K–5)

CRAIG, GERALD S., and others. Science Today and Tomorrow Series. Ginn, 1956.
Grade 1: Science near You. $2.12. (1)
Grade 2: Science around You. $2.36. (2)
Grade 3: Science Everywhere. $2.56. (3)

CRAMPTON, GERTRUDE. Tootle; pictures by Tibor Gergely. Simon & Schuster, 1945. 25c. 28p. (K–1)

CREDLE, ELLIS. Down, down the Mountain. Nelson, 1934. $2. 47p. Also Hale (Cadmus Books). (2–4)

CREEKMORE, RAYMOND. Lokoshi Learns To Hunt Seals. Macmillan, 1946. $2.75. 48p. (1–3)

CROWELL, PERS. What Can a Horse Do That You Can't Do? Whittlesey, 1954. $2.50. 32p. (1–3)

CUTRIGHT, PRUDENCE, ed. Macmillan Social Studies Series. Rev. ed. Macmillan, 1958.

Living Together Today and Yesterday. $2.28. (3)

DALGLIESH, ALICE. The Bears on Hemlock Mountain; illus. by Helen Sewell. Scribner, 1952. $2.50. 58p. (2–4)

—— Columbus Story; pictures by Leo Politi. Scribner, 1955. $2.75. 30p. (K–5)

—— The Thanksgiving Story; with illus. by Helen Sewell. Scribner, 1954. $2.75. 32p. (2–4)

DARBY, GENE. What Is a Season? pictures by Lucy and John Hawkinson. Benefic, 1959. $1.60. 48p. (1–2)

—— What Is a Turtle? pictures by Lucy and John Hawkinson. Benefic, 1959. $1.60. 48p. (1–2)

DARLING, LOUIS. Penguins. Morrow, 1956. $2.50. 64p. (1–4)

DAUGHERTY, JAMES HENRY. Andy and the Lion. Viking, 1938. $2.75. 79p. (2–4)

DAVIS, ALICE VAUGHT. Timothy Turtle; illus. by Guy Brown Wiser. Harcourt, 1940. $2.50. 32p. (K–1)

DAVIS, LAVINIA RIKER. The Wild Birthday Cake; pictures by Hildegard Woodward. Doubleday, 1949. $2.75. 50p. (2–4)

DAWSON, ROSEMARY B., and DAWSON, RICHARD. A Walk in the City. Viking, 1950. $2.25. 30p. (K–2)

DEAN, LUCILLE DENNHARDT. At the Laundry; photographer: Glenn W. Schroeder. Melmont, 1955. $2.50. 24p. (2–4)

DE ANGELI, MARGUERITE LOFFT. Ted and Nina Go to the Grocery Store. Doubleday, 1935. $1.25. 30p. (2–4)

DELAFIELD, CLELIA C. BENJAMIN. Mrs. Mallard's Ducklings; pictures by Leonard Weisgard. Lothrop, 1946. $3. 24p. (1–4)

DE LEEUW, ADELE LOUISE. Nobody's Doll; illus. by Anne Vaughan. Little, 1946. $3. 85p. (2–5)

DEMING, THERESE OSTERHELD. Indians in Winter Camp. Whitman, 1957. $2.25. 126p. (2–3)

—— Little Eagle. Whitman, 1957. $2. 96p. (1–2)

DENNIS, MORGAN. Burlap. Viking, 1945. $2. 42p. (K–2)

DENNIS, WESLEY. Flip. Viking, 1941. $2.25. 63p. (1–3)

—— Flip and the Cows. Viking, 1942. $2.25. 63p. (1–3)

DE REGNIERS, BEATRICE SCHENK. The Snow Party; drawings by Reiner Zimnik. Pantheon, 1959. $2.75. 32p. (K–1)

DILLON, INA K. Policemen; illus. by Robert Bartram. Melmont, 1957. $2.50. 30p. (1–3)

DISKA, PAT, and JENKYNS, CHRIS. Andy Says Bonjour! Vanguard, 1954. $3. 47p. (K–2)

DOBBS, ROSE. No Room: An Old Story Retold; illus. by Fritz Eichenberg. Coward-McCann, 1944. $2.50. 48p. (1–3)

———— Once upon a Time: Twenty Cheerful Tales To Read and Tell; illus. by Flavia Gág. Random, 1950. $2.95. 117p. (2–4)

DOWLING, THOMAS I., and others. The New Understanding Science Series. Winston, 1957.
The New I Wonder Why. $2.08. (1)
The New Seeing Why. $2.36. (2)
The New Learning Why. $2.44. (3)

DU BOIS, WILLIAM PÈNE. Bear Party. Viking, 1951. $2. 44p. (K–2)

———— Lion. Viking, 1956. $3. 36p. (K–3)

DURLACHER, EDWIN. The Play Party Book: Singing Games for Children; pictures by Arnold Edwin Bare; music arranged by Ken Macdonald. Devin-Adair, 1945. $3.50. 96p. (K–1)

DUVOISIN, ROGER ANTOINE. A for the Ark. Lothrop, 1952. $2.75. 40p. (K–1)

———— Christmas Whale. Knopf, 1945. $2.75. 45p. (K–2)

EATON, JEANETTE. Washington, the Nation's First Hero; illus. by Ralph Ray. Morrow, 1951. $2.50. 70p. (2–4)

EBERLE, IRMENGARDE, *see* Reading for Interest Series.

ELKIN, BENJAMIN. Gillespie and the Guards; illus. by James Daugherty. Viking, 1956. $2.50. 62p. (K–3)

———— Loudest Noise in the World; illus. by James Daugherty. Viking, 1954. $2.50. 64p. (K–3)

EMERSON, CAROLINE D., *see* History on the March Series.

ETS, MARIE HALL. In the Forest. Viking, 1944. $1.75. 45p. (K–1)

———— Mister Penny. Viking, 1935. $2. 47p. (K–1)

———— Mr. T. W. Anthony Woo: The Story of a Cat and a Dog and a Mouse. Viking, 1951. $2. 54p. (K–2)

EVANS, EVA KNOX. Araminta; illus. by Erick Berry. Putnam, 1935. $2.75. 84p. (2–4)

———— *see also* Reading for Interest Series.

FELT, SUE. Rosa-Too-Little. Doubleday, 1950. $2. 25p. (K–2)

FIEDLER, JEAN. Green Thumb Story; pictures by Barbara Latham. Holiday, 1952. $2.50. 38p. (2–4)

FISCHER, HANS ERICH. The Birthday: A Merry Tale with Many Pictures. Harcourt, 1954. $3.50. 32p. (K–1)

———— Pitschi: The Kitten Who Always Wanted To Be Something Else. Harcourt, 1953. $3. 31p. (K–2)

FISHEL, DICK, and SMITH, RED. Terry and Bunky Play Football; illus. by L. D. Warren. Putnam, 1945. $2.25. 80p. (3–5)

FITCH, FLORENCE MARY. A Book About God; illus. by Leonard Weisgard. Lothrop, 1953. $2.50. 23p. (K–3)

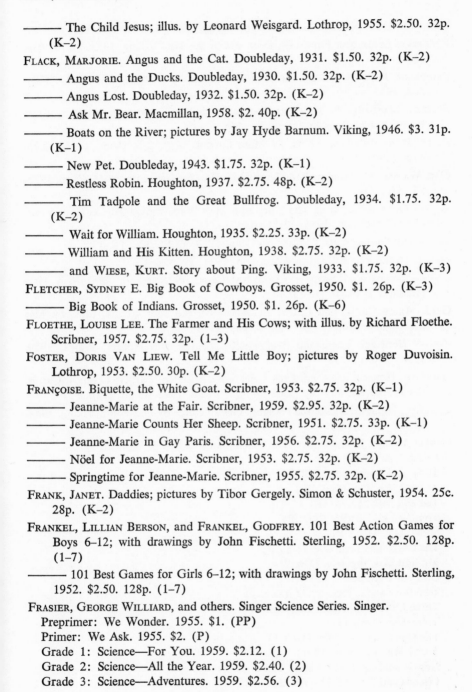

—————— The Child Jesus; illus. by Leonard Weisgard. Lothrop, 1955. $2.50. 32p. (K–2)

FLACK, MARJORIE. Angus and the Cat. Doubleday, 1931. $1.50. 32p. (K–2)

—————— Angus and the Ducks. Doubleday, 1930. $1.50. 32p. (K–2)

—————— Angus Lost. Doubleday, 1932. $1.50. 32p. (K–2)

—————— Ask Mr. Bear. Macmillan, 1958. $2. 40p. (K–2)

—————— Boats on the River; pictures by Jay Hyde Barnum. Viking, 1946. $3. 31p. (K–1)

—————— New Pet. Doubleday, 1943. $1.75. 32p. (K–1)

—————— Restless Robin. Houghton, 1937. $2.75. 48p. (K–2)

—————— Tim Tadpole and the Great Bullfrog. Doubleday, 1934. $1.75. 32p. (K–2)

—————— Wait for William. Houghton, 1935. $2.25. 33p. (K–2)

—————— William and His Kitten. Houghton, 1938. $2.75. 32p. (K–2)

—————— and WIESE, KURT. Story about Ping. Viking, 1933. $1.75. 32p. (K–3)

FLETCHER, SYDNEY E. Big Book of Cowboys. Grosset, 1950. $1. 26p. (K–3)

—————— Big Book of Indians. Grosset, 1950. $1. 26p. (K–6)

FLOETHE, LOUISE LEE. The Farmer and His Cows; with illus. by Richard Floethe. Scribner, 1957. $2.75. 32p. (1–3)

FOSTER, DORIS VAN LIEW. Tell Me Little Boy; pictures by Roger Duvoisin. Lothrop, 1953. $2.50. 30p. (K–2)

FRANÇOISE. Biquette, the White Goat. Scribner, 1953. $2.75. 32p. (K–1)

—————— Jeanne-Marie at the Fair. Scribner, 1959. $2.95. 32p. (K–2)

—————— Jeanne-Marie Counts Her Sheep. Scribner, 1951. $2.75. 33p. (K–1)

—————— Jeanne-Marie in Gay Paris. Scribner, 1956. $2.75. 32p. (K–2)

—————— Nöel for Jeanne-Marie. Scribner, 1953. $2.75. 32p. (K–2)

—————— Springtime for Jeanne-Marie. Scribner, 1955. $2.75. 32p. (K–2)

FRANK, JANET. Daddies; pictures by Tibor Gergely. Simon & Schuster, 1954. 25c. 28p. (K–2)

FRANKEL, LILLIAN BERSON, and FRANKEL, GODFREY. 101 Best Action Games for Boys 6–12; with drawings by John Fischetti. Sterling, 1952. $2.50. 128p. (1–7)

—————— 101 Best Games for Girls 6–12; with drawings by John Fischetti. Sterling, 1952. $2.50. 128p. (1–7)

FRASIER, GEORGE WILLIARD, and others. Singer Science Series. Singer.
Preprimer: We Wonder. 1955. $1. (PP)
Primer: We Ask. 1955. $2. (P)
Grade 1: Science—For You. 1959. $2.12. (1)
Grade 2: Science—All the Year. 1959. $2.40. (2)
Grade 3: Science—Adventures. 1959. $2.56. (3)

FREEMAN, DON. Norman the Doorman. Viking, 1959. $3. 64p. (K–1)

FREEMAN, LYDIA, and FREEMAN, DON. Pet of the Met. Viking, 1953. $2.75. 63p. (K–2)

FRIEDMAN, ROSE. A Whistle for Tootles; pictures by Margaret Bradfield. Abingdon, 1955. $1.50. 32p. (K–2)

FRISKEY, MARGARET R. The True Book of Birds We Know; color plates by Anna Pistorius. Childrens Pr., 1954. $2. 47p. (2–4)

FRITZ, JEAN. Fish Head; illus. by Marc Simont. Coward-McCann, 1954. $2.75. 41p. (2–4)

GÁG, WANDA. ABC Bunny; hand lettered by Howard Gág. Coward-McCann, 1933. $3. 32p. (1–3)

———— Gone Is Gone: or The Story of a Man Who Wanted To Do Housework. Coward-McCann, 1935. $1.75. 63p. (1–3)

———— Millions of Cats. Coward-McCann, 1928. $2.50. 32p. (K–1)

———— Nothing at All. Coward-McCann, 1941. $2. 32p. (K–1)

———— Snippy and Snappy. Coward-McCann, 1931. $2.50. 48p. Also Hale (Cadmus Books). (K–1)

GALL, ALICE CREW, and CREW, FLEMING. All the Year Round; illus. by Else Bostelmann. Walck, 1944. $2.50. 48p. (3–4)

———— Here and There and Everywhere; illus. by Nils Hogner. Walck, 1950. $2.50. 56p. (1–3)

GARDNER, HORACE JOHN, ed. Let's Celebrate Christmas: Parties, Legends, Carols, Poetry, Stories; illus. by Edna Potter. Ronald, 1940. $3.50. 212p. (1)

GARRETT, HELEN. Angelo, the Naughty One; pictures by Leo Politi. Viking, 1944. $2.50. 40p. (1–3)

GATES, ARTHUR I., and others. The Macmillan Readers. Macmillan, 1957.
Splash. 68c. (PP1)
Tuffy and Boots. 68c. (PP2)
At the Lake. 72c. (Sup. PP)
Ted and Sally. $1.76. (P)
Tommy Little. $1.92. (Sup. P)
Snow. 60c. (Unit P)
The Christmas Tree. 60c. (Unit P)
Mr. and Mrs. Big. 60c. (Unit P)
On Four Feet. $1.84. (1)
Two Boys and a Tree. $1.92. (Sup. 1)
Three Little Elephants. 60c. (Unit 1)
Toby. 60c. (Unit 1)
The Open Window. 60c. (Unit 1)
Today We Go. $1.96. (2–1)
New Friends and New Places. $1.96. (2–2)
Friends and Fun. $2.32. (Alt. 2)

Good Times Today. $2.20. (3–1)
Good Times Tomorrow. $2.20. (3–2)
Good Times Today and Tomorrow. $2.48. (Alt. 3)

GAY, ROMNEY, *see* Reading for Interest Series.

GAY, ZHENYA, and GAY, JAN. Pancho and His Burro. Morrow, 1930. $2.50. 35p. (K–2)

GILBERT, HELEN EARLE. Mr. Plum and the Little Green Tree; pictures by Margaret Bradfield. Abingdon, 1946. $2.50. 32p. (K–3)

GINN ENRICHMENT SERIES. Primary. Rev. ed. Ginn, 1959.
Come with Us, by Odille Ousley. 68c. (Pre–PP)
Under the Apple Tree, by Odille Ousley. $1.64. (Pre–1)
Open the Gate, by Odille Ousley. $1.75. (Pre–2)
Ranches and Rainbows, by Odille Ousley. $2. (Pre–3)
Fun and Fancy, by Eleanor Robison. $2.20. (Pre–4)

GLOVER, FLORIDA R. First Christmas; illus. by Susanne Suba. Dutton, 1943. $1.25. 10p. (K–3)

GOODSPEED, J. M. Let's Go to a Dairy; illus. by Raymond Abel. Putnam, 1957. $1.95. 46p. (2–4)

—— Let's Go to a Garage; illus. by Ruth Van Sciver. Putnam, 1958. $1.95. 48p. (2–4)

—— Let's Go To Watch a Building Go Up; illus. by Raymond Abel. Putnam, 1956. $1.95. 47p. (1–4)

GOTTLIEB, WILLIAM P. Four Seasons. Simon & Schuster, 1957. $1. 32p. (K–2)

GOUDEY, ALICE E. Good Rain; illus. by Nora S. Unwin. Dutton, 1950. $2.75. 31p. (1–4)

—— Here Come the Bears! illus. by Garry MacKenzie. Scribner, 1954. $2.50. 93p. (2–4)

—— Here Come the Deer! illus. by Garry MacKenzie. Scribner, 1955. $2.50. 92p. (1–3)

—— Here Come the Elephants! illus. by Garry MacKenzie. Scribner, 1955. $2.50. 92p. (2–4)

—— Here Come the Lions! illus. by Garry MacKenzie. Scribner, 1956. $2.50. 94p. (2–4)

—— Here Come the Whales! illus. by Garry MacKenzie. Scribner, 1956. $2.50. 94p. (2–4)

—— Here Come the Wild Dogs! illus. by Garry MacKenzie. Scribner, 1958. $2.50. 94p. (2–4)

—— Houses from the Sea; illus. by Adrienne Adams. Scribner, 1959. $2.95. 32p. (K–2)

GRAHAM, AL. Timothy Turtle; pictures by Tony Palazzo. Viking, 1949. $2.75. 30p. (K–3)

GRAMATKY, HARDIE. Hercules: The Story of an Old-fashioned Fire Engine. Putnam, 1940. $3. 72p. (K–3)

────── Little Toot. Putnam, 1939. $3. 93p. (K–3)

────── Loopy. Putnam, 1941. $3. 72p. (K–3)

GRAY, WILLIAM S., and others. Curriculum Foundation Series. The New Basic Readers. Scott, Foresman, 1956.
  The New We Look and See. 56c. (PP1)
  The New We Work and Play. 60c. (PP2)
  The New We Come and Go. 64c. (PP3)
  The New Fun with Dick and Jane. $1.48. (1–1)
  The New Our New Friends. $1.60. (1–2)
  The New Friends and Neighbors. $1.80. (2–1)
  The New More Friends and Neighbors. $1.80. (2–2)
  The New Streets and Roads. $2. (3–1)
  The New More Streets and Roads. $2. (3–2)

GREEN, IVAH E., and BROMWELL, ALICE. Woody, the Little Wood Duck; illus. by George F. Mason. Abelard-Schuman, 1955. $2.25. 63p. (2–4)

GRUENBERG, SIDONIE MATSNER, ed. Favorite Stories Old and New; illus. by Kurt Wiese. Rev. ed. Doubleday, 1955. $3.95. 512p. (K–4)

GUILFOILE, ELIZABETH. Nobody Listens to Andrew; illus. by Mary Stevens. Follett, 1957. $1. 27p. (1–2)

HADER, BERTA HOERNER, and HADER, ELMER. Big City. Macmillan, 1947. $3.50. 80p. (1–3)

────── The Big Snow. Macmillan, 1948. $3. 46p. (K–2)

────── Cock-a-Doodle Doo: The Story of a Little Red Rooster. Macmillan, 1939. $3. 56p. (K–1)

────── Farmer in the Dell. Macmillan, 1931. $3.50. 90p. (K–2)

────── Little Appaloosa. Macmillan, 1949. $3.50. 42p. (2–4)

────── Little Stone House: A Story of Building a House in the Country. Macmillan, 1944. $3.50. 63p. (1–3)

────── Little Town. Macmillan, 1941. $3.75. 87p. (K–2)

────── Runaways. Macmillan, 1956. $3. 39p. (1–3)

────── Story of Pancho and the Bull with the Crooked Tail. Macmillan, 1942. $3.50. 56p. (2–4)

HAGER, ALICE ROGERS, and MARTIN, JACKIE. Washington, City of Destiny. Macmillan, 1949. $3.50. 72p. (K–3)

HALLOCK, GRACE T., and others. Health for Better Living Series. Ginn, 1954.
  Grade 1: Health and Happy Days. $1.68. (1)
  Grade 2: Health in Work and Play. $1.80. (2)
  Grade 3: Health and Safety for You. $1.92. (3)

HANDFORTH, THOMAS. Mei Li. Doubleday, 1938. $2.75. 52p. (1–3)

HANNA, PAUL R., and others. Curriculum Foundation Series. Basic Social Studies Program. Scott, Foresman.
Primer: At Home. 1956. $1.44. (P)
Grade 1: At School. 1957. $1.52. (1)
Grade 2: In the Neighborhood. 1958. $2.28. (2)
Grade 3: In City, Town, and Country. 1959. $2.80. (3)

HARRIS, ISOBEL. Little Boy Brown; illus. by André François. Lippincott, 1949. $3. 44p. (K–2)

HARRIS, LOUISE DYER, and HARRIS, NORMAN DYER. Slim Green; illus. by Robert Candy. Little, 1955. $2.50. 53p. (2–4)

HARVEY, LOIS F. Cotton Growing; illus. by James Frew. Melmont, 1958. $2.50. 32p. (2–4)

HASTINGS, EVELYN BELMONT. All Kinds of Days; photographer: Joy Dorris Karr. Melmont, 1955. $2.50. 23p. (1–2)

——— The Dairy; illus. by Frans Van. Melmont, 1958. $2.50. 32p. (1–2)

——— The Department Store; photographer: Lewis A. Ogan. Melmont, 1956. $2.50. 22p. (1–2)

HAWKINS, QUAIL. Who Wants an Apple? illus. by David and Lolita Granahan. Holiday, 1957. $2. 40p. (1–3)

HAYS, WILMA PITCHFORD. The Story of Valentine; illus. by Leonard Weisgard. Coward-McCann, 1956. $2.50. 55p. (2–4)

HAYWOOD, CAROLYN. "B" Is for Betsy. Harcourt, 1939. $2.95. 159p. (2–4)

——— Back to School with Betsy. Harcourt, 1943. $2.95. 176p. (2–4)

——— Betsy and Billy. Harcourt, 1941. $2.95. 156p. (2–4)

——— Betsy and the Boys. Harcourt, 1945. $2.95. 175p. (2–4)

——— Betsy's Little Star. Morrow, 1950. $2.75. 157p. (2–4)

——— Eddie and Gardenia. Morrow, 1951. $2.75. 191p. (2–4)

——— Eddie and the Fire Engine. Morrow, 1949. $2.75. 189p. (2–4)

——— Eddie Makes Music. Morrow, 1957. $2.95. 191p. (2–4)

——— Here's a Penny. Harcourt, 1944. $2.95. 158p. (2–4)

——— Little Eddie. Morrow, 1947. $2.95. 160p. (2–4)

——— Penny Goes to Camp. Morrow, 1948. $2.75. 191p. (2–4)

——— Primrose Day. Harcourt, 1942. $2.95. 200p. (2–4)

——— Two and Two Are Four. Harcourt, 1940. $2.95. 171p. (2–4)

HEFFLEFINGER, JANE, and HOFFMAN, ELAINE. Firemen; illus. by Robert Bartram. Melmont, 1957. $2.50. 30p. (1–3)

HENDRICH, PAULA. Trudy's First Day at Camp; illus. by Adrienne Adams. Lothrop, 1959. $2.75. 26p. (K–3)

HEYWARD, DU BOSE, and FLACK, MARJORIE. The Country Bunny and the Little Gold Shoes. Houghton, 1939. $3.25. 48p. (1–2)

HILDRETH, GERTRUDE, and others. Easy Growth in Reading Series. Rev. ed. Winston.
  Preprimer, prelevel 1: Mary and Bill. 1951. 68c. (PP1)
  Preprimer, level 1: Mac and Muff. 1957. 68c. (PP1)
  Preprimer, level 2: The Twins, Tom and Don. 1947. 68c. (PP2)
  Preprimer, level 3: Going to School. 1947. 68c. (PP3)
  Primer, level 1: At Play. 1957. $1.68. (P–1)
  Primer, level 2: Fun in Story. 1957. $1.68. (P–2)
  Book 1, level 1: I Know a Secret. 1957. $1.76. (1–1)
  Pre-2nd: Good Stories. 1957. $1.72. (Pre–2)
  Book 2, level 1: Along the Way. 1957. $1.96. (2–1)
  Book 2, level 2: Story Road. 1957. $1.88. (2–2)
  Book 3, level 1: Faraway Ports. 1957. $2.12. (3–1)
  Book 3, level 2: Enchanting Stories. 1957. $2.04. (3–2)

HILL, MABEL BETSY. Along Comes Judy Jo. Lippincott, 1943. $2.50. 124p. (2–4)
────── Down-along Apple Market Street. Lippincott, 1934. $2.25. 32p. (2–4)
────── Jack o'Lantern for Judy Jo: An Apple Market Street Story. Lippincott, 1940. $2.50. 64p. (2–4)
────── Summer Comes to Apple Market Street. Lippincott, 1937. $2.25. 61p. (2–4)
────── Surprise for Judy Jo: An Apple Market Street Story. Lippincott, 1939. $2.50. 64p. (2–4)

HISTORY ON THE MARCH SERIES. Allan Nevins, educational consultant. Heath, 1955.
  Pioneer Children of America, by Caroline D. Emerson. $2.60. (3)

HOFF, SYD. Danny and the Dinosaur. Harper, 1958. $1.95. 64p. (1–2)
────── Julius. Harper, 1959. $1.95. 64p. (1–2)
────── Sammy the Seal. Harper, 1959. $1.95. 64p. (1–2)

HOFFMAN, ELAINE, and HEFFLEFINGER, JANE. More Friendly Helpers; photographs by Peggy Irwin. Melmont, 1954. $2.50. 23p. (1–2)
────── School Helpers; photographs by Peggy Irwin. Melmont, 1955. $2.50. 31p. (1–3)

HOGAN, INEZ. World Round. Dutton, 1949. $3. 64p. (K–3)
────── *see also* Reading for Interest Series.

HOGNER, DOROTHY CHILDS. Daisy: A Farm Fable; pictures by Nils Hogner. Walck, 1949. $2.50. 46p. (K–2)

HUGLEY, LAURA MENGERT, *see* Blended Social Studies Series.

HUMPHREYS, DENA. The Zoo Book. Holt, 1947. $2.50. 38p. (K–1)

HUNNICUTT, C. W., and GRAMBS, JEAN D. Singer Social Studies. Singer, 1957.
  Primer: I Play. $1.72. (P)
  Grade 1: I Live with Others. $2.24. (1)
  Grade 2: I Have Friends. $2.40. (2)

Grade 3: I Know People. $2.56. (3)

HUNT, MABEL LEIGH. The Double Birthday Present; illus. by Elinore Blaisdell. Lippincott, 1947. $2. 52p. (2–4)

HUNTINGTON, HARRIET E. Let's Go Outdoors; illus. by Preston Duncan. Doubleday, 1939. $3. 88p. (1–4)

—— Let's Go to the Seashore; illus. with photographs. Doubleday, 1941. $3. 88p. (1–4)

HURD, EDITH THACHER. Caboose; illus. by Clement Hurd. Lothrop, 1950. $2.50. 30p. (K–3)

—— and HURD, CLEMENT. Cat from Telegraph Hill. Lothrop, 1955. $2.50. 32p. (K–2)

—— Nino and His Fish. Lothrop, 1954. $2.50. 33p. (1–3)

HUTCHINSON, VERONICA SOMERVILLE, comp. Candle-Light Stories; illus. by Lois Lenski. Putnam, 1928. $3.95. 146p. (2–4)

—— Chimney Corner Stories; illus. by Lois Lenski. Putnam, 1925. $3.75. 149p. (2–4)

—— Fireside Stories; with drawings by Lois Lenski. Putnam, 1927. $3.75. 150p. (2–4)

IPCAR, DAHLOV ZORACH. One Horse Farm. Doubleday, 1950. $2.50. 34p. (K–2)

IRWIN, LESLIE W., and others. Health-Happiness-Success Series. Lyons & Carnahan, 1958.
  Book 1: Awake and Away. $1.36. (1)
  Book 2: Growing Day by Day. $1.88. (2)
  Book 3: Keeping Fit for Fun. $2.08. (3)

JENSEN, VIRGINIA ALLEN. Lars-Peter's Birthday; illus. by Ib Spang Olsen. Abingdon, 1959. $1.75. 36p. (K–1)

JOHNSON, CROCKETT. Harold's Circus: An Astounding, Colossal, Purple Crayon Event! Harper, 1959. $1.50. 62p. (K–1)

—— Harold's Fairy Tale: Further Adventures with the Purple Crayon. Harper, 1956. $1.50. 61p. (K–1)

—— Harold's Trip to the Sky. Harper, 1957. $1.50. 64p. (K–2)

JOHNSON, ELEANOR M., and JACOBS, LELAND B., eds. Treasury of Literature. Readtext Series. Merrill, 1954.
  Book 3: Treat Shop. $2.48. (3)

JOHNSON, MARGARET SWEET, and JOHNSON, HELEN LOSSING. Carlo, the Hound Who Thought He Was a Calf. Harcourt, 1941. $2.50. 87p. (2–4)

—— Derry the Wolfhound. Harcourt, 1943. $2.50. 74p. (2–4)

—— Joey and Patches. Morrow, 1947. $2.50. 70p. (2–4)

—— Runaway Puppy. Harcourt, 1942. $2.50. 86p. (2–4)

—— Sir Lancelot and Scamp. Harcourt, 1945. $2.50. 78p. (2–4)

—— Smallest Puppy. Harcourt, 1940. $2.50. 88p. (2–4)

—— Snowshoe Paws. Morrow, 1949. $2.50. 62p. (2–4)

—— Story of Rickey. Harcourt, 1939. $2.50. 89p. (2–4)

JOHNSTON, JOHANNA. Sugarplum; illus. by Marvin Bileck. Knopf, 1955. $2.75. 40p. (K–3)

JONES, EDWINA, and others. The Road to Health Series. Laidlaw, 1957.
Grade 1: My First Health Book. $1.56. (1)
Grade 2: My Second Health Book. $1.68. (2)
Grade 3: Easy Steps to Health. $1.80. (3)

JONES, ELIZABETH ORTON. Big Susan. Macmillan, 1947. $2.50. 82p. (2–5)

JONES, JESSIE MAE ORTON, ed. Small Rain: Selections from the Bible; illus. by Elizabeth Orton Jones. Viking, 1943. $2.50. 40p. (1–4)

—— This Is the Way: Prayers and Precepts from World Religions; illus. by Elizabeth Orton Jones. Viking, 1951. $3. 62p. (K–3)

JONES, MARY ALICE. Tell Me about God; illus. by Pelagie Doane. Rand McNally, 1943. $2.50. 69p. (1–3)

—— Tell Me about Jesus; illus. by Pelagie Doane. Rand McNally, 1944. $2.50. 69p. (1–3)

—— Tell Me about the Bible; illus. by Pelagie Doane. Rand McNally, 1945. $2.50. 91p. (1–3)

JORDAN, NINA RALSTON. Mother Goose Handicraft. Harcourt, 1945. $2.75. 149p. (1–4)

JOSLIN, SESYLE. What Do You Say, Dear? pictures by Maurice Sendak. W. R. Scott, 1958. $2.75. 48p. (K–1)

JUPO, FRANK. Nothing To Eat—but Food. Dutton, 1954. $2.75. 48p. (2–4)

KAHL, VIRGINIA. Away Went Wolfgang. Scribner, 1954. $2.50. 32p. (K–1)

—— The Duchess Bakes a Cake. Scribner, 1955. $2.50. 32p. (K–3)

—— Maxie. Scribner, 1956. $2.50. 32p. (K–2)

—— Plum Pudding for Christmas. Scribner, 1956. $2.50. 32p. (K–2)

KAY, HELEN. One Mitten Lewis; illus. by Kurt Werth. Lothrop, 1955. $2.50. 31p. (K–1)

—— Snow Birthday; illus. by Barbara Cooney. Farrar, 1955. $2.50. 46p. (2–4)

KEPES, JULIET. Five Little Monkeys. Houghton, 1952. $2.50. 32p. (K–3)

KNOX, WARREN, and others. The Wonderworld of Science Series. Rev. ed. Scribner, 1957.
Book 1: The Wonderworld of Science. $2.12. (1)
Book 2: The Wonderworld of Science. $2.24. (2)
Book 3: The Wonderworld of Science. $2.40. (3)

KOCH, DOROTHY CLARKE. Gone Is My Goose; with pictures by Doris Lee. Holiday, 1956. $2.50. 26p. (K–2)

—— I Play at the Beach; pictures by Feodor Rojankovsky. Holiday, 1955. $2.95. 28p. (K–1)

—— When the Cows Got Out; illus. by Paul Lantz. Holiday, 1958. $2.50. 36p. (1–2)

KOHL, MARGUERITE, and YOUNG, FREDERICA. Games for Children; with illus. by Phillip Miller. Wyn, 1953. $3. 184p. (K–7)

KRAUSS, RUTH. Backward Day; pictures by Marc Simont. Harper, 1950. $2. 31p. (K–2)

—— Bears; pictures by Phyllis Rowand. Harper, 1948. $1.75. 23p. (K–1)

—— Big World and the Little House; illus. by Marc Simont. Harper, 1956. $2.50. 42p. (K–2)

—— The Birthday Party; pictures by Maurice Sendak. Harper, 1957. $1.50. 29p. (K–1)

—— The Growing Story; pictures by Phyllis Rowand. Harper, 1947. $2.50. 28p. (K–3)

—— A Hole Is To Dig: A First Book of First Definitions; pictures by Maurice Sendak. Harper, 1952. $1.50. 46p. (K–2)

KUSKIN, KARLA. James and the Rain. Harper, 1957. $2.25. 48p. (K–2)

LA FONTAINE, JEAN DE. Fables; tr. by Margaret Wise Brown; illus. by André Hellé. Harper, 1940. $1.85. 39p. (1–3)

LA RUE, MABEL GUINNIP. Tiny Toosey's Birthday; pictures by Mary Stevens. Houghton, 1952. $2.75. 128p. (1–2)

LATHROP, DOROTHY PULIS. Animals of the Bible; with text selected by Helen Dean Fish from the King James Bible. Lippincott, 1937. $3. 65p. (1–4)

—— Puppies for Keeps. Macmillan, 1943. $3.50. 40p. (K–2)

—— Skittle-Skattle Monkey. Macmillan, 1945. $2.50. 48p. (2–5)

—— Who Goes There? Macmillan, 1935. $2.75. 41p. (1–3)

LATTIMORE, ELEANOR FRANCES. Bayou Boy. Morrow, 1946. $2.50. 127p. (1–4)

—— Bells for a Chinese Donkey. Morrow, 1951. $2.50. 126p. (2–4)

—— Holly in the Snow. Morrow, 1954. $2.50. 125p. (2–4)

—— Little Pear: The Story of a Little Chinese Boy. Harcourt, 1931. $2.75. 144p. (1–3)

—— Little Pear and the Rabbits. Morrow, 1956. $2.50. 125p. (2–4)

—— Story of Lee Ling. Harcourt, 1940. $2.75. 114p. (2–4)

—— Three Little Chinese Girls. Morrow, 1948. $2.50. 128p. (2–4)

LEAF, MUNRO. Arithmetic Can Be Fun. Lippincott, 1949. $2.25. 64p. (2–3)

—— Fair Play. Lippincott, 1939. $2.75. 94p. (2–3)

—— Health Can Be Fun. Lippincott, 1943. $2.25. 55p. (2–3)

—— Let's Do Better. Lippincott, 1945. $2.95. 79p. (2–3)

—— Manners Can Be Fun. Lippincott, 1936. $2.25. 45p. (2–3)

—— Safety Can Be Fun. Lippincott, 1938. $2.50. 49p. (2–3)

———— Story of Ferdinand; illus. by Robert Lawson. Viking, 1936. $1.75. 81p. (1–3)

———— Wee Gillis; illus. by Robert Lawson. Viking, 1938. $2.75. 71p. (2–4)

LEAVELL, U. W. Golden Rule Series: The Modern McGuffey Readers. American Book, 1957.
  Open Windows. $2.36. (1)
  Open Doors. $2.48. (2)
  Open Roads. $2.56. (3)

LE GRAND. Cats for Kansas. Abingdon, 1948. $2. 38p. (K–2)

———— Matilda. Abingdon, 1956. $2. 64p. (2–4)

———— Why Cowboys Sing, in Texas. Abingdon, 1950. $2. 40p. (2–4)

LENSKI, LOIS. Davy and His Dog. Walck, 1957. $1.75. 38p. (K–1)

———— Davy's Day. Walck, 1943. $1.75. 48p. (K–1)

———— A Dog Came to School. Walck, 1955. $1.75. 47p. (K–2)

———— I Like Winter. Walck, 1950. $1.75. 45p. (K–1)

———— Let's Play House. Walck, 1944. $2. 40p. (K–1)

———— Little Airplane. Walck, 1938. $2. 48p. (K–1)

———— Little Auto. Walck, 1934. $2. 45p. (K–1)

———— Little Farm. Walck, 1942. $2. 48p. (K–1)

———— Little Sail Boat. Walck, 1937. $2. 48p. (K–1)

———— Little Train. Walck, 1940. $2. 45p. (K–1)

———— Mr. and Mrs. Noah. Crowell, 1948. $1.75. 46p. (K–1)

———— Papa Small. Walck, 1951. $2. 45p. (K–1)

———— Project Boy. Lippincott, 1954. $2.50. 128p. (2–4)

———— Spring Is Here. Walck, 1945. $1.75. 48p. (1–3)

———— Surprise for Davy. Walck, 1947. $1.50. 46p. (1–3)

———— Surprise for Mother. Lippincott, 1934. $1.50. 91p. (1–3)

———— We Live by the River. Lippincott, 1956. $2.50. 127p. (2–4)

LEWELLEN, JOHN BRYAN. Tommy Learns To Drive a Tractor; illus. by Leonard Kessler. Crowell, 1958. $2.75. 45p. (2–4)

———— Tommy Learns To Fly; illus. by Leonard Kessler. Crowell, 1956. $2.75. 48p. (2–5)

———— The True Book of Farm Animals; illus. by Dwight Mutchler. Childrens Pr., 1954. $2. 47p. (1–3)

LIANG, YEN. Tommy and Dee-Dee. Walck, 1953. $2.25. 32p. (K–1)

LIEBERS, RUTH, and ROTHENBERG, LILLIAN. Stevie Finds a Way; illus. by Robert Doremus. Abingdon, 1958. $1.75. 48p. (1–3)

LIFTON, BETTY JEAN. Joji and the Dragon; illus. by Eiichi Mitsui. Morrow, 1957. $2.50. 69p. (K–2)

McCLOSKEY, ROBERT. Blueberries for Sal. Viking, 1948. $3. 54p. (K–2)

—— Lentil. Viking, 1940. $3.50. 61p. (2–4)

—— Make Way for Ducklings. Viking, 1941. $3. 67p. (K–1)

—— One Morning in Maine. Viking, 1952. $3. 64p. (K–2)

McCLUNG, ROBERT M. Green Darner: The Story of a Dragonfly. Morrow, 1956. $2.50. 48p. (1–5)

—— Major: The Story of a Black Bear. Morrow, 1956. $2.50. 64p. (2–4)

—— Sphinx: The Story of a Caterpillar. Morrow, 1949. $2.50. 48p. (2–4)

—— Stripe: The Story of a Chipmunk. Morrow, 1951. $2.50. 48p. (2–4)

MacDONALD, GOLDEN. Little Lost Lamb; with illus. by Leonard Weisgard. Doubleday, 1945. $3. 40p. (K–1)

—— Red Light, Green Light; illus. by Leonard Weisgard. Doubleday, 1944. $2.50. 40p. (1–3)

—— Whistle for the Train; illus. by Leonard Weisgard. Doubleday, 1956. $2.50. 30p. (K–2)

McGAW, JESSIE BREWER. How Medicine Man Cured Paleface Woman: An Easy-Reading Story in Indian Picture Writing and Paleface Words. W. R. Scott, 1956. $2.75. 62p. (1–4)

McGINLEY, PHYLLIS LOUISE. All around the Town; illus. by Helen Stone. Lippincott, 1948. $2.75. 55p. (K–2)

—— The Horse Who Had His Picture in the Paper; pictures by Helen Stone. Lippincott, 1951. $2.75. 48p. (K–2)

—— The Horse Who Lived Upstairs; illus. by Helen Stone. Lippincott, 1944. $2.95. 48p. (K–2)

—— The Year without a Santa Claus; pictures by Kurt Werth. Lippincott, 1957. $3. 32p. (K–1)

MacGREGOR, ELLEN. Theodore Turtle; pictures by Paul Galdone. Whittlesey, 1955. $2.50. 32p. (K–2)

McINTIRE, ALTA, and HILL, WILHELMINA. Follett New Unified Social Studies Series. Follett.
Grade 1: Billy's Friends. 1957. $2.28. (1)
Grade 2: Billy's Neighbors. 1957. $2.44. (2)
Grade 3: Working Together. 1959. $3.16. (3)

McKEE, PAUL, and others. Reading for Meaning Series. Houghton, 1957.
Preprimer: Tip and Mitten. 64c. (PP2)
Preprimer: The Big Show. 64c. (PP3)
Grade 1: Jack and Janet. $1.56. (1–1)
Grade 2: Come Along. $1.84. (2–1)
Grade 2: On We Go. $1.84. (2–2)
Grade 3: Looking Ahead. $2.04. (3–1)
Grade 3: Climbing Higher. $2.04. (3–2)

MAROKVIA, MIREILLE. Jannot, a French Rabbit; with drawings by Artur Marokvia. Lippincott, 1959. $3. 47p. (2–4)

MARTIN, PATRICIA MILES. The Pointed Brush; illus. by Roger Duvoisin. Lothrop, 1959. $2.75. 29p. (1–3)

MASON, MIRIAM EVANGELINE. Happy Jack; illus. by George and Doris Hauman. Macmillan, 1945. $2.50. 136p. (2–4)

———— Little Jonathan; illus. by George and Doris Hauman. Macmillan, 1944. $2.50. 127p. (2–4)

———— Matilda and Her Family; illus. by Meg Wohlberg. Macmillan, 1942. $2.75. 144p. (2–4)

———— Timothy Has Ideas; illus. by Berta and Elmer Hader. Macmillan, 1943. $2.50. 127p. (2–4)

MASSEY, JEANNE. The Littlest Witch; illus. by Adrienne Adams. Knopf, 1959. $2.75. 34p. (K–2)

MASSOGLIA, ELINOR. Fun-Time Paper Folding; illus. by George Rhoads. Childrens Pr., 1959. $2.50. 32p. (2–4)

MATHIESEN, EGON. Blue-eyed Pussy; tr. by Karen Rye. Doubleday, 1951. $2.50. 111p. (K–2)

MATIAS. A Little Donkey—Un Petit Âne. Walck, 1959. $1.75. 18p. (K–2)

MEIGS, CORNELIA LYNDE. Wonderful Locomotive; illus. by Berta and Elmer Hader. Macmillan, 1928. $3.50. 104p. (1–3)

MERRILL, JEAN. The Travels of Marco; drawings by Ronni Solbert. Knopf, 1956. $3. 42p. (K–3)

MILHOUS, KATHERINE. Appolonia's Valentine. Scribner, 1954. $2.75. 32p. (2–4)

———— The Egg Tree. Scribner, 1950. $2.75. 28p. (2–4)

———— With Bells On: A Christmas Story. Scribner, 1955. $2.75. 32p. (K–3)

MILLER, JOHN P., illus. The Little Red Hen. Simon & Schuster, 1954. 25c. 28p. (K–1)

MILNE, ALAN ALEXANDER. House at Pooh Corner; with decorations by Ernest H. Shepard. Dutton, 1928. $2.50. 178p. (1–3)

———— Winnie-the-Pooh; with decorations by Ernest H. Shepard. Dutton, 1950. $2.50. 159p. (1–3)

MINARIK, ELSE HOLMELUND. Father Bear Comes Home; pictures by Maurice Sendak. Harper, 1959. $1.95. 62p. (1–2)

———— Little Bear; pictures by Maurice Sendak. Harper, 1957. $1.95. 63p. (1–2)

MINER, OPAL IRENE SEVREY. The True Book of Policemen and Firemen; pictures by Irene Miner and Mary Salem. Childrens Pr., 1954. $2. 44p. (1–2)

MITCHELL, LUCY SPRAGUE, ed. Another Here and Now Story Book; illus. by Rosalie Slocum. Dutton, 1937. $3.50. 369p. (K–3)

———— Here and Now Story Book: Two-to-Seven Year Olds; illus. by Hendrik Willem Van Loon and Christine Price. New ed. rev. and enl. Dutton, 1948. $3. 256p. (K–3)

———— and others. Our Growing World. Rev. ed. Heath, 1955.

Book I: Farm and City. $2.08. (1)

Book II: Animals, Plants, and Machines. $2.36. (2)

Book III: Our Country. $2.56. (3)

MONROE, MARION, and others. Curriculum Foundation Series. Reading for Independence. Scott, Foresman, 1959.

New We Three. $1.56. (1)

New What Next. Part One. $1.44. (2–1)

New Tall Tales. Part One. $1.44. (3–1)

MOON, GRACE PURDIE, and MOON, CARL. One Little Indian. Whitman, 1950. $2. 32p. (K–2)

MOORE, LILIAN. My First Counting Book; pictures by Garth Williams. Simon & Schuster, 1956. $1.25. 22p. (K–1)

———— Wobbly Wheels; pictures by Beth Krush. Abingdon, 1956. $1.50. 47p. (1–2)

MORROW, ELIZABETH CUTLER. Painted Pig: A Mexican Picture Book; pictures by René d'Harnoncourt. Knopf, 1942. $3. 32p. (1–3)

MYERS, GRAYCE SILVERTON. The Fishing Cat; pictures by Paul Galdone. Abingdon, 1953. $1.25. 24p. (1–3)

NEVINS, ALLAN, *see* History on the March Series.

NEWBERRY, CLARE TURLEY. April's Kittens. Harper, 1940. $2.75. 30p. (K–3)

———— Babette. Harper, 1937. $2.50. 30p. (K–3)

———— Barkis. Harper, 1938. $2.50. 30p. (K–3)

———— Mittens. Harper, 1936. $2.50. 28p. (K–3)

———— Pandora. Harper, 1944. $2.95. 35p. (K–3)

———— Smudge. Harper, 1948. $2.50. 32p. (K–2)

———— T-Bone, the Baby Sitter. Harper, 1950. $2.50. 26p. (K–2)

NOLEN, BARBARA, *see* Reading for Interest Series.

NORLING, JOSEPHINE STEARNS, and NORLING, ERNEST RALPH. Pogo's Fishing Trip: A Story of Salmon. Holt, 1942. $1.75. 40p. (2–4)

———— Pogo's House: The Story of Lumber. Holt, 1941. $1.75. 42p. (2–4)

———— Pogo's Lamb: A Story of Wool. Holt, 1947. $2. 44p. (2–4)

———— Pogo's Letter: A Story of Paper. Holt, 1946. $1.75. 42p. (2–4)

———— Pogo's Mining Trip: A Story of Gold. Holt, 1945. $2. 40p. (2–4)

———— Pogo's Sea Trip: A Story of Boats. Holt, 1949. $1.75. 50p. (1–3)

———— Pogo's Sky Ride: A Story of Airplanes. Holt, 1943. $1.75. 44p. (2–4)

———— Pogo's Train Ride: A Story of Freight Trains. Holt, 1944. $1.75. 40p. (2–4)

O'DONNELL, MABEL, and others. The Alice and Jerry Basic Reading Program. Row, Peterson, 1957.

Skip Along. 48c. (PP1)

Under the Sky. 60c. (PP2)
Open the Door. 60c. (PP3)
High on a Hill. 48c. (PP4)
Day In and Day Out. $1.56. (Basic P)
The Wishing Well. $1.44. (Par. P)
Round About. $1.72. (Basic 1)
Anything Can Happen. $1.72. (Par. 1)
Down the River Road. $1.68. (Read. 2)
Friendly Village. $1.80. (Basic 2)
Neighbors on the Hill. $1.80. (Par. 2)
Through the Green Gate. $1.80. (Read. 3)
If I Were Going. $2.08. (Basic 3)
The Five-and-a-Half Club. $1.80. (Par. 3)

OFTEDAL, LAURA, and JACOB, NINA. My First Dictionary: The Beginner's Picture Word Book; illus. by Pelagie Doane. Grosset, 1948. $1.50. 140p. (K–2)

O'KEEFE, PATTRIC RUTH, and others. Winston Health Series. Winston, 1954.
Grade 1: From Head to Toe. $1.80. (1)
Grade 2: Side by Side. $2. (2)
Grade 3: How We Grow. $2.08. (3)

OLDS, ELIZABETH. Big Fire. Houghton, 1945. $3.75. 32p. (K–2)

OLDS, HELEN DIEHL. The Silver Button; illus. by Harold Berson. Knopf, 1958. $2.50. 32p. (1–3)

ORTON, HELEN FULLER. Grandmother's Cooky Jar; illus. by M. L. Frantz. Lippincott, 1930. $2.25. 129p. (1–3)

———— The Little Lost Pigs; illus. by Luxor Price. Lippincott, 1925. $2.25. 96p. (1–3)

———— Prancing Pat; illus. by Maurice Day. Lippincott, 1927. $2.25. 119p. (1–3)

———— Queenie: Story of a Cow; illus. by Maurice Day. Lippincott. 1929. $2.25. 119p. (1–3)

OSSWALD, EDITH, and REED, MARY M. Golden Picture Book of Numbers; illus. by Corinne Malvern. Simon & Schuster, 1954. $1.50. 80p. (1–2)

OTTO, MARGARET. The Little Brown Horse; illus. by Barbara Cooney. Knopf, 1959. $2.50. 40p. (K–1)

OUSLEY, ODILLE, *see* Ginn Enrichment Series.

PALMER, ROBIN, *see* Reading for Interest Series.

PARKER, BERTHA MORRIS, *see* Blough, Glenn O., Basic Science Education Series, Primary.

PARTCH, DOROTHEA WEIN, *see* Basic Social Studies Series.

PAULL, GRACE A. Come to the City. Abelard-Schuman, 1959. $2.75. 40p. (K–1)

———— Pancakes for Breakfast. Doubleday, 1946. $2. 28p. (K–3)

PERERA, LYDIA. Frisky; illus. by Oscar Liebman. Holiday, 1955. $2.25. 48p. (2–4)

PETERSHAM, MAUD FULLER, and PETERSHAM, MISKA. American ABC. Macmillan, 1941. $3. 56p. (1–3)

—— Box with Red Wheels. Macmillan, 1949. $2.75. 28p. (K–2)

—— Christ Child: As Told by Matthew and Luke. Doubleday, 1931. $3. 63p. (K–3)

—— The Circus Baby. Macmillan, 1950. $2.50. 28p. (K–2)

PETERSON, BARBARA (BURNS), and PETERSON, RUSSELL F. Whitefoot Mouse; illus. by Russell F. Peterson. Holiday, 1959. $2.50. 53p. (2–4)

PHILLIPS, ESTHER, *see* Reading for Interest Series.

PINE, TILLIE S., and LEVINE, JOSEPH. Sounds All Around; illus. by Bernice Myers. Whittlesey, 1959. $2.50. 48p. (3–5)

PIPER, WATTY. Little Engine That Could; retold from the Pony Engine by Mabel C. Bragg; illus. by George and Doris Hauman. Platt & Munk, 1954. $1.25. 28p. (K–1)

PISTORIUS, ANNA. What Butterfly Is It? Follett, 1949. $2. 24p. (2–5)

PODENDORF, ILLA. The True Book of Pebbles and Shells; pictures by Mary Gehr. Childrens Pr., 1954. $2. 47p. (2–4)

—— The True Book of Pets; illus. by Bill Armstrong. Childrens Pr., 1954. $2. 46p. (2–4)

—— The True Book of Rocks and Minerals; pictures by George Rhoads. Childrens Pr., 1958. $2. 48p. (2–4)

—— The True Book of Space; pictures by Robert Borja. Childrens Pr., 1959. $2. 48p. (2–4)

—— The True Book of Trees; illus. by Richard Gates. Childrens Pr., 1954. $2. 43p. (1–3)

—— The True Book of Weeds and Wildflowers; pictures by Mary Gehr. Childrens Pr., 1955. $2. 48p. (1–3)

POLITI, LEO. A Boat for Peppe. Scribner, 1950. $2.50. 30p. (2–4)

—— Juanita. Scribner, 1948. $2.50. 30p. (K–2)

—— Little Leo. Scribner, 1951. $2.50. 28p. (2–4)

—— Pedro, the Angel of Olvera Street. Scribner, 1946. $2.25. 32p. (1–4)

—— Song of the Swallows. Scribner, 1949. $2.75. 30p. (K–2)

POTTER, BEATRIX. Tailor of Gloucester. Warne, 1931. $1. 85p. (K–2)

—— Tale of Peter Rabbit. Warne, 1904. $1. 81p. (K–1)

PURCELL, JOHN WALLACE. The True Book of African Animals; pictures by Katherine Evans. Childrens Pr., 1954. $2. 46p. (2–4)

PYNE, MABLE MANDEVILLE. Little History of the United States. Houghton, 1940. $3.95. 35p. (2–4)

QUINLAN, MYRTLE BANKS. Quinlan Basic Readers. Allyn & Bacon.
First Preprimer: Before Winky. 1950. 68c. (1st PP)
Preprimer: Winky. 1950. 68c. (PP)
Readiness Primer: Happy Days. 1949. $2.04. (Read. P)
Basic Primer: Day by Day. 1949. $2.44. (P)
Book 1: To and Fro. 1950. $2.60. (1)
Book 2: Faces and Places. 1950. $2.88. (2)
Book 3: Busy World. 1949. $2.96. (3)

RAPAPORT, STELLA F. A Whittle Too Much. Putnam, 1955. $2. 46p. (2–4)

READING FOR INTEREST SERIES; educational consultants: Paul Witty and others.
Rev. ed. Heath, 1955.
Preprimer 1: Ned and Nancy, by Inez Hogan. 60c. (PP1)
Preprimer 2: Bigger and Bigger, by Inez Hogan. 60c. (PP2)
Preprimer 3: Little Lost Dog, by Lula Wright. 60c. (PP3)
Preprimer 4: Molly, Pete, and Ginger, by Esther Phillips. 72c. (PP4)
Primer 1: Home for Sandy, by Romney Gay. $1.64. (P)
Primer 2: Rain and Shine, by Ardra Soule Wavle. $1.64. (P)
Book 1: Something Different, by Eva Knox Evans. $1.92. (1)
Book 2–1: Lost and Found, by Robin Palmer. $2.12. (2–1)
Book 2–2: Secrets and Surprises, by Irmengarde Eberle. $2.12. (2–2)
Book 3–1: Fun and Frolic, ed. by Barbara Nolen. $2.28. (3–1)
Book 3–2: Do and Dare, ed. by Barbara Nolen. $2.28. (3–2)

REESE, THELMA KIER, *see* Basic Social Studies Series.

RENICK, MARION LEWIS. Jimmy's Own Basketball; illus. by Pru Herric. Scribner,
1952. $2.50. 119p. (2–4)

――――― Todd's Snow Patrol; illus. by Pru Herric. Scribner, 1955. $2.50. 123p.
(2–4)

REY, HANS AUGUSTO. Cecily G. and the Nine Monkeys. Houghton, 1942. $3.25.
31p. (K–2)

――――― Curious George. Houghton, 1941. $3.25. 55p. (1–3)

――――― Curious George Gets a Medal. Houghton, 1957. $3.25. 47p. (K–2)

――――― Curious George Rides a Bike. Houghton, 1952. $3.25. 48p. (2–4)

――――― Curious George Takes a Job. Houghton, 1947. $3.25. 47p. (1–3)

REYHER, REBECCA HOURWICH. My Mother Is the Most Beautiful Woman in the
World: A Russian Folktale Retold; pictures by Ruth Gannett. Lothrop, 1945.
$2.50. 39p. (1–3)

RICKERT, EDITH. Bojabi Tree; illus. by Anna Braune. Doubleday, 1958. $2. 48p.
(1–3)

ROBINSON, THOMAS PENDELTON, and WIESE, KURT. Mr. Red Squirrel. Viking,
1943. $2.50. 32p. (1–3)

ROBINSON, WILLIAM WILCOX. At the Seashore; pictures by Irene Bowen Robinson.
Macmillan, 1942. $3. 40p. (1–3)

——— and ROBINSON, IRENE BOWEN. Picture Book of Animal Babies. Macmillan, 1947. $3. 40p. (K–1)

ROBISON, ELEANOR, *see* Ginn Enrichment Series.

ROSS, DIANA. The Little Red Engine Gets a Name; pictures by Lewitt-Him. Transatlantic Arts, 1945. $2.50. 32p. (1–4)

ROTHSCHILD, ALICE. Bad Trouble in Miss Alcorn's Class; illus. by Irwin Rosenhouse. W. R. Scott, 1959. $2.75. 101p. (2–4)

ROWAND, PHYLLIS. George. Little, 1956. $2.75. 42p. (K–3)

RUSSELL, BETTY. Big Store—Funny Door; pictures by Mary Gehr. Whitman, 1955. $1.25. 33p. (1–2)

——— Run Sheep, Run; pictures by Mary Gehr. Whitman, 1952. $1.25. 32p. (1–2)

RUSSELL, DAVID HARRIS, and others. Ginn Basic Readers. Rev. ed. Ginn.
My Little Red Story Book. 1957. 64c. (PP1)
My Little Green Story Book. 1957. 64c. (PP2)
My Little Blue Story Book. 1957. 68c. (PP3)
Little White House. 1957. $1.60. (P)
On Cherry Street. 1957. $1.72. (1)
We Are Neighbors. 1957. $1.92. (2–1)
Around the Corner. 1958. $1.92. (2–2)
Finding New Neighbors. 1957. $2.12. (3–1)
Friends Far and Near. 1957. $2.12. (3–2)

SCHLEIN, MIRIAM. Amazing Mr. Pelgrew; illus. by Harvey Weiss. Abelard-Schuman, 1957. $2.75. 48p. (K–2)

——— Deer in the Snow; illus. by Leonard Kessler. Abelard-Schuman, 1956. $2.75. 42p. (K–3)

——— How Do You Travel? pictures by Paul Galdone. Abingdon, 1954. $1.50. 23p. (K–1)

——— Little Rabbit, the High Jumper; illus. by Theresa Sherman. W. R. Scott, 1957. $2.50. 48p. (K–1)

——— Something for Now, Something for Later; illus. by Leonard Weisgard. Harper, 1956. $2.50. 44p. (2–4)

——— When Will the World Be Mine? The Story of a Snowshoe Rabbit; lithographs by Jean Charlot. W. R. Scott, 1953. $2.25. 33p. (K–1)

SCHLOAT, GEORGE WARREN. Playtime for You. Scribner, 1950. $2.75. 63p. (K–2)

——— The Wonderful Egg. Scribner, 1952. $2.75. 46p. (K–5)

SCHNEIDER, HERMAN, and SCHNEIDER, NINA. Heath Elementary Science Series. Heath, 1954.
Grade 1: Science for Work and Play. $2.04. (1)
Grade 2: Science for Here and Now. $2.24. (2)
Grade 3: Science Far and Near. $2.56. (3)

—— How Big Is Big?—From Stars to Atoms; with illus. by Symeon Shimin. Rev. ed. W. R. Scott, 1950. $2.50. 40p. (2–4)

—— Let's Find Out: A Picture Science Book; pictures by Jeanne Bendick. W. R. Scott, 1946. $2.50. 38p. (1–4)

—— Let's Look under the City; illus. by Bill Ballantine. W. R. Scott, 1954. $2. 70p. (2–4)

—— Now Try This; pictures by Bill Ballantine. W. R. Scott, 1947. $2.50. 40p. (2–4)

—— You among the Stars; illus. by Symeon Shimin. W. R. Scott, 1951. $3. 58p. (2–4)

SCHNEIDER, NINA. While Susie Sleeps; pictures by Dagmar Wilson. W. R. Scott, 1948. $2.75. 31p. (K–2)

SCHREIBER, GEORGES. Bambino Goes Home. Viking, 1959. $3. 32p. (2–4)

—— Bambino the Clown. Viking, 1947. $2.50. 30p. (2–4)

SCHWARTZ, ELIZABETH REEDER, and SCHWARTZ, CHARLES. Cottontail Rabbit. Holiday, 1957. $2.50. 46p. (1–3)

SCHWARTZ, JULIUS. Now I Know; pictures by Marc Simont. Whittlesey, 1955. $2.25. 32p. (K–2)

SCOTT, SALLY. Molly and the Tool Shed; illus. by Ellen Segner. Harcourt, 1943. $2.25. 40p. (3)

—— Rip and Royal; pictures by Beth Krush. Harcourt, 1950. $2.25. 58p. (2–4)

—— Tippy; pictures by Beth Krush. Harcourt, 1950. $2.25. 48p. (2–4)

SEARS, PAUL McCUTCHEON. Firefly; illus. by Glen Rounds. Holiday, 1956. $2.50. 37p. (1–4)

—— Tree Frog; illus. by Barbara Latham. Holiday, 1954. $2. 45p. (2–4)

SELSAM, MILLICENT ELLIS. All about Eggs and How They Change into Animals; illus. by Helen Ludwig. W. R. Scott, 1952. $2.50. 64p. (K–2)

—— Nature Detective; pictures by Theresa Sherman. W. R. Scott, 1958. $2.75. 48p. (2–4)

—— Seeds and More Seeds; pictures by Tomi Ungerer. Harper, 1959. $1.95. 62p. (1–3)

—— A Time for Sleep; How the Animals Rest; illus. by Helen Ludwig. W. R. Scott, 1953. $2.25. 58p. (K–5)

SEUSS, DR. And To Think That I Saw It on Mulberry Street. Vanguard, 1937. $2.95. 32p. (K–3)

—— The Cat in the Hat. Random, 1957. $1.95. 61p. (1)

—— The Cat in the Hat Comes Back. Random, 1958. $1.95. 64p. (1)

—— The 500 Hats of Bartholomew Cubbins. Vanguard, 1938. $2.95. 47p. (1–3)

SEWELL, HELEN MOORE. Blue Barns: The Story of Two Big Geese and Seven Little Ducks. Macmillan, 1933. $2.75. 46p. (K–1)

SHACKELFORD, JANE DABNEY. My Happy Days; photographs by Cecil Vinson. Associated Pub., 1944. $2.65. 121p. (1–3)

SHARP, ADDA MAI, and YOUNG, EPSIE. Secret Places; illus. by Elizabeth Rice. Steck, 1955. $1.75. 48p. (1–2)

SHARPE, STELLA GENTRY. Tobe; photographs by Charles Farrell. Univ. of North Carolina Pr., 1939. $2.50. 121p. (1–3)

SHELDON, WILLIAM D., and others. Sheldon Basic Reading Series. Allyn & Bacon, 1957.
  Preprimer: At Home. 60c. (PP1)
  Preprimer: Here and Near. 68c. (PP2)
  Preprimer: Here and Away. 72c. (PP3)
  Senior Preprimer: At Home and Away. $1.52. (SPP)
  Primer: Our School. $1.72. (P)
  Book 1: Our Town. $1.84. (1)
  Book 2: Fields and Fences. $2.04. (2–1)
  Book 2: Town and Country. $2.04. (2–2)
  Book 3: Magic Windows. $2.36. (3–1)
  Book 3: Story Caravan. $2.36. (3–2)

SILVERMAN, MEL. Ciri-biri-bin. World, 1957. $2.50. 40p. (1–3)

SIMON, RUTH CORABEL SHIMER. Mat and Mandy and the Big Dog, Bigger; with pictures by Lisl Weil. Crowell, 1954. $2.50. 93p. (1–2)

SLOBODKIN, LOUIS. Clear the Track for Michael's Magic Train. Macmillan, 1945. $3. 48p. (K–2)

—— Friendly Animals. Vanguard, 1944. $2.95. 25p. (K–2)

—— Horse with the High-heeled Shoes. Vanguard, 1954. $2.95. 30p. (K–1)

—— Magic Michael. Macmillan, 1944. $2.75. 48p. (K–1)

SLOBODKINA, ESPHYR. Caps for Sale: A Tale of a Peddler, Some Monkeys & Their Monkey Business. W. R. Scott, 1947. $2.50. 42p. (K–3)

—— Wonderful Feast. Lothrop, 1955. $2.35. 24p. (K–1)

SMILEY, VIRGINIA KESTER. Little Boy Navajo; pictures by Tom Two Arrows. Abelard-Schuman, 1954. $2.95. 58p. (K–3)

SMITH, J. RUSSELL, and SORENSON, FRANK E. Our Neighbors Geographies. Winston, 1954. $3.52.
  Our Neighbors at Home. (3)

SMITH, MARIE ELIZABETH. Social Learnings Readers. Scribner, 1951.
  Bill's Story of the Wholesale Produce Market. $1.48. (2–4)
  Bob's Story of the Retail Food Market. $1.48. (2–4)
  Joe's Story of the Airport. $1.48. (2–4)
  Mother's Story of Dairying. $1.48. (2–4)

SMITH, VICTOR C., and others. Science for Modern Living Series. Lippincott, 1956.

Grade 1: Science along the Way. $2. (1)
Grade 2: Science under the Sun. $2.20. (2)
Grade 3: Science around the Clock. $2.40. (3)

SOOTIN, LAURA. Let's Go to an Airport; pictures by George Wilde. Putnam, 1957. $1.95. 48p. (2–4)

SORENSEN, CLARENCE WOODROW. Man's Ways and Times Series. Silver Burdett. Ways of Our Land. 1954. $2.60. (3)

STEINER, CHARLOTTE. A Friend Is "Amie." Knopf, 1956. $2.75. 30p. (2–4)

———— Kiki Loves Music. Doubleday, 1954. $1.50. 32p. (K–2)

STOLZ, MARY SLATTERY. Emmett's Pig; pictures by Garth Williams. Harper, 1959. $1.95. 62p. (1–2)

SWIFT, HILDEGARDE HOYT, and WARD, LYND KENDALL. The Little Red Lighthouse and the Great Gray Bridge. Harcourt, 1942. $2.75. 56p. (K–3)

TARRY, ELLEN. The Runaway Elephant; pictures by Oliver Harrington. Viking, 1950. $2. 40p. (2–4)

TENSEN, RUTH MARJORIE. Come to the City. Reilly & Lee, 1951. $2. 37p. (1–2)

———— Come to the Farm. Reilly & Lee, 1949. $2. 35p. (K–2)

THOMAS, ELEANOR, *see* Tiegs-Adams Social Studies Series.

THORN, SAMUEL A., and others. Science and Conservation Series. Benefic, 1957.
Preprimer: Let's Go. $1.36. (PP)
Primer: Let's Try. $1.52. (P)
Grade 1: Let's Find Out. $1.68. (1)
Grade 2: Let's Look Around. $1.92. (2)
Grade 3: Let's See Why. $2. (3)

THURBER, WALTER A. Exploring Science Series. Allyn & Bacon, 1955.
Exploring Science One. $2.12. (1)
Exploring Science Two. $2.28. (2)
Exploring Science Three. $2.40. (3)

TIEGS-ADAMS SOCIAL STUDIES SERIES. Ginn, 1960.
Stories about Linda and Lee, by Eleanor Thomas. $2.32. (1)
Stories about Sally, by Eleanor Thomas. $2.48. (2)
Your Town and Mine, by Eleanor Thomas. $2.16. (3)

TITUS, EVA. Anatole; pictures by Paul Galdone. Whittlesey, 1956. $2.50. 32p. (K–3)

———— Anatole and the Cat; pictures by Paul Galdone. Whittlesey, 1957. $2.50. 32p. (K–2)

TOBA SOJO. The Animal Frolic. Putnam, 1954. $2.75. 48p. (K–3)

TRESSELT, ALVIN R. Autumn Harvest; illus. by Roger Duvoisin. Lothrop, 1951. $2.75. 23p. (1–3)

———— Follow the Wind; illus. by Roger Duvoisin. Lothrop, 1950. $2.75. 26p. (K–2)

—— "Hi, Mister Robin"; illus. by Roger Duvoisin. Lothrop, 1950. $2.75. 26p. (K–2)

—— I Saw the Sea Come In; illus. by Roger Duvoisin. Lothrop, 1954. $2.75. 24p. (K–1)

—— Sun Up; pictures by Roger Duvoisin. Lothrop, 1949. $2.75. 26p. (K–2)

—— Wake Up, Farm! illus. by Roger Duvoisin. Lothrop, 1955. $2.75. 30p. (K–1)

—— White Snow, Bright Snow; illus. by Roger Duvoisin. Lothrop, 1947. $2.75. 33p. (K–2)

TRUE, BARBARA, and HENRY, MARGUERITE. Their First Igloo on Baffin Island; illus. by Gladys Rourke Blackwood. Whitman, 1943. $1.75. 28p. (1–3)

TUDOR, TASHA. Dolls' Christmas. Walck, 1950. $2.50. 29p. (1–4)

—— Pumpkin Moonshine. Walck, 1938. $1.75. 41p. (K–2)

—— Tale for Easter. Walck, 1941. $2.75. 33p. (K–2)

—— Thistly B. Walck, 1949. $2.50. 27p. (K–2)

TURPIN, EDNA HENRY LEE. Three Circus Days; pictures by George and Doris Hauman. Macmillan, 1935. $2.50. 96p. (1–3)

UDRY, JANICE MAY. A Tree Is Nice; pictures by Marc Simont. Harper, 1956. $2.50. 32p. (K–2)

UNGERER, TOMI. The Mellops Go Diving for Treasure. Harper, 1957. $2. 32p. (K–1)

UNITED NATIONS. Department of Public Information. A Garden We Planted Together. Whittlesey, 1952. $2. 48p. (2–4)

UNWIN, NORA S. Poquito, the Little Mexican Duck. McKay, 1959. $2.75. 32p. (1–3)

URELL, CATHERINE, and others. The Big City Series. Follett.
  The Big City Book of Conservation. 1956. $3. (3)
  Big City Fun. 1953. $3. (3)
  Big City Homes. 1954. $3. (3)
  Big City Neighbors. 1955. $3. (3)
  Big City Water Supply. 1953. $3. (3)
  Big City Workers. 1953. $3. (3)

VREEKEN, ELIZABETH. The Boy Who Would Not Say His Name; illus. by Leonard Shortall. Follett, 1959. $1. 29p. (2–4)

WALPOLE, ELLEN WALES. Golden Dictionary; illus. by Gertrude Elliot. Simon & Schuster, 1944. $2.95. 94p. (K–3)

WALTERS, MARGUERITE. The Real Santa Claus; illus. by Meg Wohlberg. Lothrop, 1950. $2. 31p. (K–2)

WARD, LYND KENDALL. The Biggest Bear. Houghton, 1952. $3. 84p. (K–3)

WARD, NANDA WEEDON. Black Sombrero; pictures by Lynd Ward. Farrar, 1952. $1.75. 27p. (K–1)

WATTERS, GARNETTE, and COURTIS, STUART. The Picture Dictionary for Children; completely rev. and with new pictures by Doris and Marion Henderson and Barry Bart. Grosset, 1948. $1.95. 383p. (1–6)

WATTS, MABEL. A Cow in the House; illus. by Katherine Evans. Follett, 1956. $2. 31p. (K–2)

—— Patchwork Kilt; illus. by Winifred Bromhall. Dutton, 1954. $2.75. 42p. (1–3)

WAVLE, ARDRA SOULE, *see* Reading for Interest Series.

WEBB, ADDISON. Song of the Seasons; illus. by Charles L. Ripper. Morrow, 1950. $2.75. 127p. (2–4)

WEBB, CLIFFORD. Animals from Everywhere. Warne, 1952. $2.75. 64p. (K–2)

WEBB, MARIAN AGNES. Games for Younger Children. Morrow, 1947. $2.75. 124p. (K–2)

WEBBER, IRMA ELEANOR SCHMIDT. Bits That Grow Big: Where Plants Come From. W. R. Scott, 1949. $2.25. 64p. (1–3)

—— Travelers All: The Story of How Plants Go Places. W. R. Scott, 1957. $1.75. 32p. (1–3)

—— Up Above and Down Below. W. R. Scott, 1957. $1.75. 31p. (1–3)

WEIL, LISL. I Wish, I Wish. Houghton, 1957. $2.75. 40p. (K–2)

WEISGARD, LEONARD. Whose Little Bird Am I? Crowell, 1944. $1. 39p. (1–3)

WERNER, JANE. The Golden Picture Book of Words: How They Look and What They Tell; pictures by Cornelius De Witt. Simon & Schuster, 1954. $1.50. 64p. (1–3)

WHIPPLE, GERTRUDE, and JAMES, PRESTON E. Basal Geographies. Macmillan. Our Earth. Rev. 1954. $3.28. (3)

WIESE, KURT. Fish in the Air. Viking, 1948. $2.50. 26p. (2–4)

—— You Can Write Chinese. Viking, 1945. $2. 64p. (2–4)

WILCOX, CHARLOTTE E., and others. Health Action Series. Benefic, 1955.
  Grade 1: Come On. $1.60. (1)
  Grade 2: Here We Go. $1.76. (2)
  Grade 3: Step Lively. $1.92. (3)

WILL and NICOLAS. Chaga. Harcourt, 1955. $2.50. 40p. (K–2)

—— Circus Ruckus. Harcourt, 1954. $2.75. 44p. (1–3)

—— Even Steven. Harcourt, 1952. $2.50. 48p. (K–3)

—— Finders Keepers. Harcourt, 1951. $2.95. 28p. (2–4)

WILLIAMS, GARTH. The Golden Animal ABC. Simon & Schuster, 1954. $1.25. 24p. (K–1)

WITTY, PAUL, *see* Reading for Interest Series.

WOOLLEY, CATHERINE. David's Railroad; illus. by Iris Beatty Johnson. Morrow, 1949. $2.75. 159p. (2–4)

―――― I Like Trains; illus. by Doris Spiegel. Harper, 1944. $1.75. 32p. (1–3)

WRIGHT, ETHEL BELLE, and ROSE, RICHARD. Saturday Walk. W. R. Scott, 1954. $2. 32p. (K–2)

WRIGHT, LULA, *see* Reading for Interest Series.

WRIGHT, WENDELL WILLIAM, ed., assisted by Helene Laird. Rainbow Dictionary; illus. by Joseph Low. World, 1947. $4.95. 433p. (2–4)

WYNKOOP, MARGARET L. Mac Goes to School; photographs by Robert Yarnall Richie. Doubleday, 1942. $2.50. 40p. (1–3)

YLLA, illus. Animal Babies; story by Arthur Gregor; designed by Luc Bouchage. Harper, 1959. $2.75. 37p. (K–2)

YOAKAM, GERALD A., and others. Laidlaw Basic Readers. Laidlaw, 1955.
Primer: On the Way to Storyland. $1.52. (P)
Book I: Making Storybook Friends. $1.52. (1)
Book II: Stories We Like. $2.16. (2)
Book III: Children Everywhere. $2.36. (3)

ZAFFO, GEORGE J. The Big Book of Real Building and Wrecking Machines. Grosset, 1951. $1. 24p. (2–4)

―――― The Big Book of Real Fire Engines. Grosset, 1950. $1. 22p. (K–3)

―――― The Big Book of Real Trains. Grosset, 1949. $1. 24p. (1–5)

ZIM, HERBERT SPENCER. Elephants; pictures by Joy Buba. Morrow, 1946. $2.50. 63p. (2–4)

―――― Goldfish; pictures by Joy Buba. Morrow, 1947. $2.50. 64p. (2–5)

ZION, EUGENE. All Falling Down; pictures by Margaret Bloy Graham. Harper, 1951. $2.50. 26p. (K–1)

―――― Dear Garbage Man; pictures by Margaret Bloy Graham. Harper, 1957. $2.50. 32p. (K–1)

―――― Harry the Dirty Dog; illus. by Margaret Bloy Graham. Harper, 1956. $2.50. 28p. (K–1)

―――― The Plant Sitter; pictures by Margaret Bloy Graham. Harper, 1959. $2.50. 32p. (K–3)

―――― Really Spring; pictures by Margaret Bloy Graham. Harper, 1956. $2.50. 32p. (K–1)

―――― The Summer Snowman; pictures by Margaret Bloy Graham. Harper, 1955. $2.50. 32p. (K–2)

ZOLOTOW, CHARLOTTE S. Indian Indian; pictures by Leonard Weisgard. Simon & Schuster, 1952. 25c. 28p. (K–1)

―――― One Step, Two . . . ; illus. by Roger Duvoisin. Lothrop, 1955. $2.50. 30p. (K–1)

―――― Park Book; pictures by H. A. Rey. Harper, 1944. $2.50. 32p. (K–1)

―――― The Storm Book; illus. by Margaret Bloy Graham. Harper, 1952. $2.50. 32p. (K–3)

SUBJECT INDEX
TO BOOKS
FOR PRIMARY GRADES

ACORNS: *see also* Oak Trees; Seeds
Buff, Dash and Dart, p.48–53
RA; In (3)

ADAMS, JOHN QUINCY
Leavell, Open Roads, p.142–47   *3

ADOPTION
Haywood, Here's a Penny, p.3–18,
131–45   *In (3)

AFRICA: *see also* Egypt
Association for Childhood Education,
Told under the Magic Umbrella,
p.3–49, 101-12 (Bojabi Tree)
*RA

Carpenter, Our Little Neighbors at
Work and Play: Here, There,
Then, and Now, p.194–201   3+

Hildreth, Faraway Ports, p.76–81
*3–1

O'Donnell, If I Were Going, p.270–
73, *274–328   Basic 3

Purcell, True Book of African Animals   In (3)

Rickert, Bojabi Tree   *RA; In (3)

AGRICULTURE: *see* Animals, Domestic; Barns; Farm Life; Food;
Soils

AIR
Barnard, Macmillan Science-Life Series, Bk.1, p.86–90   1

—— Macmillan Science-Life Series, Bk.2, p.58–61   2

Craig, Science around You, p.24–39
2

—— Science Everywhere, p.87–95
3

—— Science near You, p.43–49
1

Dowling, New Seeing Why, p.113–36
2

Frasier, Science—All the Year, p.61–
72   2

—— Science—For You, p.68–79
1

—— We Wonder, p.27   PP

Schneider, H., Let's Find Out, p.28–
38   In (3)

—— Science for Work and Play,
p.145–49   1

Thorn, Let's Find Out, p.29–31   1

—— Let's Look Around, p.71–
81   2

AIRPLANES
Betts, ABC All in a Day, p.26–29
(carnival)   PP3

—— ABC Beyond Treasure Valley, p.208–15   *3–1

—— ABC Time To Play, p.34–37;
52–57 (toy)   PP2

Bond, G. L., Ride with Us, p.58–61
PP4

Cavanah, Our Country's Story, p.66–
67   In (3)

Eberle, Secrets and Surprises, p.210–
18   2–2
Gates, Friends and Fun, p.149–68
(helicopter)   *Alt. 2
────── Good Times Today, p.96–
102   *3–1
────── New Friends and New Places,
p.59–78 (helicopter)   *2–2
────── Today We Go, p.162–71
                                 *2–1
Gramatky, Loopy   *RA
Gray, New Streets and Roads, p.106–
13   *3–1
Hildreth, At Play, p.69   P–1
────── I Know a Secret, p.132–37
                                 *1–1
Johnson, E. M., Treat Shop, p.155–
63   *3
Lenski, Little Airplane *RA (K–2)
Lewellen, Tommy Learns To Fly
                                 *In (3)
McIntire, Working Together, p.153–
61   3
Mitchell, Animals, Plants, and Ma-
chines, p.144–47   2
────── Another Here and Now Story
Book, p.175–78   *RA
Nolen, Do and Dare, p.3–11   *3–2
Norling, Pogo's Sky Ride   *In (3)
O'Donnell, High on a Hill, p.32–40
                                 *PP4
Palmer, Lost and Found, p.214–33
                                 *2–1
Quinlan, Faces and Places, p.210–13,
221–29   2
────── To and Fro, p.3–16   *1
Russell, D. H., Around the Corner,
p.102–20, 126–31   *2–2
────── My Little Blue Story Book,
p.3–18   *PP3
Sheldon, Here and Away, p.59–62
                                 *PP3
────── Town and Country, p.43–54,
71–74   *2–2

Smith, M. E., Joe's Story of the Air-
port   2+
Smith, V. C., Science around the
Clock, p.129–37   3
Thomas, Stories about Sally, p.67–71
                                 2

AIRPLANES—MODELS
Gray, New More Streets and Roads,
p.41–50   *3–2

AIRPORTS
Colonius, At the Airport   In (3)
Eberle, Secrets and Surprises, p.122–
38   2–2
Frasier, Science—All the Year, p.6–
7   2
Hunnicutt, I Have Friends, p.160–65
                                 2
────── I Know People, p.102–16   3
McIntire, Working Together, p.153–
60   3
Palmer, Lost and Found, p.220–28
                                 *2–1
Quinlan, Faces and Places, p.214–
19   2
────── To and Fro, p.3–5   *1
Reese, Basic Social Studies, p.118–
25   2
Russell, D. H., Around the Corner,
p.121–25   *2–2
Smith, M. E., Joe's Story of the Air-
port   2+
Sootin, Let's Go to an Airport
                                 In (3)
Sorensen, Ways of Our Land, p.150–
53   3
Thomas, Stories about Sally, p.67–
9   2

ALASKA
Johnson, M. S., Smallest Puppy
                                 *In (3)

ALPHABET BOOKS: *see also* Dic-
tionaries; Words
Adams, ABC Picture Book   In (1)
Duvoisin, A for the Ark   RA (K–1)

Gág, ABC Bunny RA (K–1); In (2)
McGinley, All around the Town
                         RA (K–2)
Petersham, American ABC   In (3)
Williams, Golden Animal ABC
                         RA (K–1)

AMERICAN REVOLUTION: *see also* Adams, John Quincy; Fourth of July; United States—History; Washington, George
Cavanah, Our Country's Story, p.26–31   In (3)

ANIMAL TRACKS
Deming, Little Eagle, p.68–69, 76
                         *In (2)
Lathrop, Who Goes There?   In (3)
Selsam, Nature Detective   In (3)
Thurber, Exploring Science Three, p.76–82   3

ANIMALS: *see also* Hibernation; Pets; Zoos; also names of groups of animals, as Birds
Association for Childhood Education, Told under the Magic Umbrella
                         *RA
Baker, A. O., In Your Neighborhood, p.18–25   3
Barnard, Macmillan Science-Life Series, Bk.2, p.106–11, 115, 127–37   2
——— Macmillan Science-Life Series, Bk.3, p.19–23, 53   3
Beauchamp, All around Us, p.3–28   2
——— How Do We Know? p.3–36   3
——— Look and Learn, p.3–24   1
Betts, ABC Along Friendly Roads, p.89–104, 299–306   *3–2
——— ABC Beyond Treasure Valley, p.162–76   *3–1
——— ABC Over a City Bridge, p.155–60, 243–47   *2–2

Bond, A. D., Knowing about Science, p.39–40 (hamsters), 41–44, 172–89   3
——— Looking at Science, p.64–77   1
——— Thinking about Science, p.55–79, 155–65   2
Bond, G. L., Down Our Way, p.88–126, 242–47   *2–1
——— Happy Times, p.158–85   *1
——— Once upon a Storytime, p.64–98   *3–2
Brock, To Market! To Market!
                       *RA (K–2)
Brown, M. W., Big Red Barn
                       *RA (K–1)
Clark, A. N., In My Mother's House
                    *RA; In (2)
Craig, Science around You, p.18–21, 66–69, 92–97, 100–1, 136–37   2
——— Science Everywhere, p.4–45
                          3
——— Science near You, p.10–23, 88–91   1
Deming, Indians in Winter Camp
                       In (3)
——— Little Eagle   *In (2)
Dowling, New Learning Why, p.65–69, 191–217   3
——— New Seeing Why, p.67–75 (growth)   2
Duvoisin, A for the Ark RA (K–1)
Ets, In the Forest   *RA
——— Mister Penny   *RA
Flack, Ask Mr. Bear   *RA (K–2)
Foster, Tell Me Little Boy
                    *RA; In (2)
Frasier, Science—Adventures, p.67–85, 182–204   3
——— Science—All the Year, p.36–38, 41–42, 45–54, 109–17, 144–85   2
——— Science—For You, p.40–46, 138–57   1
——— We Ask, p.30–33   P

———— We Wonder, p.7–8, 10–11, 28–29   PP

Gall, All the Year Round   In (3)

———— Here and There and Everywhere   In (2)

Gates, On Four Feet, p.93–105 (Baby Monkey and the Elephant)   *1

Gray, New Friends and Neighbors, p.78–176   *2–1

———— New More Friends and Neighbors, p.206–35   *2–2

———— New More Streets and Roads, p.98–127, 135–43   *3–2

———— New Our New Friends, p. 156–84   *1–2

———— New Streets and Roads, p. 124–86 (Ride to Animal Town; Tippy Elephant's Hat; Sojo; Noisy Mr. Redhead; Story of White Satin; Brother Rabbit and Tar Baby; Paddy's Christmas), 188–248   *3–1

Gruenberg, Favorite Stories Old and New   *RA

Hader, Runaways   *RA; In (2)

Hogan, World Round   RA; In (2)

Humphreys, Zoo Book   RA

Irwin, Growing Day by Day, p.12–15, 30–35   2

———— Keeping Fit for Fun, p.62–66 (circus)   3

Johnson, E. M., Treat Shop, p.8–11 (horse), p.28–71, 150–54   *3

Knox, Wonderworld of Science, Bk. 2, p.7–56, 111–50   2

Lathrop, Animals of the Bible   RA

McKee, Climbing Higher, p.256–67   3–2

———— Come Along, p.40–58 (kangaroo)   *2–1

———— Looking Ahead, p.272–81 (fox)   *3–1

———— Up and Away, p.6–52   *1–2

Miller, Little Red Hen   *RA (K–1); In (2)

Mitchell, Animals, Plants, and Machines, p.3–12   *2

Nolen, Do and Dare, p.46–74, 156–60 (How the Leopard Chose a Prince), 161–74, 187–94, 210–20   *3–2

———— Fun and Frolic, p.3–9, 19–98, 213–25, 244–65 (Tortoise and the Elephant; Elephant and the Whale; Monkey and the Crocodile), 266–72   *3–1

O'Donnell, Day In and Day Out, p.78–104   *Basic P

O'Keefe, How We Grow, p.1–10 (farm), 11–18 (circus)   3

Petersham, Box with Red Wheels   *RA (K–1); In (2)

Purcell, True Book of African Animals   In (3)

Rickert, Bojabi Tree   *RA; In (3)

Robinson, W. W., Picture Book of Animal Babies   RA (K–1)

Russell, D. H., Around the Corner, p.162–88, 200–14   *2–2

———— Friends Far and Near, p. 110–17 (Rabbit and the Pine Gum Wolf)   *3–2

———— On Cherry Street, p.174–219   *1

———— We Are Neighbors, p.123–32, 150–62   *2–1

Schlein, How Do You Travel?   RA (K–1)

———— When Will the World Be Mine?   *RA (K–1)

Schneider, H., How Big Is Big?   In (3)

———— Science Far and Near, p.24–30 (desert)   3

———— Science for Here and Now, p.164–73   *2

Selsam, All about Eggs   RA (K–1); In (2)

———— Time for Sleep   RA; In (3)

Sharp, Secret Places   In (2)

Sheldon, Magic Windows, p.117–54, 237–51 (jackal and alligator), 252–67 (bears) *3–1
—— Story Caravan, p.192–232 (Eddie and Gardenia) *3–2
—— Town and Country, p.76–126, 189–97 (deer) *2–2
Thorn, Let's Find Out, p.55–9, 103–6 1
Webb, C., Animals from Everywhere RA (K–2)
Whipple, Our Earth, p.107–11 3
Williams, Golden Animal ABC RA (K–1)
Ylla, Animal Babies RA
Yoakam, Making Storybook Friends, p.30–45, 48–53 (Bee and the Goats; Timid Rabbit), 56–65 (Mouse Sisters), 68–89, 99–103, 106–11 (Red Hen and Sly Fox), 112–25 (Peter Rabbit) *1

ANIMALS—CARE: *see also* Animals —Houses; Cats—Care; Dogs— Care and Training; Kindness to Animals; Pets—Care
Barnard, Macmillan Science-Life Series, Bk.1, p.45 1
—— Macmillan Science-Life Series, Bk.2, p.127–28 2
—— Macmillan Science-Life Series, Bk.3, p.24–30 3
Craig, Science around You, p.134 2
—— Science near You, p.16–23 2

ANIMALS—CHARACTERISTICS
Barnard, Macmillan Science-Life Series, Bk.3, p.114–16 (eyes) 3
Craig, Science Everywhere, p.5–28, 31–37, 39–45 3

ANIMALS—FEEDING
Baker, A. O., Around the Corner, p.14–15 2
Craig, Science Everywhere, p.31–37 3

Gray, New Friends and Neighbors, p.219–24 *2–1
—— New Our New Friends, p.114–18 *1–2
Irwin, Keeping Fit for Fun, p.62–66 3
Robinson, T. P., Mr. Red Squirrel *In (2)
Slobodkina, Wonderful Feast RA (K–1)
Smith, V. C., Science under the Sun, p.16–21, 24–27 2

ANIMALS—HOUSES: *see also* Aquariums; Bird Houses
Barnard, Macmillan Science-Life Series, Bk.1, p.104–7 1
Craig, Science around You, p.136–37 2
—— Science near You, p.10–15 1
Dowling, New Seeing Why, p.90–95 2
Frasier, Science—All the Year, p.165–80 2
Hildreth, Faraway Ports, p.98–105 3–1

ANIMALS—PICTURES
Slobodkin, Friendly Animals RA (K–1)
Toba Sojo, Animal Frolic RA

ANIMALS—PROTECTION: *see also* Animals—Care; Birds—Protection; Pets—Care
Baker, A. O., Around the Corner, p.21 2
Craig, Science Everywhere, p.39–45 3
Frasier, Science—Adventures, p.80–85 3
Knox, Wonderworld of Science, Bk.2, p.31–33 2

ANIMALS, DOMESTIC: *see also* Animals—Care; Dairy; Kindness to Animals; Pets; also names of domestic animals, as Dogs

Blough, Useful Plants and Animals, p.3–12, 16–19   3

Knox, Wonderworld of Science, Bk.2, p.144–48   2

Lewellen, True Book of Farm Animals   In (2)

ANIMALS, PREHISTORIC: *see also* Dinosaurs; Fossils

Bond, A. D., Knowing about Science, p.57–73   3

ANIMALS, WILD

Baker, A. O., Around the Corner, p.16–20   2

Bond, G. L., Happy Times, p.91–95, 142–48   *1

ANIMALS IN WINTER: *see also* Hibernation

Blough, Animals round the Year, p.20–25   3

Bond, A. D., Knowing about Science, p.32–38, 41–44   3

Bond, G. L., Happy Times, p.108–13   1

Buff, Dash and Dart, p.34–57   RA; In (3)

Craig, Science around You, p.66–69   2

Frasier, Science—Adventures, p.71–74   3

Gates, Good Times Today and Tomorrow, p.111–13   *Alt. 3

Knox, Wonderworld of Science, Bk.2, p.50–55   *2

Schneider, H., Science for Here and Now, p.101–8   2

Sheldon, Fields and Fences, p.99–105, 128–34   *2–1

Thurber, Exploring Science Three, p.76–92   3

Yoakam, Stories We Like, p.178–83   2

ANTS

Barnard, Macmillan Science-Life Series, Bk.1, p.106–7   1

Blough, Animals That Live Together, p.25–31   3

Bond, G. L., Down Our Way, p.237–41   *2–1

Gruenberg, Favorite Stories Old and New   *RA

Huntington, Let's Go Outdoors, p.30–37   In (3)

Thorn, Let's See Why, p.132–36   3

APARTMENT HOUSES

Haywood, Two and Two Are Four, p.3–13   *In (3)

Hunnicutt, I Live with Others, p.108–14   1

McIntire, Working Together, p.28–29   3

Mitchell, Farm and City, p.80–83   1

——— Our Country, p.102–5   3

Palmer, Lost and Found, p.59–76   *2–1

Russell, D. H., Around the Corner, p.31–35   *2–2

Urell, Big City Homes, p.6–8, 16–21 (building)   3+

APPLE TREES

Gates, Two Boys and a Tree   *Sup. 1

Hildreth, Story Road, p.92–100   *2–2

Russell, D. H., Friends Far and Near, p.22–31   *3–2

Thorn, Let's Look Around, p.115–19   2

APPLES

Betts, ABC Beyond Treasure Valley, p.266–73   *3–1

Gray, New Friends and Neighbors, p.192–96   2–1

McIntire, Working Together, p.46–51   *3

Ousley, Come with Us, p.27–30   *Pre-P

Russell, D. H., My Little Green Story Book, p.12–14   *PP2

Smith, J. R., Our Neighbors at Home, p.51–58, 60–64   3

APRIL FOOL'S DAY
  Child Study Association of America,
    Holiday Storybook   *RA
  Sheldon, Story Caravan, p.89–105
                                 *3–2

AQUARIUMS: *see also* Fish; Gold-
    fish; Snails
  Barnard, Macmillan Science-Life Se-
    ries, Bk.2, p.20–24   2
  ——— Macmillan Science-Life Se-
    ries, Bk.3, p.44–52   3
  Blough, Aquarium   3
  Dowling, New Seeing Why, p.100–
    11   2
  Frasier, Science—All the Year, p.168–
    73   2
  Schneider, H., Science Far and Near,
    p.172–79   3
  Thorn, Let's Look Around, p.83–85
                                   2

AQUEDUCTS
  Urell, Big City Water Supply, p.18–
    19   3+

ARBOR DAY: *see also* Trees; also
    names of trees, as Oak Trees
  Burkhardt, Our Home and School,
    p.109–15   1
  Child Study Association of America,
    Holiday Storybook   *RA
  Thorn, Let's See Why, p.127–29   3

ARITHMETIC: *see also* Numbers
  Leaf, Arithmetic Can Be Fun In (3)

ARMISTICE DAY
  Child Study Association of America,
    Holiday Storybook   *RA

ART: *see also* Color; Painting
  Cohn, Little People in a Big Country
                                 *RA
  Freeman, D., Norman the Doorman
                                 *RA
  Massoglia, Fun-Time Paper Folding
                                  RA
  Toba Sojo, Animal Frolic   RA

ART MUSEUMS
  Freeman, D., Norman the Doorman
                                 *RA
ARTISTS
  Gruenberg, Favorite Stories Old and
    New, p.253–56 (Boy Who Drew
    Cats)   *RA
ASTRONOMY: *see also* Earth; Gravi-
    tation; Moon; Seasons; Sky; Stars;
    Sun; Tides
  Baker, A. O., In Your Neighborhood,
    p.81–88   3
  Frasier, Science—Adventures, p.86–
    118   3
  ——— Science—For You, p.8–13,
    86–89   1
AUSTRALIA
  Gruenberg, Favorite Stories Old and
    New, p.121–27 (Karoo, the Kan-
    garoo)   *RA
AUSTRIA
  Bemelmans, Hansi   *RA
  Kahl, Away Went Wolfgang   *RA
AUTOMOBILES: *see also* Buses; Fill-
    ing Stations; Garages; Trucks
  Beim, J., Twelve o'Clock Whistle
                                 *RA
  Evans, Something Different, p.72–96
                                  *1
  Lenski, Little Auto
                        *RA (K–1); In (2)
  McIntire, Working Together, p.134–
    37   3
  Mitchell, Another Here and Now
    Story Book   *RA
  ——— Farm and City, p.98–101   1
  Monroe, New We Three, p.40–44 *1
  O'Donnell, Round About, p.89–97
                             *Basic 1
  Ousley, Open the Gate, p.116–20
                               *Pre–2
  Russell, D. H., Friends Far and Near,
    p.260–68   *3–2

AUTOMOBILES—TRAILERS
Bond, G. L., Down Our Way, p.36–42 *2–1
Cutright, Living Together Today and Yesterday, p.53–61 3
Hildreth, Faraway Ports, p.152–83 *3–1
McIntire, Working Together, p.30–32 3
Nolen, Do and Dare, p.12–21 *3–2
Sheldon, Our Town, p.30–36 *1

AUTUMN
Association for Childhood Education, Told under the Blue Umbrella, p.18–20 *RA
Baker, A. O., Around the Corner, p.113–18 2
——— In Your Neighborhood, p.150–54 3
Blough, Animals round the Year, p.3–13, 18–19 3
Bond, A. D., Getting Ready, p.59–79 P
Craig, Science around You, p.12–22 2
Frasier, Science—All the Year, p.35–54 2
——— We Wonder, p.18 PP
Gates, Two Boys and a Tree, p.38–40 *Sup. 1
Knox, Wonderworld of Science, Bk.3, p.29–31 3
O'Donnell, Round About, p.72–74 *Basic 1
Parker, Fall Is Here 1
Quinlan, To and Fro, p.174–78 *1
Schneider, H., Science for Here and Now, p.29–31 2
Smith, V. C., Science along the Way, p.89–91 1
Tresselt, Autumn Harvest RA; In (3)

BABIES
Hanna, At School, p.12–16 1

Mitchell, Farm and City, p.141–44 1
Newberry, T-Bone, the Baby Sitter *RA; In (3)

BABIES—CARE
Flack, New Pet *RA
Hill, Jack o'Lantern for Judy Jo *In (3)
O'Donnell, Friendly Village, p.12–15 *Basic 2
Russell, D. H., Friends Far and Near, p.76–84 *3–2

BABOONS: *see also* Monkeys
Bond, G. L., Stories from Everywhere, p.50–60 3–1

BACON, SIR FRANCIS
Dowling, New Learning Why, p.135–38 3

BACTERIA: *see* Germs

BAKERS—TRUCKS
Russell, D. H., We Are Neighbors, p.183–86 *2–1

BAKERY: *see also* Bread; Factories and Mills; Stores
Burkhardt, Our Neighborhood, p.39–44 *2
Hugley, Around the Home, p.55–57 3
Thomas, Stories about Sally, p.86–91 2

BALANCE OF NATURE: *see* Aquariums

BALL: *see also* Baseball; Basketball; Football; Playing Ball
Bond, G. L., Fun with Us, p.17–26 *PP3
Brownell, All Day, Every Day, p.17–21 1
——— Come Rain, Come Shine, p.69–72 3
Hunnicutt, I Live with Others, p.30–34 1

McKee, Big Show, p.2–19   *PP3
Monroe, New We Three, p.61–65 *1
Russell, D. H., My Little Green Story
  Book, p.34–36, 44–46   *PP2
Sheldon, Here and Away, p.43–46
  (water)   *PP3

BALLOONS
Betts, ABC Over a City Bridge, p.24–
  29   *2–2
——— ABC Up the Street and
  Down, p.139–43   P
Gay, R., Home for Sandy, p.64–74
                                *P–1
Nolen, Fun and Frolic, p.172–79
                                *3–1

BANKS AND BANKING: *see also*
  Money
Monroe, New We Three, p.23–27
  (piggy bank)   *1
Thomas, Your Town and Mine,
  p.54–56   3

BARNACLES
Huntington, Let's Go to the Seashore,
  p.64–71   In (3)

BARNS
Association for Childhood Educa-
  tion, Told under the Blue Um-
  brella, p.120–25   *RA
Brown, M. W., Big Red Barn
                            *RA (K–1)
Smith, M. E., Mother's Story of
  Dairying, p.16–23   P

BASEBALL: *see also* Ball; Basketball;
  Football; Playing Ball
Betts, ABC Over a City Bridge,
  p.188–94 (baseball)   *2–2
Russell, D. H., Around the Corner,
  p.64–69 (baseball)   *2–2
——— Finding New Neighbors,
  p.208–16 (sandlot)   *3–1

BASEBALL FIELDS
Betts, ABC Over a City Bridge,
  p.182–87 (vacant lot)   *2–2

BASKETBALL: *see also* Ball; Baseball;
  Football; Playing Ball
Renick, Jimmy's Own Basketball
                              *In (3)

BASKETS AND BASKETRY
Clark, A. N., Little Indian Basket
  Maker   RA; In (2)

BATHS: *see* Cleanliness

BATS
O'Donnell, Neighbors on the Hill,
  p.149–54   *Par. 2
Thorn, Let's See Why, p.29–32   3

BEARS
Association for Childhood Education,
  Told under the Green Umbrella
  (Scrapefoot)   *RA
Baker, A. O., Around the Corner,
  p.18–20   *2
Betts, ABC Around Green Hills,
  p.30–35   *1
——— ABC Beyond Treasure Val-
  ley, p.258–65   *3–1
Bond, G. L., Happy Times, p.108–9,
  113–47   *1
——— Just for Fun, p.21–29, *122–
  30, 143–54   *2–2
Buff, Dash and Dart, p.27–33, 62–
  63   RA; In (3)
Charushin, Baby Bears   In (3)
Du Bois, Bear Party   *RA (K–2)
Gates, Good Times Today, p.230–
  40 (Tuffy Bear's Sugar Party)
                                *3–1
Goudey, Here Come the Bears!
                              In (3)
Gray, New Friends and Neighbors,
  p.138–41, 158–62   *2–1
——— New More Friends and
  Neighbors, p.206–9   *2–2
——— New More Streets and Roads,
  p.160–66   *3–2
——— New Streets and Roads,
  p.220–25   *3–1

Gruenberg, Favorite Stories Old and New, p.83–85 (from Max)   *RA

Hildreth, Fun in Story, p.60–76   *P–2

—————— I Know a Secret, p.65–77, 81–91, 167–83   *1–1

—————— Story Road, p.130–37   *2–2

Hutchinson, Chimney Corner Stories (Three Bears)   *RA

Johnson, E. M., Treat Shop, p.254–60   *3

Krauss, Bears   *RA (K–1)

Leavell, Open Roads, p.50–56 (wooden)   *3

McCloskey, Blueberries for Sal   *RA (K–2)

McClung, Major; The Story of a Black Bear   In (3)

Minarik, Father Bear Comes Home   *In (1–2)

—————— Little Bear   *In (1)

O'Donnell, Five-and-a-Half Club, p.176–88   *Par. 3

Ousley, Open the Gate, p.49–55   *Pre–2

Quinlan, Busy World, p.30–38   *3

Robison, Fun and Fancy, p.87–95   Pre–4

Russell, D. H., Around the Corner, p.200–7   *2–2

—————— Finding New Neighbors, p.110–17   *3–1

—————— On Cherry Street, p.215–19   *1

Sheldon, Fields and Fences, p.151–58   *2–1

—————— Magic Windows, p.252–67   *3–1

—————— Our Town, p.172–77 (toy)   *1

Ward, L. K., Biggest Bear   *RA; In (3)

Yoakam, Stories We Like, p.178–83   2

BEAVERS

Blough, Animals That Live Together, p.14–24   3

Bond, G. L., Stories from Everywhere, p.176–206   *3–1

Burton, W. H., Our Good Neighbors, p.237–44   3

Gray, New Streets and Roads, p.234–40 (from Beaver Twins)   *3–1

Russell, D. H., Around the Corner, p.169–72   *2–2

BEDTIME

Association for Childhood Education, Told under the Blue Umbrella, p.13–16   *RA

Barnard, Macmillan Science-Life Series, Bk.1, p.115–20   1

Bauer, Being Six, p.92–97   1

—————— From Eight to Nine, p.128–30   3

—————— Seven or So, p.64–67   2

Brownell, All Day, Every Day, p.47–48, 104–5   1

Gates, Toby, p.30–32   *Unit 1

Hallock, Health in Work and Play, p.22–25, 110–15   2

Jones, E., Easy Steps to Health, p.57–67   3

Mitchell, Another Here and Now Story Book, p.157–62   *RA

O'Donnell, Day In and Day Out, p.150–57   *Basic P

O'Keefe, Side by Side, p.59–60   2

Quinlan, Faces and Places, p.45   *2

Schneider, N., While Susie Sleeps   RA (K–2)

Selsam, Time for Sleep   RA; In (3)

Thomas, Stories about Linda and Lee, p.37–39   1

BEES: *see also* Honey

Betts, ABC Along Friendly Roads, p.114–20   3–2

Blough, Animals That Live Together, p.3–13   3

———— Insect Parade, p.28–29   3

Huntington, Let's Go Outdoors
                                    In (3)

McIntire, Working Together, p.69–
70   3

Quinlan, Busy World, p.61–66   3

Sheldon, Our Town, p.88–93   *1

Smith, J. R., Our Neighbors at Home,
p.28–30   3

BEETLES
Huntington, Let's Go Outdoors
                                    In (3)

BELLS
McKee, Looking Ahead, p.246–63
                                  *3–1

Mitchell, Farm and City, p.66–68
(sleigh)   1

BERRIES
McCloskey, Blueberries for Sal
                             *RA (K–2)

McKee, Climbing Higher, p.5–25
                                  *3–2

BIBLE STORIES
Duvoisin, A for the Ark RA (K–1)

Gruenberg, Favorite Stories Old and
New, p.293–317 (Noah's Ark;
Joseph; Moses; David and Goliath;
Nativity; Jesus in the Temple;
Jesus Healing the Blind; Loaves
and the Fishes; Three Parables)
                                   RA

Jones, J. M. O., Small Rain   RA

Jones, M. A., Tell Me about God
                                   RA

———— Tell Me about Jesus   RA

———— Tell Me about the Bible RA

Lathrop, Animals of the Bible   RA

Leavell, Open Windows, p.160–65
(Daniel)   1

Lenski, Mr. and Mrs. Noah
                         RA (K–1); In (2)

Petersham, Christ Child   RA

BICYCLES
Gruenberg, Favorite Stories Old and
New, p.44–52   *RA

Hunnicutt, I Know People, p.23–32
                                  3

Jensen, Lars-Peter's Birthday
                           *RA; In (2)

McIntire, Working Together, p.132–
33   3

Moore, Wobbly Wheels   *In (2)

Nolen, Do and Dare, p.132–38 (invention of bicycle)   3–2

BIRD BATHS
Dowling, New Seeing Why, p.87–89
                                  2

Smith, V. C., Science under the Sun,
p.54–58   2

BIRD HOUSES
Dowling, New Seeing Why, p.90–
93   2

Hanna, At School, p.51–55   1

Hildreth, I Know a Secret, p.34–37
                                 *1–1

Ousley, Under the Apple Tree, p.29–
32   *Pre–1

Sheldon, Our Town, p.106–11 (blue-
bird)   *1

BIRDS: *see also* Water Birds; also
names of birds, as Blue Jays,
Canaries

Baker, A. O., In Your Neighborhood,
p.7–16   3

Betts, ABC Around Green Hills, p.6–
11 (parakeets)   *1

Blough, Birds in the Big Woods   3

———— Useful Plants and Animals,
p.20–23   3

Bond, A. D., Thinking about Science,
p.35, 62–65, 73–79, 161–65   2

Bond, G. L., Happy Times, p.77–81
                                 *1

Burton, W. H., Meet Our Friends,
p.184–89   *2

———— Our Good Neighbors, p.262–70   *3

Craig, Science around You, p.20–21, 69, 75, 92–95   2

Davis, L. R., Wild Birthday Cake   *In (3)

Dowling, New Learning Why, p.110–15   3

Frasier, We Ask, p.75–82   P

Friskey, True Book of Birds We Know   In (2)

Gall, All the Year Round   In (3)

Gruenberg, Favorite Stories Old and New, p.162–66   *RA

McKee, On We Go, p.65, 232–33   2–2

O'Donnell, Day In and Day Out, p.124–33   *Basic P

Parker, Birds in Your Backyard   2

Quinlan, Happy Days, p.86–90   *Read. P

———— Winky, p.6–21   *PP

Sheldon, Our Town, p.94–99 (parakeets)   *1

Smith, J. R., Our Neighbors at Home, p.38–40   3

Smith, V. C., Science under the Sun, p.133–56   2

Thorn, Let's Find Out, p.83–85   1

———— Let's Go, p.32–34   PP

———— Let's Try, p.20–24, 29–33 P

Urell, Big City Book of Conservation, p.73–78, 81–82   3+

Weisgard, Whose Little Bird Am I?   *RA

BIRDS—BANDING
Thorn, Let's See Why, p.181–86   3

BIRDS—CARE
Barnard, Macmillan Science-Life Series, Bk.2, p.131–36   2

———— Macmillan Science-Life Series, Bk.3, p.31–35   3

BIRDS—EGGS AND NESTS
Blough, Birds in the Big Woods, p.18–23   3

Flack, Restless Robin   *RA; In (3)

Frasier, Science—Adventures, p.187–93   3

Gates, Two Boys and a Tree, p.24–27   *Sup. 1

Gray, New More Friends and Neighbors, p.86–91   *2–2

Jones, M. A., Tell Me about the Bible, p.20–24   *RA

Knox, Wonderworld of Science, Bk.2, p.123–26   2

Quinlan, Winky, p.15–19   *PP

Smith, V. C., Science under the Sun, p.135–47   2

Thorn, Let's Look Around, p.107–10   2

Thurber, Exploring Science Two, p.146–58   2

BIRDS—FEEDING: *see also* Pigeons —Feeding
Blough, Animals round the Year, p.23–25   3

———— Birds in the Big Woods, p.30–33   3

Dowling, New Seeing Why, p.83–85   2

Frasier, Science—All the Year, p.109–14   2

Gates, Two Boys and a Tree, p.28–29   *Sup. 1

Smith, V. C., Science under the Sun, p.151–56   2

Thorn, Let's Look Around, p.65–69   2

BIRDS—MIGRATION
Betts, ABC Over a City Bridge, p.195–98   2–2

Flack, Restless Robin   *RA; In (3)

Frasier, Science—Adventures, p.67–70   3

Gates, Good Times Today, p.186–94 3–1

Quinlan, To and Fro, p.176–78 *1

Urell, Big City Book of Conservation, p.81 3+

BIRDS—PROTECTION: *see also* Bird Baths; Birds—Feeding

Smith, V. C., Science under the Sun, p.154–55 2

BIRDS—TRACKS

Thurber, Exploring Science Three, p.82–83 3

BIRDS IN WINTER

Blough, Animals round the Year, p.23–25 3

—— Birds in the Big Woods, p.24–27 3

Smith, V. C., Science under the Sun, p.148–56 2

Urell, Big City Book of Conservation, p.63–66 3+

BIRTHDAYS

Association for Childhood Education, Told under the Magic Umbrella, p.1–4 (Ask Mr. Bear), 180–88 *RA

Averill, Jenny's Birthday Book *RA (K–1)

Beim, L. L., Lucky Pierre *In (3)

Betts, ABC Over a City Bridge, p.211–16 2–2

Bond, G. L., Many Surprises, p.28–58 *P

Burton, W. H., Our Happy Ways, p.28–34 *1

Charters, Health Secrets, p.10 3

Child Study Association of America, Holiday Storybook *RA

—— Read-to-Me Storybook, p.7–8 *RA

Cutright, Living Together Today and Yesterday, p.113–21 3

Davis, L. R., Wild Birthday Cake *In (3)

Eberle, Secrets and Surprises, p.140–54 *2–2

Fischer, Birthday *RA (K–1)

Flack, Ask Mr. Bear *RA (K–2)

Gates, Good Times Today, p.75–86 *3–1

—— Good Times Today and Tomorrow, p.57–68 *Alt. 3

Gray, New Friends and Neighbors, p.37–42 *2–1

Gruenberg, Favorite Stories Old and New, p.321–23 (Ask Mr. Bear) *RA

Hanna, At Home, p.61–64 P

—— In the Neighborhood, p.124–32 2

Haywood, "B" Is for Betsy, p.60–75 *In (3)

—— Primrose Day, p.106–24 *In (3)

Hildreth, Along the Way, p.152–62 *2–1

—— At Play, p.50–51 *P–1

—— I Know a Secret, p.94–100 *1–1

Hunt, Double Birthday Present *In (3)

Hurd, Nino and His Fish *In (2)

Jensen, Lars-Peter's Birthday *RA; In (2)

Jones, E., My Second Health Book, p.16–19 2

Kay, Snow Birthday *In (3)

Krauss, Birthday Party *RA (K–1)

La Rue, Tiny Toosey's Birthday *In (2)

Leavell, Open Windows, p.137–42 *1

Lenski, Surprise for Davy *RA (K–1); In (2)

—— Surprise for Mother *RA

McIntire, Billy's Friends, p.22–24, 71–73 1

McKee, Jack and Janet, p.133–45
*1–1
——— Looking Ahead, p.73–93
*3–1
O'Donnell, Anything Can Happen, p.38–42, 54–66   *Par. 1
——— Five-and-a-Half Club, p.79–109   *Par. 3
——— Round About, p.62–67
*Basic 1
O'Keefe, From Head to Toe, p.70–75   1
Orton, Grandmother's Cooky Jar, p.123–29   *RA
Ousley, Under the Apple Tree, p.37–41   Pre–1
Quinlan, Busy World, p.138–49   *3
——— Happy Days, p.68–72
*Read. P
Russell, D. H., Around the Corner, p.31–35   *2–2
——— Little White House, p.60–86
*P
Sheldon, At Home and Away, p.54–56   *SPP
——— Our Town, p.144–49, 178–83   *1

BLACKBIRDS
Betts, ABC Over a City Bridge, p.50–55   2–2
Russell, D. H., Friends Far and Near, p.186–93   *3–2

BLACKSMITHS
Emerson, Pioneer Children of America, p.258–59   3
Mitchell, Another Here and Now Story Book, p.97–98   *RA

BLOOD: see Circulatory System

BLUE JAYS
Monroe, New What Next, p.53–60
*2–1

BOATS: see also Canoes and Canoeing; Sailing; Steamships

Agle, Three Boys and a Tugboat
*In (3)
Allison, Fishing for Tuna   In (3)
Betts, ABC Down Singing River, p.60–65 (fireboat), 105–11   2–1
Bond, G. L., Ride with Us, p.54–57
*PP4
Burchard, *Carol Moran*   *In (2)
Burton, W. H., Our Good Neighbors, p.169–76   *3
Carpenter, Our Little Neighbors at Work and Play: Here, There, Then, and Now, p.45–48 (canoe), 97–99 (dugout)   3+
Eberle, Secrets and Surprises, p.103–21 (ferryboat)   *2–2
Emerson, Pioneer Children of America, p.24–25 (sailing vessel)   3
Flack, Boats on the River
RA (K–1)
Gates, New Friends and New Places, p.102–5 (houseboat)   *2–2
——— On Four Feet, p.112–17 *1
——— Ted and Sally, p.95–98 *P
——— Three Little Elephants, p.15–18   *Unit 1
——— Tuffy and Boots, p.41–63
*PP2
Gramatky, Little Toot   *RA (K–2)
Gruenberg, Favorite Stories Old and New, p.14–17 (tugboat), 37–40 (Tabby and the Boat Fire)   *RA
Hildreth, At Play, p.68   *P–1
Hunnicutt, I Know People, p.118–28 (ocean vessels)   3
Leavell, Open Windows, p.15–20 (toy)   *1
Lenski, Little Sail Boat *RA (K–2)
McIntire, Working Together, p.149–52 (liner)   3
McKee, Up and Away, p.56–71 *1–2
Mitchell, Animals, Plants, and Machines, *p.152–67, 172–77   2
——— Another Here and Now Story Book, p.100–4 (ferry)   *RA

————— Farm and City, p.103–10   1

————— Here and Now Story Book, p.167–75   *RA

Monroe, New We Three, p.14–17 (sailboat)   *1

Nolen, Do and Dare, p.251–59 (boat in bottle)   *3–2

————— Fun and Frolic, p.101–14 (sailboat)   *3–1

Norling, Pogo's Fishing Trip *In (3)

————— Pogo's Sea Trip   *In (2)

O'Donnell, Wishing Well, p.72–80 (houseboat), 101–16   Par. P

Ousley, Under the Apple Tree, p.104–8 (toy), 109–13, 118–25 (toy)   *Pre–1

Palmer, Lost and Found, p.46–50   *2–1

Politi, Boat for Peppe   *In (3)

Sheldon, At Home and Away, p.50–52   *Pre–P

————— Magic Windows, p.19–30 (fireboat)   *3–1

Thomas, Stories about Sally, p.116–23   2

Whipple, Our Earth, p.119–23 (canoes and sailboats)   3

BOBOLINKS
Frasier, Science—Adventures, p.67–69   3

BOBWHITES: *see* Partridges and Quails

BODY: *see* Physiology

BONES
Barnard, Macmillan Science-Life Series, Bk.2, p.38–41   2

BONFIRES
Gray, New Friends and Neighbors, p.187–91   *2–1

Leavell, Open Windows, p.82–87 *1

Yoakam, On the Way to Storyland, p.67–73   *P

BOOKS: *see also* Libraries; Paper
Brownell, Come Rain, Come Shine, p.74–76 (picture album)   3

Gates, Friends and Fun, p.29–38 (picture album)   *Alt. 2

————— On Four Feet, p.76–79 *1

————— Today We Go, p.29–38 *2–1

Hanna, At School, p.66–70   1

McIntire, Billy's Friends, p.130–31 1

————— Working Together, p.177–78   3

Sheldon, Our School, p.67–71 *P

————— Our Town, p.100–1   *1

Thomas, Stories about Linda and Lee, p.19–20   1

BOONE, DANIEL
Betts, ABC Along Friendly Roads, p.74–80   3–2

Cavanah, Our Country's Story, p.32–34   In (3)

Nolen, Do and Dare, p.272–82 *3–2

BOSTON
McCloskey, Make Way for Ducklings   *RA; In (2)

BOWS AND ARROWS
Deming, Little Eagle, p.35–44   *In (2)

BOXES
Brownell, Come Rain, Come Shine, p.21–24   3

O'Donnell, Round About, p.26–28 (music)   *Basic 1

Russell, D. H., Around the Corner, p.13–18   *2–2

BRAVERY
Gates, Good Times Today, p.46–54, 96–102   *3–1

Gruenberg, Favorite Stories Old and New, p.243–45 (Dutch Boy and the Dike)   *RA

Jones, M. A., Tell Me about Jesus, p.36–38   *RA

Leavell, Open Doors, p.95–101 *2

———— Open Roads p.10–16, 100–6
*3

———— Open Windows, p.52–57 *1

McKee, Climbing Higher, p.56–67
*3–2

BRAZIL

Baker, A. B., Talking Tree   *RA

BREAD: *see also* Bakery

Hugley, Around the Home, p.54–55
3

McIntire, Working Together, p.63–68
68   3

Mitchell, Animals, Plants, and Machines, p.117–20   2

Partch, Basic Social Studies, p.34–35
3

BREAKFAST: *see also* Lunch

Barnard, Macmillan Science-Life Series, Bk.1, p.4–10   1

Bauer, Being Six, p.11–13   1

———— Just Like Me, p.26–27   P

———— Seven or So, p.26–29   2

Charters, Health Secrets, p.17–20 3

Hallock, Health in Work and Play, p.10–11   2

Jones, E., My First Health Book, p.20–22   1

———— My Second Health Book, p.9–12   2

Mitchell, Farm and City, p.29–30 1

O'Keefe, How We Grow, p.111–17
3

Quinlan, Day by Day, p.6–10   *P

———— Winky, p.28–32   *PP

Wilcox, Here We Go, p.97–100   2

BRICKS: *see also* Clay

Partch, Basic Social Studies, p.198–99   3

Thomas, Your Town and Mine, p.104–8   3

BRIDGES

Bate, Who Built the Bridge?
RA; In (2)

Betts, ABC Along Friendly Roads, p.33–39   *3–2

BRITTANY

Beim, L. L., Lucky Pierre   *In (3)

Bond, G. L., Stories from Everywhere, p.252–65 (Lucky Pierre)
*3–1

O'Donnell, If I Were Going, p.146–51, *152–204   Basic 3

BROWNIES: *see* Fairies

BUFFALOES

Mitchell, Our Country, *p.68–88, 89–91   3

BUGS: *see* Insects

BUILDING MATERIALS: *see also* names of materials, as Glass, Iron, Steel

Hanna, In City, Town, and Country, p.160–66   3

McIntire, Working Together, p.16–20   3

Partch, Basic Social Studies, p.191–207   3

Schneider, H., Science for Here and Now, p.43–80   2

Thomas, Your Town and Mine, p.100–15   3

Urell, Big City Homes, p.27–31 (construction), 32–37 (interior)   3+

Whipple, Our Earth, p.232–35   3

BUILDINGS

Alain, Magic Stones   RA (2–3)

Goodspeed, Let's Go To Watch a Building Go Up   In (3)

Liebers, Stevie Finds a Way *In (2)

Zaffo, Big Book of Real Building and Wrecking Machines   In (3)

BULBS

Frasier, Science—For You, p.134–37
1

———— We Ask, p.87–93   P

Thorn, Let's Find Out, p.77–82   1

BULLS
  Gruenberg, Favorite Stories Old and
    New, p.336–38 (Story of Ferdi-
    nand)   *RA
  Hader, Story of Pancho   *RA
  Leaf, Story of Ferdinand   *In (3)

BUNYAN, PAUL
  Gruenberg, Favorite Stories Old and
    New, p.355–58   *RA

BURROS: *see* Donkeys

BUS STATIONS
  Reese, Basic Social Studies, p.106–
    11   2

BUSES
  Beim, J., Andy and the School Bus
                                  *In (2)
  Betts, ABC Down Singing River,
    p.118–23   2–1
  Burton, W. H., Meet Our Friends,
    p.105–7   *2
  Child Study Association of America,
    Read-to-Me Storybook, p.66–68
                                     *RA
  Gates, Friends and Fun, p.108–21
                                  *Alt. 2
  ——— Today We Go, p.129–42
                                    *2–1
  Hugley, Around the Home, p.35–39
    (sight-seeing)   3
  Hunnicutt, I Have Friends, p.113–18
    (school)   2
  Jones, E., My First Health Book,
    p.26–29 (school)   1
  McIntire, Working Together, p.139–
    40   3
  O'Donnell, If I Were Going, p.94–
    120   *Basic 3
  Ousley, Open the Gate, p.102–7
    (school)   *Pre–2
  ——— Ranches and Rainbows, p.75–
    79 (school)   *Pre–3
  Reese, Basic Social Studies, p.86–
    104   2

  Russell, D. H., On Cherry Street,
    p.29–34 (school)   *1
  Sheldon, Our School p.105–9 (school)
                                      *P

BUSINESS: *see* Banks and Banking;
    Earning Money; Industries; Mar-
    kets; Money; Shopping; Stores;
    also names of industries and trades
    as Dairy; Shoemakers

BUSINESS CENTERS
  Hanna, In City, Town, and Country,
    p.18–19, 112–13   3

BUTCHERS: *see* Stores

BUTTER
  Carpenter, Our Little Neighbors at
    Work and Play: Here, There,
    Then, and Now, p.83–84   3+
  Emerson, Pioneer Children of Ameri-
    ca, p.96–97   3
  Hugley, Around the Home, p.51–53
    (creamery)   3
  Mitchell, Farm and City, p.19–23 3
  Thomas, Your Town and Mine, p.37
                                       3

BUTTERFLIES: *see also* Caterpillars;
    Cocoons; Moths
  Barnard, Macmillan Science-Life Se-
    ries, Bk.2, p.18–19   2
  Blough, Animals and Their Young,
    p.12–13 (monarch)   3
  ——— Insect Parade, p.13–18   3
  Frasier, Science—All the Year, p.45–
    50   2
  Hildreth, Along the Way, p.132–36
                                    *2–1
  Huntington, Let's Go Outdoors, p.76–
    79   In (3)
  Parker, Six-legged Neighbors, p.17–
    25   2
  Pistorius, What Butterfly Is It? In (3)
  Sheldon, Our Town, p.102–5   1

CACTUS
Betts, ABC Beyond Treasure Valley,
p.234–41   *3–1

CAFETERIAS: *see* Restaurants, Lunch
Rooms, etc.

CAKE
Gray, New More Friends and Neigh-
bors, p.146–51   *2–2
Leavell, Open Roads, p.198–204 *3
――――― Open Windows, p.68–73 *1
Russell, D. H., My Little Blue Story
Book, p.40–44   *PP3
――――― My Little Green Story Book,
p.60–63   *PP2
Sheldon, Our School, p.137–41   *P

CALIFORNIA
Harvey, Cotton Growing   In (3)
Mitchell, Our Country, p.198–205 3
Sorensen, Ways of Our Land, p.132–
40, 138–39 (Los Angeles)   3

CAMELS
Blough, Useful Plants and Animals,
p.12   3
Gates, Friends and Fun, p.194–205
*Alt. 2
――――― New Friends and New
Places, p.136–48   *2–2
O'Donnell, If I Were Going, p.280–
328   *Basic 3

CAMPING: *see also* Automobiles—
Trailers
Baker, M. E., Tammy Camps Out
*In (3)
Bond, G. L., Down Our Way, p.25–
42   *2–1
Charters, Health Secrets, p.182–87 3
Gray, New More Streets and Roads,
p.245–51   *3–2
Haywood, Penny Goes to Camp
*In (3)
Hendrick, Trudy's First Day at
Camp   *RA; In (3)

Monroe, New We Three, p.50–55
(back yard)   *1
O'Donnell, Five-and-a-Half Club,
p.110–22 (back yard)   Par. 3
Wilcox, Step Lively, p.171–75   3
Yoakam, Stories We Like, p.9–26 *2

CANADA
Gray, New More Streets and Roads,
p.245–51   *3–2
Hildreth, Faraway Ports, p.243–57
*3–1
Nolen, Do and Dare, p.251–59 (Gas-
pé)   *3–2
Rapaport, A Whittle Too Much
*In (3)

CANALS: *see also* Irrigation
Haywood, Two and Two Are Four,
p.56–76   *In (3)

CANARIES
Gruenberg, Favorite Stories Old and
New, p.59–64   *RA
Tudor, Thistly B   *RA (K–2)

CANARIES—CARE
Blough, Pet Show, p.23–26   3

CANDLES
Hildreth, Faraway Ports, p.116–25
*3–1

CANDY
Betts, ABC Around Green Hills,
p.118–23   *1
Brownell, Come Rain, Come Shine,
p.146–48   3
Buchheimer, Let's Go to a Candy
Factory   In (3)
Hildreth, I Know a Secret, p.101–5
*1–1
Nolen, Do and Dare, p.196–203
(Magic Lollipop)   *3–2

CANNING: *see* Factories and Mills

CANOES AND CANOEING: *see also*
Boats

Emerson, Pioneer Children of America, p.102–21   3

CARAVANS: *see* Camels

CARDINAL BIRDS
Frasier, Science—For You, p.150–55
   1
Hildreth, Along the Way, p.64–74
   *2–1
—— Good Stories, p.45–48
   *Pre–2

CARE OF ANIMALS: *see* Animals—Care; Animals, Domestic; Kindness to Animals; Pets—Care

CAREERS: *see* Occupations

CAREFULNESS
Jones, M. A., Tell Me about God, p.17–18   *RA

CARPENTRY: *see also* Bird Houses; Doll Houses; Houses; Tools; Wood Carving
Gray, New Friends and Neighbors, p.178–82   *2–1
Mitchell, Here and Now Story Book, p.177–83   *RA
Partch, Basic Social Studies, p.181–82   3

CARROTS
Thorn, Let's Look Around, p.93–96
   2

CATBIRDS
McKee, On We Go, p.232–33   2–2

CATERPILLARS: *see also* Butterflies; Cocoons; Moths
Barnard, Macmillan Science-Life Series, Bk.2, p.8–16, 18   2
Blough, Insect Parade, p.13–26   3
Frasier, Science—All the Year, p.45–50   2
—— We Ask, p.50–51   P
Hildreth, Along the Way, p.126–36
   *2–1
Huntington, Let's Go Outdoors, p.72–75   In (3)

McClung, Sphinx   In (3)

CATS
Association for Childhood Education, Told under the Blue Umbrella, p.101–8 (Seven White Cats) *RA
Averill, Jenny's Adopted Brothers
   *RA; In (3)
—— Jenny's Birthday Book
   *RA (K–1)
—— Jenny's Moonlight Adventure
   *RA; In (3)
—— School for Cats *RA; In (3)
Beattie, In Came Horace *RA (K–2)
Betts, ABC Beyond Treasure Valley, p.60–66, 300–7   *3–1
—— ABC Down Singing River, p.157–62   *2–1
—— ABC Over a City Bridge, p.231–36   *2–2
—— ABC Up the Street and Down, p.50–53   *P
Birnbaum, Green Eyes   RA (K–1)
Blough, Animals and Their Young, p.26–29   3
—— Pet Show, p.19–22, *32–35
   3
Bond, G. L., Down Our Way, p.231–36   *2–1
—— Just for Fun, p.42–50 *2–2
—— Many Surprises, p.2–26 *P
Bradbury, Muggins   *In (3)
—— One Kitten Too Many
   *In (3)
Brown, M. W., Seven Stories about a Cat Named Sneakers   *RA
—— Willie's Adventures
   *RA; In (2)
Burton, W. H., Meet Our Friends, p.76–80 (stuffed toy)   *2
—— Our Good Neighbors, p.10–18, 185–92, 254–60   *3
Child Study Association of America, Read-to-Me Storybook, p.48–53, 92–96   *RA

Clymer, Yard for John   *RA
Cook, Curious Little Kitten   *RA
Diska, Andy Says Bonjour!
                               *RA (K–2)
Ets, Mr. T. W. Anthony Woo
                               *RA (K–2)
Evans, Something Different, p.42–70,
   92–96   *1
Fischer, Birthday   *RA (K–1)
——— Pitschi   *RA (K–2)
Flack, Angus and the Cat
                               *RA (K–2)
——— William and His Kitten *RA
Fritz, Fish Head   *In (3)
Gág, Millions of Cats   *RA
Gates, Good Times Today and To-
   morrow, p.212–16   *Alt. 3
——— Good Times Tomorrow,
   p.68–72   *3–2
——— Open Window, p.21–24
                               *Unit 1
——— Tuffy and Boots   *PP2
Gay, R., Home for Sandy, p.9–12,
   42–50   *P–1
Gray, New Friends and Neighbors,
   p.237–41   *2–1
——— New More Friends and
   Neighbors, p.81–85   *2–2
——— New More Streets and
   Roads, p.32–40   *3–2
——— New Our New Friends, p.90–
   93   *1–2
Gruenberg, Favorite Stories Old and
   New, p.37–43 (Tabby and the
   Boat Fire; Twins and Tabiffa),
   140–42 (Lion-hearted Kitten) *RA
Haywood, Here's a Penny, p.19–63
                               *In (3)
Hildreth, Mac and Muff   *Pre–PP
Hurd, Cat from Telegraph Hill
                               *RA (K–2)
Johnson, E. M., Treat Shop, p.150–
   54   *3
Johnson, M. S., Joey and Patches
                               *In (3)

——— Snowshoe Paws   *In (3)
Le Grand, Cats for Kansas
                               *RA (K–2)
McKee, Climbing Higher, p.157–58
                                 *3–2
——— Jack and Janet, p.100–12,
   166–83   *1–1
——— On We Go, p.66–83 *2–2
——— Tip and Mitten, p.22–40
                                *PP2
——— Up and Away, p.6–21 *1–2
Mason, Matilda and Her Family
                               *In (3)
Mathiesen, Blue-eyed Pussy
                               *RA (K–2)
Mitchell, Animals, Plants, and Ma-
   chines, p.213–25   *2
——— Another Here and Now
   Story Book, p.187–91   *RA
——— Here and Now Story Book,
   p.103–6, 121–29   *RA
Myers, Fishing Cat   *RA; In (2)
Newberry, April's Kittens
                               *RA (K–2)
——— Babette   *RA
——— Mittens   *RA
——— Pandora   *RA
——— Smudge   *RA (K–2)
——— T-Bone, the Baby Sitter
                          *RA; In (3)
Nolen, Do and Dare, p.187–94 *3–2
——— Fun and Frolic, p.3–9, 46–
   57   *3–1
O'Donnell, Wishing Well, p.51–59
                               *Par. P
Phillips, Molly, Pete, and Ginger,
   p.48–60   *PP1
Quinlan, To and Fro, p.110–20 *1
Robison, Fun and Fancy, p.69–75
                               *Pre–4
Russell, D. H., Finding New Neigh-
   bors, p.84–89   *3–1
——— Little White House, p.142–
   46   *P
——— On Cherry Street, p.49–58 *1

———— We Are Neighbors, p.65–69, 150–56   *2–1
Scott, Tippy   *In (3)
Seuss, Cat in the Hat   *In (1)
Sheldon, Our Town, p.24–29, 68–73   *1
———— Town and Country, p.141–49 (glass)   *2–2
Thorn, Let's See Why, p.81–87   3
Weil, I Wish, I Wish   *RA (K–2)
Yoakam, On the Way to Storyland, p.13–17   *P

CATS—CARE
Blough, Pet Show, p.19–22   3
Brownell, All Day, Every Day, p.52–57   1

CATTLE: *see also* Cows
Hanna, In the Neighborhood, p.19–24   2
Hugley, Around the Home, p.74–83   3
Hunnicutt, I Know People, p.188–97   3
Mitchell, Our Country, p.44–49   3
O'Donnell, Five-and-a-Half Club, p.165–75   *Par. 3
Sorensen, Ways of Our Land, p.104–5, 108–14   3
Thomas, Your Town and Mine, p.50–54, 346   3

CAVES
Frasier, Science—Adventures, p.45–49   3
Hildreth, Faraway Ports, p.67–68   *3–1
Nolen, Do and Dare, p.232–40   *3–2

CEMENT: *see* Concrete

CEREALS: *see* Grain

CHANGES
Craig, Science Everywhere, p.47–56 (physical-chemical), 57–62 (growth)   3

Frasier, Science—Adventures, p.136–37 (growth); 176–81 (physical-chemical)   3

CHARACTER BUILDING: *see also* Home Life
Beskow, Pelle's New Suit (service to others)   *RA; In (3)
Gruenberg, Favorite Stories Old and New, p.7–8 (Pelle's New Suit), 18–20 (sharing)   *RA
Haywood, "B" Is for Betsy, p.109–25   *In (3)
———— Betsy and the Boys   *In (3)
Hill, Summer Comes to Apple Market Street (doing things for others)   *In (3)
Hunnicutt, I Live with Others, p.82–86 (sharing)   1
Leavell, Open Doors   2
———— Open Roads   3
———— Open Windows   1
Newberry, Barkis   *RA
O'Donnell, Five-and-a-Half Club, p.17–26, 189–98, 236–54   *Par. 3
Wilcox, Step Lively, p.117–21, 123–27 (self-reliance)   3

CHEESE
Carpenter, Our Little Neighbors at Work and Play: Here, There, Then, and Now, p.85   3+
Thomas, Your Town and Mine, p.63   3

CHERRIES
Smith, J. R., Our Neighbors at Home, p.58–59   3

CHICKENS
Association for Childhood Education, Told under the Blue Umbrella, p.48–51   *RA
Bond, G. L., Down Our Way, p.88–109   *2–1
———— Just for Fun, p.2–11, 69–83   *2–2
Brown, M. W., Little Chicken   *RA

Gray, New Friends and Neighbors, p.87–91, 116–20, 126–30   *2–1
Hader, Cock-a-Doodle Doo   *RA
Hallock, Health and Happy Days, p.116–17   1
Haywood, Back to School with Betsy, p.156–76   *In (3)
Hildreth, At Play, p.53–59   *P–1
———— Enchanting Stories, p.29–43   *3–2
———— Fun in Story, p.25-46   *P–2
———— Good Stories, p.50–70 *Pre–2
———— Story Road, p.26–42   *2–2
Johnson, E. M., Treat Shop, p.28–35 (rooster)   *3
McIntire, Billy's Neighbors, p.143–45   2
McKee, Looking Ahead, p.73–93   *3–1
Mitchell, Farm and City, p.136–37   1
———— Here and Now Story Book, p.107–14   *RA
Palmer, Lost and Found, p.129–34   *2–1
Partch, Basic Social Studies, p.50–53   3
Quinlan, To and Fro, p.46–56   *1
Robison, Fun and Fancy, p.59–67   *Pre–4
Russell, D. H., Finding New Neighbors, p.18–27   *3–1
———— Little White House, p.153–59   *P
———— On Cherry Street, p.84–88, 93–96, 209–14   *1
Sheldon, Our School, p.28–32   *P
Smith, J. R., Our Neighbors at Home, p.19–22   3
Yoakam, Making Storybook Friends, p.76–89   *1

CHIMPANZEES: *see also* Baboons; Monkeys
McKee, Climbing Higher, p.258–67   3–2

Russell, D. H., Finding New Neighbors, p.64–69   3–1

CHINA
Baker, A. B., Talking Tree   *RA
Bishop, Five Chinese Brothers   *RA; In (3)
Bond, G. L., Stories from Everywhere, p.238–51   *3–1
Carpenter, Our Little Neighbors at Work and Play: Here, There, Then, and Now, p.175–84   3+
Flack, Story about Ping   *RA
Gruenberg, Favorite Stories Old and New, p.18–20 (from Little Pear), p.233–36 (Girl Who Could Think), p.268–73 (Ah Tcha the Sleeper)   *RA
Handforth, Mei Li   *RA: In (2)
Hildreth, Faraway Ports, p.72–73, *258–73   3–1
Lattimore, Bells for a Chinese Donkey   *In (3)
———— Little Pear   *In (3)
———— Little Pear and the Rabbits   *In (3)
———— Story of Lee Ling   *In (3)
———— Three Little Chinese Girls   *In (3)
Liang, Tommy and Dee-Dee   RA (K–1); In (2)
McKee, Climbing Higher, p.47–53   *3–2
Martin, Pointed Brush   *RA
Russell, D. H., Finding New Neighbors, p.224–33   *3–1
Wiese, Fish in the Air   *In (3)
———— You Can Write Chinese   In (3)
Yoakam, Children Everywhere, p.34–44 (from Little Pear and His Friends)   *3

CHIPMUNKS
Gall, All the Year Round, p.14–19   In (3)

Gates, Good Times Today, p.123–34 *3–1

—— Good Times Today and To-morrow, p.89–100 *Alt. 3

Gray, New Streets and Roads, p.202–10 *3–1

McClung, Stripe In (3)

Russell, D. H., Around the Corner, p.162–68 *2–2

Sheldon, Town and Country, p.106–26 *2–2

Thorn, Let's Look Around, p.111–13 2

CHRISTMAS

Adshead, Brownies—It's Christmas *RA (K–1)

Alden, Christmas Tree Forest *RA

Association for Childhood Education, Told under the Green Umbrella (Elves and the Shoemaker; Wee Robin's Christmas Day; Fulfilled; First Christmas) *RA

—— Told under the Magic Umbrella, p.68–85 (A Happy Christmas Tree; Gissing and the Telephone) *RA

Bond, G. L., Once upon a Story-time, p.222–33 *3–2

Brown, M. W., Little Fir Tree *RA

Brunhoff, Babar and Father Christmas *RA

Burton, W. H., Our Good Neighbors, p.178–84 *3

—— Our Happy Ways, p.43–52 *1

Child Study Association of America, Holiday Storybook *RA

—— Read Me Another Story *RA

—— Read-to-Me Storybook, p. 106–8 *RA

Duvoisin, Christmas Whale *RA (K–2)

Françoise, Noël for Jeanne-Marie *RA (K–2)

Gardner, Let's Celebrate Christmas T

Gates, Good Times Tomorrow, p.221–29 *3–2

Gray, New Streets and Roads, p.172–79 (Paddy's Christmas) *3–1

Hanna, In the Neighborhood, p.171–79 2

Haywood, Betsy and Billy, p.62–91 *In (3)

—— Betsy and the Boys, p.124–41 *In (3)

Hildreth, Along the Way, p.170–81 (Christmas Hatchet) *2–1

—— At Play, p.118–48 *P–1

—— Enchanting Stories, p.63–96 (Welcome House; Runaway Christmas Trees) *3–2

—— Fun in Story, p.106–20 *P–2

—— Good Stories, p.95–106 (Christmas Stocking) *Pre–2

Hutchinson, Chimney Corner Stories (Elves and the Shoemaker) *RA

Jones, E. O., Big Susan *In (3)

Jones, M. A., Tell Me about Jesus, p.21–27 *RA

Kahl, Plum Pudding for Christmas *RA (K–2)

Leavell, Open Doors, p.120–26 *2

Milhous, With Bells On *RA; In (3)

Mitchell, Farm and City, p.84–92 1

Newberry, Babette, p.24–30 *RA

Piper, Little Engine That Could *RA

Potter, Tailor of Gloucester *RA

Russell, D. H., Finding New Neighbors, p.254–64 *3–1

—— We Are Neighbors, p.265–68 (Wee Robin's Christmas Song) *2–1

Sheldon, Magic Windows, p.252–67 *3–1

Tudor, Dolls' Christmas *In (3)

CHRISTMAS—CAROLS

Betts, ABC Along Friendly Roads, p.221–27 *3–2

CHRISTMAS—MEXICO
Hildreth, Faraway Ports, p.202–30
*3–1

CHRISTMAS—PARTIES
Gardner, Let's Celebrate Christmas
T
Gray, New Streets and Roads, p.114–
22   *3–1

CHRISTMAS—PLAYS
Betts, ABC Beyond Treasure Valley,
p.145–52   3–1

CHRISTMAS—SANTA CLAUS
Betts, ABC Down Singing River,
p.151–56   *2–1
——— ABC Over a City Bridge,
p.129–34   *2–2
Hildreth, Along the Way, p.182–91
*2–1
McGinley, Year without a Santa
Claus   *RA
O'Donnell, Wishing Well, p.117–27
*Par. P
Walters, Real Santa Claus
*RA (K–2)

CHRISTMAS—TOYS
Betts, ABC Over a City Bridge,
p.123–28   *2–2

CHRISTMAS—TREES: *see also* Ever-
green Trees
Betts, ABC Along Friendly Roads,
p.189–96   *3–2
Burton, W. H., Meet Our Friends,
p.91–96   *2
Gates, Christmas Tree   Unit P
Gray, New Friends and Neighbors,
p.202–8   *2–1
Thorn, Let's Try, p.46–50   P
Urell, Big City Neighbors, p.40–46
3+

CHURCH: *see also* Prayers; Religion
Burkhardt, Our Community, p.110–
16   3
——— Our Family, p.41–45   P

Hanna, In the Neighborhood, p.63–
68   2
Urell, Big City Neighbors, p.66–76
3+
Yoakam, Making Storybook Friends,
p.14–22   *1

CIRCULATORY SYSTEM (BLOOD)
Frasier, Science—Adventures, p.119–
22   3
Thurber, Exploring Science Two,
p.72–75   2

CIRCUS: *see also* Clowns; also names
of circus animals, as Elephants
Betts, ABC Around Green Hills,
p.42–62   *1
Bond, G. L., Down Our Way, p.14–
24   *2–1
——— Happy Times, p.34–64 (back
yard)   *1
Burkhardt, Our Home and School,
p.102–8   1
Burton, W. H., Our Happy Ways,
p.88–100   *1
Eberle, Secrets and Surprises, p.33–
86   *2–2
Flack, Wait for William *RA (K–2)
Gates, Good Times Today, p.3–54
*3–1
——— Good Times Today and To-
morrow, p.1–36   *Alt. 3
Gray, New Friends and Neighbors,
p.163–69   *2–1
——— New More Friends and
Neighbors, p.36–40   *2–2
Gruenberg, Favorite Stories Old and
New, p.98–102 (Casey Joins the
Circus)   *RA
Haywood, Two and Two Are Four,
p.6–91   *In (3)
Hildreth, Good Stories, p.16–24
*Pre–2
——— I Know a Secret, p.106–31
*1–1
Hoff, Julius   *In (1–2)

Irwin, Keeping Fit for Fun, p.62–
71   3
Johnson, C., Harold's Circus   *RA
Johnson, E. M., Treat Shop, p.150–
54   3
McKee, Big Show, p.21–39   *PP3
———— Up and Away, p.118–26
                                                      *1–2
Mason, Happy Jack, p.7–44   *In (3)
Meigs, Wonderful Locomotive, p.48–
60   *RA
O'Donnell, Friendly Village, p.32–
44   *Basic 2
———— Through the Green Gate,
p.165–91   *Read. 3
Petersham, Circus Baby *RA (K–2)
Quinlan, Faces and Places, p.230–31
                                                          *2
Russell, D. H., Around the Corner,
p.38–61   *2–2
Sheldon, Magic Windows, p.41–104
                                                       *3–1
Turpin, Three Circus Days   *RA
Will, Circus Ruckus   *RA; In (3)
Yoakam, Stories We Like, p.28–36
                                                          *2

CITIZENSHIP: *see also* Community
Life; Conservation; Election Day;
Flag Day; Patriotism; Respon-
sibility; Safety
Burkhardt, Our Neighborhood, p.128–
36 (voting), p.137–45 (respect,
reverence, patriotism)   2
Hanna, In City, Town, and Country,
p.82–87   3
Leaf, Fair Play, p.57–59   In (3)

CITY DEVELOPMENT
Gates, Two Boys and a Tree, p.95–
102   *Sup. 1

CITY LIFE: *see also* Apartment Houses
Association for Childhood Education,
Told under the Blue Umbrella,
p.87–88   *RA

Betts, ABC Down Singing River,
p.112–17, 135–41   *2–1
———— ABC Over a City Bridge,
p.6–11, 18–23, 204–9   2–2
Bulla, Old Charlie   *In (3)
Burkhardt, Our Community, p.149–
61   3
Burton, V. L., Little House   *RA
Burton, W. H., Our Happy Ways,
p.132–52   *1
Carpenter, Our Little Neighbors at
Work and Play: Here, There, Then,
and Now, p.136–61   3+
Dawson, Walk in the City
                                               *RA (K–2)
Eberle, Secrets and Surprises, p.89–
138   *2–2
Gates, Tommy Little   *Sup. P
Goudey, Good Rain   In (3)
Hader, Big City   In (2)
Hanna, In City, Town, and Country,
p.6–51   3
———— In the Neighborhood, p.70–
143   2
Harris, I., Little Boy Brown
                                               *RA (K–2)
Hugley, Around the Home, p.25–39
                                                          3
Hunnicutt, I Know People, p.201–7
                                                          3
———— I Live with Others, p.27–29,
104–18   1
La Rue, Tiny Toosey's Birthday
                                                   *In (2)
McGinley, All around the Town
                                               RA (K–2)
———— Horse Who Had His Picture
in the Paper   *RA (K–2)
———— Horse Who Lived Upstairs
                                                       *RA
Merrill, Travels of Marco   *RA
Mitchell, Another Here and Now
Story Book, p.157–62, 165–67,
303–9   *RA
———— Farm and City, p.95–124 1

———— Our Country, p.94–107   3
Palmer, Lost and Found, p.58–116
    *2–1
Paull, Come to the City   RA
Russell, D. H., Around the Corner,
    p.8–36, 64–100, 216–21   *2–2
Schneider, H., Let's Look under the
    City   In (3)
Sheldon, Town and Country, p.55–
    70   *2–2
Smith, J. R., Our Neighbors at Home,
    p.193–234   3
Sorensen, Ways of Our Land, p.160–
    76   3
Tensen, Come to the City   In (2)
Thomas, Stories about Sally, p.114–
    16   2
Urell, Big City Homes (also all other
    titles in this series)   3
Zolotow, One Step, Two . . .
    *RA (K–1); In (2)

CIVIL WAR, U.S.
Cavanah, Our Country's Story, p.50–
    53   In (3)

CLAMS
Huntington, Let's Go to the Sea-
    shore, p.76–77   In (3)

CLAY: see also Bricks; Pottery
Schneider, H., Science Far and Near,
    p.46–55   3

CLAY MODELING: see also Pottery
Bond, G. L., Down Our Way, p.187–
    92 (animals)   *2–1
Monroe, New We Three, p.19–22 *1

CLEANLINESS: see also Laundry
Barnard, Macmillan Science-Life Se-
    ries, Bk.1, p.91–97   1
———— Macmillan Science-Life Se-
    ries, Bk.3, p.84–100   3
Bauer, From Eight to Nine, p.154–
    55 (bathing)   3
———— Seven or So, p.114–17   2
Brownell, All Day, Every Day, p.100–
    3 (bath)   1

———— Blue Skies, p.13–14 (per-
    sonal), 122–27 (spring cleaning) 2
Charters, Health Secrets, p.2–5   3
Frasier, Science—For You, p.52–53
    1

Hallock, Health and Safety for You,
    p.94–98, 103–8, 107–11, 112–14 3
———— Health in Work and Play,
    p.6–9   2
Irwin, Keeping Fit for Fun, p.79–
    85   3
Jones, E., Easy Steps to Health, p.9–
    24   3
———— My First Health Book, p.12–
    16   1
Leaf, Health Can Be Fun, p.27–42
    In (3)
Mitchell, Another Here and Now
    Story Book, p.42–46, 93–95 *RA
———— Here and Now Story Book,
    p.219–27   *RA
Quinlan, Busy World, p.*164–72,
    174–79   3–2
Schneider, H., Science for Here and
    Now, p.195–99   2
Thomas, Stories about Linda and
    Lee, p.30, 39–40   1
Wilcox, Here We Go, p.111–26,   2
Yoakam, On the Way to Storyland,
    p.29–35   *3–2

CLEMENS, SAMUEL LANGHORNE
Leavell, Open Roads, p.116–22   *3

CLEVERNESS
Gray, New Streets and Roads, p.140–
    47   *3–1

CLOCKS: see also Telling Time
Betts, ABC Around Green Hills,
    p.168–73   *1
Bond, G. L., Just for Fun, p.79–84
    (alarm)   *2–2
Brownell, Blue Skies, p.90–91   2
Burton, W. H., Meet Our Friends,
    p.178–83   *2

Gray, New More Friends and Neighbors, p.172–77   *2–2

Orton, Grandmother's Cooky Jar, p.50–55   *RA

Sheldon, Story Caravan, p.6–24 *3–2

CLOTHING: *see also* Knitting; Laundry; also names of articles of clothing, as Hats; also names of clothing material, as Cotton

Association for Childhood Education, Told under the Blue Umbrella, p.23–25 (Pelle's New Suit) *RA

Barnard, Macmillan Science-Life Series, Bk.2, p.65 (rain)   2

Bauer, From Eight to Nine, p.19–23   3

Beskow, Pelle's New Suit
                            *RA; In (3)

Betts, ABC Over a City Bridge, p.199–203   *2–2

Brownell, All Day, Every Day, p.80–84   1

——— Blue Skies, p.101–6   2

Burkhardt, Our Community, p.62–78   3

——— Our Home and School, p.7–9 (coat)   1

Burton, W. H., Meet Our Friends, p.27–31 (gloves)   *2

Carpenter, Our Little Neighbors at Work and Play: Here, There, Then, and Now, p.25–31 (Indian), 87–96   3+

Charters, Health Secrets, p.6–9   3

Child Study Association of America, Read-to-Me Storybook, p.81–86
                                   *RA

Emerson, Pioneer Children of America, p.168–69   3

Gates, On Four Feet, p.56–70 (mittens and boots)   *1

Gruenberg, Favorite Stories Old and New, p.7–8 (Pelle's New Suit), 21–24 (Cap That Mother Made)
                                   *RA

Hallock, Health and Safety for You, p.77–92   3

Hanna, In City, Town, and Country, p.156–59   3

Hugley, Around the Home, p.102–34   3

Irwin, Growing Day by Day, p.93–97   2

——— Keeping Fit for Fun, p.96–100   3

Jones, E., Easy Steps to Health, p.95–102   3

Kay, One Mitten Lewis *RA (K–1)

Leaf, Health Can Be Fun   In (3)

Lenski, Surprise for Mother   *RA

McIntire, Working Together, p.91–120, 121–23 (other lands)   3

McKee, Jack and Janet, p.47–53 (mittens)   *1–1

Mitchell, Animals, Plants, and Machines p.57–96   2

——— Another Here and Now Story Book, p.85–90   *RA

——— Here and Now Story Book, p.229–35   *RA

Monroe, New What Next, p.16–20 (mittens)   *2

O'Donnell, Anything Can Happen, p.87–94 (cap)   *Par. 1

——— Day In and Day Out, p.22–28 (coat)   *Basic P

——— Wishing Well, p.34–50
                              *Par. P

O'Keefe, How We Grow, p.43–55 3

Partch, Basic Social Studies, p.102–62   3

Robison, Fun and Fancy, p.98–103 (cowboy)   Pre–4

Schneider, H., Science Far and Near, p.75–97   3

Sheldon, Fields and Fences, p.8–15 (boots)   *2–1

Thomas, Your Town and Mine, p.68–98   3

Whipple, Our Earth, p.228–31   3

CLOTHING—CARE
McIntire, Working Together, p.117–
19   3

CLOTHING STORE: *see* Stores

CLOUDS
Baker, A. O., Around the Corner,
p.39   2
Barnard, Macmillan Science-Life Se-
ries, Bk.2, p.62–64   2
Blough, Water Appears and Disap-
pears, p.28–29   3
Smith, V. C., Science under the Sun,
p.75–83   2
Thurber, Exploring Science Three,
p.103, 106–11   3
——— Exploring Science Two, p.26–
29   2
Urell, Big City Water Supply, p.37–
40   3+

CLOWNS: *see also* Circus
Betts, ABC Around Green Hills,
p.36–40, 63–68   *1
Bond, G. L., Many Surprises, p.79–
90   *P
Gates, Good Times Today, p.37–44
                                              *3–1
Gray, New Streets and Roads, p.75–
85   *3–1
McKee, On We Go, p.189–216 *2–2
Monroe, New Tall Tales, p.4–8 *3–1
Russell, D. H., Around the Corner,
p.49–54   *2–2
Schreiber, Bambino Goes Home
                                          *RA; In (3)
——— Bambino the Clown
                                          *RA; In (3)
Sheldon, Magic Windows, p.43–73
                                              *3–1
Yoakam, Stories We Like, p.28–36
                                               *2

CLUBS
Hanna, In City, Town, and Country,
p.120–26   3

McIntire, Billy's Neighbors, p.63–
68 (reading)   2
O'Donnell, Five-and-a-Half Club
(play)   *3–3
Quinlan, Faces and Places, p.145–
48 (book club)   *2
Smith, J. R., Our Neighbors at Home,
p.189–91   3
Thomas, Your Town and Mine, p.24,
37, 130–36   3

COAL
Mitchell, Animals, Plants, and Ma-
chines, p.42–44   2
Smith, J. R., Our Neighbors at Home,
p.122–30   3
Sorensen, Ways of Our Land, p.60–
71   3

COASTING: *see* Winter Sports

COBBLERS: *see* Shoemakers

COCKS: *see* Chickens

COCOONS: *see also* Butterflies; Cat-
erpillars; Moths; Silkworms
Barnard, Macmillan Science-Life Se-
ries, Bk.2, p.8–15   2
Frasier, Science—For You, p.146–
47   1
——— We Ask, p.54–55   P
Thorn, Let's Find Out, p.97–99   1

COLD: *see* Weather

COLDS: *see also* Germs
Barnard, Macmillan Science-Life Se-
ries, Bk.1, p.74–79   1
——— Macmillan Science-Life Se-
ries, Bk.2, p.29   2
Bauer, Being Six, p.100–7   1
——— From Eight to Nine, p.94–
103   3
——— Seven or So, p.124–25   2
Brownell, All Day, Every Day, p.60–
64   1
——— Blue Skies, p.107–9   2
——— Come Rain, Come Shine,
p.129–31   3

Burton, W. H., Meet Our Friends, p.20–26 *2

Charters, Health Secrets, p.100–111 3

Hallock, Health and Happy Days, p.68–70 1

—————— Health in Work and Play, p.58–62 2

Leaf, Health Can Be Fun, p.45–49 In (3)

O'Keefe, Side by Side, p.65–70 2

Wilcox, Here We Go, p.39–41 2

COLONIAL PERIOD, U.S.: *see also* Pilgrims; School Life—Colonial Period, U.S.; Thanksgiving Day; Washington, George

Aulaire, George Washington In (3)

Cavanah, Our Country's Story, p.12–25 In (3)

Emerson, Pioneer Children of America, p.2–121 (Jamestown), p.4–23 (Spanish in Florida), 54–73 (Pilgrims at Plymouth), 78–95 (Dutch at New Amsterdam), 104–19 (French) 3

Hildreth, Faraway Ports, p.114–49 *3–1

Leavell, Open Roads, p.134–40, 142–47 *3

COLOR: *see also* Rainbow

Brown, M. W., Color Kittens *RA; In (2)

Quinlan, Day by Day, p.92–94 *P

Sheldon, Here and Away, p.23–30 *PP3

COLOR OF ANIMALS: *see* Animals —Protection

COLORADO

Johnson, M. S., Sir Lancelot and Scamp *In (3)

COLUMBUS, CHRISTOPHER

Burkhardt, Our Community, p.193–200 *3

Cavanah, Our Country's Story, p.10–11 In (3)

Child Study Association of America, Holiday Storybook *RA

Dalgliesh, Columbus Story RA; In (3)

Russell, D. H., Finding New Neighbors, p.236–40 *3–1

COMMUNICATION: *see also* Language; Newspapers; Radio; Reading; Signals and Signaling; Telegraph; Telephone; Television; Transportation

Burkhardt, Our Community, p.117–41 3

Hanna, In City, Town, and Country, p.171–74 3

Hunnicutt, I Know People, p.229–35 3

McIntire, Working Together, p.165–96 3

COMMUNITY LIFE: *see also* City Life; Farm Life; Helpers; Houses; Maps; Neighbors; Safety; School Life; Village Life; also such phases of community life as Banks and Banking; Garbage; Police

Burkhardt, Our Community 3

—————— Our Neighborhood 2

Burton, V. L., Katy and the Big Snow *RA

Carpenter, Our Little Neighbors at Work and Play: Here, There, Then, and Now, p.106–9 3+

Cutright, Living Together Today and Yesterday 3

Frank, Daddies RA (K–2)

Gilbert, Mr. Plum and the Little Green Tree *RA (K–3)

Hader, Little Town In (3)

Hanna, In City, Town, and Country 3

—————— In the Neighborhood 2

Hoffman, More Friendly Helpers

In (2)

Hugley, Around the Home   3

Hunnicutt, I Have Friends, p.92–97, 105–11   2

Lenski, Project Boy   *In (3)

———— We Live by the River *In (3)

McIntire, Billy's Neighbors   2

Russell, D. H., We Are Neighbors, p.163–93   *2–1

Shackelford, My Happy Days

*In (3)

Smith, J. R., Our Neighbors at Home

3

Sorensen, Ways of Our Land   3

Thomas, Your Town and Mine   3

Urell, Big City Fun   3+

———— Big City Homes   3+

———— Big City Neighbors   3+

———— Big City Water Supply   3+

———— Big City Workers   3+

Zolotow, Park Book   RA (K–1)

CONCRETE

Partch, Basic Social Studies, p.202– 3   3

Thomas, Your Town and Mine, p.110–11   3

CONSERVATION: *see also* Animals —Protection; Birds—Protection; Floods; Forests and Forestry; Irrigation

Hanna, In City, Town, and Country, p.77–79 (soil), 90–94 (forests) 3

Hunnicutt, I Know People, p.129– 35 (water)   3

Thorn, Let's See Why, p.20–23 (soil)

3

Urell, Big City Book of Conservation

3+

CONTAGION: *see also* Colds; Germs

Baker, A. O., In Your Neighborhood, p.110–14   3

Brownell, Come Rain, Come Shine, p.129, 151   *3

Charters, Health Secrets, p.111–13, 117–18   3

Hunnicutt, I Have Friends, p.132–35

2

Jones, E., My Second Health Book, p.57–58   2

McKee, On We Go, p.23–26 (mumps)   *2–2

O'Donnell, Through the Green Gate, p.130–47   *Read. 3

O'Keefe, How We Grow, p.121–38

3

CONTENTMENT: *see also* Happiness

Association for Childhood Education, Told under the Magic Umbrella, p.189–96   *RA

Charles, Roundabout Turn   *RA

Gates, Good Times Today, p.135– 43   *3–1

Hildreth, Enchanting Stories, p.154– 59 (Never Worked and Never Will)   *3–1

McKee, On We Go, p.113–32   *2–2

Robison, Fun and Fancy, p.178–87 (Cow in the Kitchen)   *Pre–4

Watts, Cow in the House *RA (K–2)

CONTINENTS

Whipple, Our Earth, p.203–6   3

COOKIES

Burton, W. H., Our Happy Ways, p.35–42   *1

Gray, New Friends and Neighbors, p.26–30   *2–1

Hildreth, Along the Way, p.28–36

*2–1

Orton, Grandmother's Cooky Jar

*RA

Sheldon, At Home and Away, p.30– 32   *SPP

———— Our School, p.84–88   *P

———— Our Town, p.12–17   *1

COOKING: *see also* Bakery; Food; also names of food, as Bread

Deming, Little Eagle   *In (2)
Haywood, Betsy and Billy, p.92–107
    *In (3)
———— Betsy and the Boys, p.3–19
    *In (3)
Lenski, Surprise for Mother   *RA

COONS: *see* Raccoons

COOPERATION: *see also* Community
  Life; Interdependence
Beim, L. L., Two Is a Team
    *RA; In (3)
Burkhardt, Our Home and School   1
———— Our Neighborhood, p.89–107
    2
Cavanah, Our Country's Story, p.70–
72   In (3)
Charters, Health Secrets, p.88–90   3
Hanna, In the Neighborhood, p.26–
30, 165–69   2
Hunnicutt, I Have Friends, p.154–59
    2
———— I Live with Others, p.40–44
    1
Leaf, Let's Do Better   In (3)
Leavell, Open Roads, p.33–38   *3
———— Open Windows, p.68–73, 82–
93, 137–42, 151–56   *1
O'Keefe, How We Grow, p.167–73 3
Smith, J. R., Our Neighbors at Home,
p.14–17   3

CORN: *see also* Grain
Baker, A. O., In Your Neighborhood,
p.27–30   3
Clark, A. N., In My Mother's House,
p.14–18   RA; In (2)
Hanna, In the Neighborhood, p.26–
30 (harvesting)   2
Mitchell, Animals, Plants, and Ma-
chines, p.111–16 (seed)   2
Thorn, Let's See Why, p.55–58   3
Whipple, Our Earth, p.75–89   3

COSTUME: *see* Clothing

COTTON: *see also* (The) South
Betts, ABC Along Friendly Roads,
p.106–13   *3–2
Blough, Useful Plants and Animals,
p.28–29   3
Burkhardt, Our Community, p.70 3
Burton, W. H., Our Good Neighbors,
p.155–62   *3
Harvey, Cotton Growing   In (3)
Hugley, Around the Home, p.112–21
    3
Hunnicutt, I Know People, p.136–48
    3
McIntire, Working Together, p.95–
96   3
Mitchell, Animals, Plants, and Ma-
chines, p.62–68   *2
Partch, Basic Social Studies, p.111–
13   3
Quinlan, Faces and Places, p.162–66
    *2
Sorensen, Ways of Our Land, p.55–
59   *3
Thomas, Your Town and Mine, p.77–
80   *3

COUNTING: *see also* Arithmetic;
  Numbers
Françoise, Jeanne-Marie Counts Her
Sheep   *RA (K–1); In (2)
Kuskin, James and the Rain
    *RA (K–2)
Moore, My First Counting Book
    RA (K–1)

COUNTRY LIFE: *see* Farm Life

COURAGE: *see* Bravery

COVERED WAGONS
Betts, ABC Beyond Treasure Valley,
p.97–104   *3–1
Bond, G. L., Stories from Everywhere, p.116–22, 141–68   *3–1
Cavanah, Our Country's Story, p.46–
49   In (3)

Emerson, Pioneer Children of America, p.198–219   *3
Yoakam, Children Everywhere, p.96–112   *3

COWBIRDS
Blough, Birds in the Big Woods, p.21–22   3

COWBOYS: *see also* Cattle; Rodeo
Anglund, Brave Cowboy *RA (K–1)
Barr, Texas Pete, Little Cowboy
                                        *In (2)
Betts, ABC Along Friendly Roads, p.214–20, 236–43, 258–64   *3–2
——— ABC Beyond Treasure Valley, p.216–23   *3–1
Bracken, Rodeo   In (3)
Cavanah, Our Country's Story, p.58–59   In (3)
Eberle, Secrets and Surprises, p.189–218   2–2
Fletcher, Big Book of Cowboys RA
Gates, Good Times Tomorrow, p.173–81   *3–2
Gray, New More Streets and Roads, p.235–44   *3–2
Gruenberg, Favorite Stories Old and New, p.88–91   *RA
Haywood, Eddie and Gardenia
                                        *In (3)
Le Grand, Why Cowboys Sing, in Texas   *RA; In (3)
O'Donnell, Friendly Village, p.124–48   *Basic 2
O'Keefe, Side by Side, p.132–49   2
Quinlan, Faces and Places, p.73–76, 88–118   *2
Robison, Fun and Fancy, p.116–25
                                      *Pre–4
Sheldon, Our Town, p.132–37 (show)
                                        *1
——— Town and Country, p.168–73   *2–2
Sorensen, Ways of Our Land, p.108–14   3

Thomas, Stories about Sally, p.105–7
                                         2
Will, Even Steven   *RA
COWGIRLS
Robison, Fun and Fancy, p.104–15
                                      *Pre–4

COWS: *see also* Butter; Cheese; Milk
Bond, A.D., Knowing about Science, p.179–83   3
Boreman, Mooloo, the Calf   In (2)
Brownell, Blue Skies, p.139–44   2
Burton, W. H., Meet Our Friends, p.166–71   *2
——— Our Good Neighbors, p.87–92   *3
Carpenter, Our Little Neighbors at Work and Play: Here, There, Then, and Now, p.81–82   3+
Clark, A. N., In My Mother's House, p.33   RA; In (2)
Emerson, Pioneer Children of America, p.80–93   *3
Floethe, Farmer and His Cows
                                    In (3)
Gates, Good Times Tomorrow, p.87–95   *3–2
Gray, New Friends and Neighbors, p.92–97 (calves)   *2–1
McKee, Climbing Higher, p.249–55
                                      *3–2
——— Up and Away p.42–52 (calves)   *1–2
Mitchell, Animals, Plants, and Machines, p.31–33   2
——— Another Here and Now Story Book, p.123–24   *RA
——— Farm and City, p.10–18, 129–35   1
——— Here and Now Story Book, p.203–10   *RA
Monroe, New Tall Tales, p.28–33
                                      *3–1
Nolen, Fun and Frolic, p.31–42 *3–1
Orton, Queenie   *RA

Ousley, Open the Gate, p.41–48
  (calves)   *Pre–2
Quinlan, To and Fro, p.68–80   *1
Russell, D. H., We Are Neighbors,
  p.236–39   *2–1
Sheldon, Story Caravan, p.167–90
                                        *3–2
Thomas, Your Town and Mine,
  p.34–36   3
Thorn, Let's Look Around, p.121–26
                                        2
Watts, Cow in the House *RA (K–2)
Whipple, Our Earth, p.59–67   2
Yoakam, Children Everywhere, p.22–
  31   *3

COYOTES
  Bronson, Coyotes   In (3)

CRABS
  Adrian, Fiddler Crab   In (3)
  Huntington, Let's Go to the Sea-
    shore, p.32–55   In (3)
  O'Donnell, Friendly Village, p.182–
    90   *Basic 2
  Robinson, W. W., At the Seashore
                                  In (3)

CRAYFISH
  Thorn, Let's See Why, p.159–63   3

CREAMERY: see Butter

CREATIVE EXPRESSION: see Art;
  Games; Handicraft; Music; Plays;
  Puppet Shows

CREEK
  Bond, G. L., Once upon a Storytime,
    p.100–12   *3–2

CRICKETS
  Bond, G. L., Stories from Every-
    where, p.303–12   *3–1

CROWS
  Blough, Birds in the Big Woods,
    p.12–13, 19   3+
  Bond, G. L., Once upon a Storytime,
    p.244–57   *3–2

Brownell, Blue Skies, p.8–12   2
Gray, New Friends and Neighbors,
  p.98–102   *2–1
Hildreth, Story Road, p.149–58 *2–2

CRYSTALS: see Salt; Sugar

CUBA
  Carpenter, Our Little Neighbors at
    Work and Play: Here, There,
    Then, and Now, p.166–74   *3+

DACRON AND ORLON
  McIntire, Working Together, p.104–
    5   3

DADDY LONGLEGS
  Huntington, Let's Go Outdoors,
    p.50–53   In (3)

DAIRY: see also Butter; Cheese; Cows;
  Milk
  Bond, G. L., Down Our Way, p.66–
    76   *2–1
  Goodspeed, Let's Go to a Dairy
                                  In (3)
  Hallock, Health in Work and Play,
    p.82–87   2
  Hanna, In City, Town, and Country,
    p.142–53   3
  Hastings, Dairy   In (2)
  Hugley, Around the Home, p.42–53
                                  3
  Hunnicutt, I Have Friends, p.58–65 2
  McIntire, Working Together, p.57–
    63   *3
  Mitchell, Animals, Plants, and Ma-
    chines, p.34–37   2
  ———— Here and Now Story Book,
    p.339–51   *RA
  Partch, Basic Social Studies, p.17–22
                                  3
  Smith, J. R., Our Neighbors at
    Home, p.33–38   3
  Smith, M. E., Mother's Story of
    Dairying   2+
  Thomas, Stories about Sally, p.81–
    85   2

DAMS: *see also* Floods; Irrigation; Water Supply
Cutright, Living Together Today and Yesterday, p.11–18   3
Mitchell, Our Country, p.23–31   3
Thomas, Your Town and Mine, p.119–20   3

DANCES
Urell, Big City Neighbors, p.63–65 (Greek, Russian, Austrian)   3+

DAVID: *see* Bible Stories

DAYS: *see* Birthdays; Holidays; also names of holidays, as Mother's Day

DEATH
Gruenberg, Favorite Stories Old and New, p.143–44 (Blue Silver) *RA

DEER: *see also* Moose
Betts, ABC Along Friendly Roads, p.20–25   *3–2
Blough, Animals and Their Young, p.34–35   3
Bond, G. L., Once upon a Storytime, p.161–72   *3–2
Buff, Dash and Dart   RA; In (3)
Goudey, Here Come the Deer!   In (2)
Gray, New Streets and Roads, p.211–19   *3–1
Hildreth, Faraway Ports, p.1–15   *3–1
O'Donnell, Round About, p.140–58   *Basic 1
Russell, D. H., Around the Corner, p.173–76   *2–2
Schlein, Deer in the Snow RA; In (3)
Sheldon, Magic Windows, p.117–34   *3–1

DENMARK
Baker, A. B., Talking Tree   *RA
Collin, Wind Island   *In (3)
Jensen, Lars-Peter's Birthday   *RA; In (2)

DENTISTS: *see also* Teeth
Barnard, Macmillan Science-Life Series, Bk.1, p.64–65   1
Brownell, Blue Skies, p.92–95   2
————— Come Rain, Come Shine, p.98–101   3
Hallock, Health and Happy Days, p.104–5   1
————— Health and Safety for You, p.134–36   3
————— Health in Work and Play, p.97–101   2
Irwin, Growing Day by Day, p.43–47   2
————— Keeping Fit for Fun, p.115–21   3
O'Keefe, From Head to Toe, p.84–88   1
————— How We Grow, p.33–39   3
————— Side by Side, p.103–8   2
Wilcox, Come On, p.92–98   1

DEPARTMENT STORES: *see* Shopping; Stores

DESERTS: *see also* Cactus; Camels; Indians of North America; Irrigation
Buff, Elf Owl   RA; In (2)
Carpenter, Our Little Neighbors at Work and Play: Here, There, Then, and Now, p.194–201   3+
Cutright, Living Together Today and Yesterday, p.50   3
Frasier, Science—Adventures, p.21–26   3
Mitchell, Our Country, p.227–32   3
Schneider, H., Science Far and Near, p.23–36   3
Whipple, Our Earth, p.98–111   3

DICTIONARIES: *see also* Words
Oftedal, My First Dictionary In (1)
Walpole, Golden Dictionary   In (3)
Watters, Picture Dictionary for Children   In (3)

Wright, W. W., Rainbow Dictionary
In (3)
DIKES: *see* Netherlands
DINOSAURS: *see also* Animals, Pre-
historic; Fossils; Reptiles
Hoff, Danny and the Dinosaur
*RA (K–1); In (2)
DISEASES: *see also* Colds; Contagion;
Germs; Health
Frasier, Science—All the Year, p.96–
99   2
Leaf, Fair Play, p.30–33, 91   In (3)

DISHES: *see* Pottery

DOCTORS: *see also* Dentists; Health
Barnard, Macmillan Science-Life Se-
ries, Bk.1, p.58–63   1
Bauer, Being Six, p.54–55   1
——— From Eight to Nine, p.160–
63   3
Frasier, We Ask, p.64–65   P
Gruenberg, Favorite Stories Old and
New, p.138–39 (from Dr. Dolit-
tle)   *RA
Hallock, Health and Happy Days,
p.94–97   1
——— Health and Safety for You,
p.126–29 (school), 130–33   3
Hill, Surprise for Judy Jo   *In (3)
McIntire, Billy's Friends, p.75–77   1
O'Keefe, From Head to Toe, p.89–93
1
——— How We Grow, p.69–77   3
Russell, D. H., Finding New Neigh-
bors, p.77–83 (animal)   3–1
Wilcox, Come On, p.101–13   1

DOGS
Association for Childhood Education,
Told under the Blue Umbrella,
p.32–36, 41–43 (Angus and the
Ducks)   *RA
——— Told under the Magic Um-
brella, p.33–38, 79–85   *RA
Beim, L. L., Little Igloo   *In (3)

Bemelmans, Madeline's Rescue
*RA; In (2)
Bettina, Pantaloni   *RA (K–2)
Betts, ABC Along Friendly Roads,
p.68–73   *3–2
——— ABC Beyond Treasure Val-
ley, p.46–53, 75–82, 122–28 *3–1
——— ABC Down Singing River,
p.72–77   2–1
——— ABC Over a City Bridge,
p.62–66, 112–18   *2–2
Black, Dusty and His Friends
*In (3)
Blough, Useful Plants and Animals,
p.7–10   3
Bond, G. L., Down Our Way, p.206–
9   *2–1
——— Happy Times, p.73–76   *1
——— Just for Fun, p.90–100 *2–2
Bontemps, Fast Sooner Hound
*In (3)
Brann, Patrick Was His Name   *RA
Brown, M. W., Country Noisy Book
RA
——— Indoor Noisy Book   RA
——— Seashore Noisy Book   RA
Burton, W. H., Meet Our Friends,
p.32–38   *2
——— Our Happy Ways, p.16–27
*1
Carroll, Scuffles   *RA
——— Where's the Bunny?
*RA (K–1); In (2)
Child Study Association of America,
Read-to-Me Storybook, p.42–46,
54–58   *RA
Dennis, M., Burlap   *RA (K–2)
Ets, Mr. T. W. Anthony Woo
*RA (K–2)
Flack, Angus and the Cat *RA (K–2)
——— Angus and the Ducks
*RA (K–2)
——— Angus Lost   *RA (K–2)
Friedman, Whistle for Tootles
*RA (K–2)

Gág, Nothing at All   *RA
Gates, Friends and Fun, p.40–53,
82–94 (from There Was Tammie),
p.95–106 (from Smoky and the
Red Fire Engine)   *Alt. 2
——— Good Times Today and To-
morrow, p.206–11   *Alt. 3
——— Good Times Tomorrow,
p.62–67, 81–86   *3–2
——— On Four Feet   *1
——— Splash   *PP1
——— Today We Go, p.41–55, 101–
14 (from There Was Tammie),
115–26 (from Smoky and the Red
Fire Engine)   *2–1
——— Tuffy and Boots   *PP2
Gay, R., Home for Sandy, p.2–50,
64–119   *P–1
Gray, New Friends and Neighbors,
p.242–47   *2–1
——— New Fun with Dick and
Jane, p.65–68, 101–4   *1–1
——— New More Friends and
Neighbors, p.41–50, 58–63 (tricks
on), 92–96   *2–2
——— New More Streets and
Roads, p.26–31   *3–2
——— New Our New Friends, p.85–
89, 104–8   *1–2
——— New Streets and Roads, p.58–
66, 188–92   *3–1
Gruenberg, Favorite Stories Old and
New, p.98–102 (Casey Joins the
Circus)   *RA
Hanna, At Home, p.38–45   P
Haywood, "B" Is for Betsy *In (3)
——— Betsy and Billy   *In (3)
Hildreth, Along the Way, p.6–26 *2–1
——— At Play, p.149–51   *P–1
——— I Know a Secret, p.19–22,
121–29, 138–42   *1–1
——— Mac and Muff   *PP1
Hill, Surprise for Judy Jo   *In (3)
Johnson, E. M., Treat Shop, p.20–26,
36–41, 45–52   *3

Johnson, M. S., Carlo, the Hound
Who Thought He Was a Calf
                                  *In (3)
——— Derry the Wolfhound
                                  *In (3)
——— Runaway Puppy   *In (3)
——— Sir Lancelot and Scamp
                                  *In (3)
——— Smallest Puppy   *In (3)
——— Story of Rickey   *In (3)
Kahl, Away Went Wolfgang   *RA
——— Maxie   *RA
Lathrop, Puppies for Keeps *In (3)
Lenski, Davy and His Dog
                         *RA (K–1); In (1)
——— Dog Came to School
                         *RA (K–1); In (2)
McKee, Big Show, p.49–50, 60–63
                                  *PP3
——— Climbing Higher, p.161–83,
205–31   *3–2
——— Come Along, p.6–22, 24–38
                                  *2–1
——— Jack and Janet, p.50–66,
115–31   *1–1
——— On We Go, p.5–22   *2–2
——— Tip and Mitten, p.1–20 *PP2
——— Up and Away, p.142–63
                                  *1–2
Mason, Timothy Has Ideas *In (3)
Mitchell, Another Here and Now
Story Book, p.225–29   *RA
——— Farm and City, p.3–7   1
——— Here and Now Story Book,
p.147–52   *RA
——— Our Country, p.138–45   3
Monroe, New What Next, p.27–33
                                   *2
Newberry, Barkis   *RA
O'Donnell, Anything Can Happen,
p.162–91   *Par. 1
——— Day In and Day Out, p.16–
21, 43–48, 144–46   *Basic P
——— If I Were Going, p.64–88
                              *Basic 3

———— Through the Green Gate, p.72–128   *Read. 3

Ousley, Come with Us, p.32–40, 60–63   *Pre–P

Quinlan, Faces and Places, p.158–60   *2

———— Happy Days, p.74–78, 92–95   *Read. P

———— To and Fro, p.59–65   *1

Robison, Fun and Fancy, p.50–58 (Necessary Nellie)   *Pre–4

Rowand, George   *RA

Russell, D. H., Around the Corner, p.23–30   *2–2

———— Finding New Neighbors, p.44–54   *3–1

———— On Cherry Street, p.155–60   *1

———— We Are Neighbors, p.25–29, 157–62, 168–78   *2–1

Scott, Rip and Royal   *In (3)

Sheldon, Fields and Fences, p.37–42   *2–1

———— Our School, p.116–21   *P

———— Our Town, p.160–65   *1

———— Town and Country, p.6–15   *2–2

Simon, Mat and Mandy and the Big Dog, Bigger   *In (2)

Will, Finders Keepers   *In (3)

Wright, L., Little Lost Dog   *PP3

Wynkoop, Mac Goes to School   *RA

Yoakam, Children Everywhere, p.221–25   *3

———— Making Storybook Friends, p.30–35   *1

———— On the Way to Storyland, p.5–17, 48–75   P

———— Stories We Like, p.54–60 *2

Zion, Harry the Dirty Dog   *RA (K–1)

DOGS—CARE AND TRAINING

Blough, Pet Show, p.4–13   3

DOLL HOUSES

Hill, Surprise for Judy Jo   *In (3)

Urell, Big City Homes, p.53–60 (furniture)   3+

DOLLS

Association for Childhood Education, Told under the Blue Umbrella, p.109–13   *RA

Bell, Pawnee   *In (3)

Betts, ABC Up the Street and Down, p.86–90   *P

Bianco, Little Wooden Doll *In (3)

Brownell, All Day, Every Day, p.65–70   1

De Leeuw, Nobody's Doll   *In (3)

Emerson, Pioneer Children of America, p.104–19   *3

Gates, Ted and Sally, p.39–44   *P

Gray, New Our New Friends, p.138–42   *1–2

Hildreth, I Know a Secret, p.51–54   *1–1

Johnston, Sugarplum   *RA

Jones, E. O., Big Susan   *In (3)

O'Donnell, Day In and Day Out, p.106–22   *Basic P

———— Round About, p.22–25   *Basic 1

Sheldon, Our Town, p.6–11   *1

Tudor, Dolls' Christmas   *In (3)

Yoakam, On the Way to Storyland, p.20–59   *P

DOMESTIC ANIMALS: *see* Animals, Domestic; Farm Animals; Pets; also names of animals, as Goats

DONKEYS

Association for Childhood Education, Told under the Magic Umbrella, p.145–53, 197–204   *RA

Beim, L. L., Burro That Had a Name   *In (3)

Bettina, Cocolo Comes to America   *In (3)

Betts, ABC Beyond Treasure Valley,
  p.242–48   *3–1
Bond, G. L., Many Surprises, p.92–
  116   *P
Bulla, Donkey Cart   *In (2)
Cutright, Living Together Today and
  Yesterday, p.256–63 (burro)   *3
Gates, Friends and Fun, p.54–65
                                  *Alt. 2
———— Today We Go, p.56–69
  (from Burro That Had a Name)
                                   *2–1
Gay, Z., Pancho and His Burro *RA
Johnson, E. M., Treat Shop, p.144–
  48   *3
Matias, A Little Donkey—Un Petit
  Âne   *RA; In (2)
O'Donnell, Down the River Road,
  p.56–76   *Read. 2
Quinlan, Busy World, p.17–26   *3

DOVES: *see* Pigeons

DRAGONFLIES
Huntington, Let's Go Outdoors, p.80–
  89   In (3)
McClung, Green Darner   In (3)

DRAWING: *see also* Painting
Ousley, Come with Us, p.36–40
                                *Pre–P
Quinlan, Day by Day, p.40–44   *P

DREAMS
Association for Childhood Education,
  Told under the Magic Umbrella,
  p.165–71 (Bean Boy)   *RA
Brownell, Come Rain, Come Shine,
  p.62–63   3
Burton, W. H., Meet Our Friends,
  p.39–47 (animals)   *2
———— Our Happy Ways, p.101–5
  (circus)   *1
Hildreth, Along the Way, p.28–36
                                  *2–1
Jones, E., My Second Health Book,
  p.5–8   2

Mitchell, Another Here and Now
  Story Book, p.175–78, 309–12
                                    *RA
Russell, D. H., Friends Far and
  Near, p.279–89   *3–2
Schwartz, J., Now I Know   In (2)

DRESSING
Mitchell, Here and Now Story Book,
  p.79–88   *RA

DRESSING UP
Gray, New Friends and Neighbors,
  p.109–14   *2–1
Haywood, Two and Two Are Four,
  p.46–51   *In (3)
Hunnicutt, I Have Friends, p.168–75,
  184–87   2
McKee, Come Along, p.196–214
                                   *2–1

DUCKS
Association for Childhood Education,
  Told under the Blue Umbrella,
  p.30–32, 41–43 (Angus and the
  Ducks)   *RA
Betts, ABC Around Green Hills,
  p.96–102   *1
———— ABC Down Singing River,
  p.31–35, 144–50   *2–1
———— ABC Up the Street and
  Down, p.10–18, 54–58, 96–100,
  134–38   *P
Bond, G. L., Happy Times, p.82–86
                                    *1
Burton, W. H., Meet Our Friends,
  p.141–45   *2
Child Study Association of America,
  Read-to-Me Storybook, p.88–90
                                    *RA
Delafield, Mrs. Mallard's Ducklings
                                  In (3)
Evans, Something Different, p.139–
  83   *1
Flack, Angus and the Ducks
                             *RA (K–2)
———— Story about Ping   *RA

Gray, New Friends and Neighbors,
  p.82–86   *2–1
———— New Our New Friends,
  p.164–67   *1–2
Green, Woody, the Little Wood Duck
                                  In (3)
Gruenberg, Favorite Stories Old and
  New, p.86–87 (from Peppi) *RA
Hildreth, Faraway Ports, p.16–34
                                    *3–1
———— Fun in Story, p.36–46 *P–2
———— Good Stories, p.72–80
                                  *Pre–2
———— I Know a Secret, p.1–18
                                    *1–1
———— Story Road, p.2–12   *2–2
McCloskey, Make Way for Ducklings
                              *RA; In (2)
O'Donnell, Day In and Day Out,
  p.84–89   *Basic P
———— Neighbors on the Hill, p.129–
  41, 155–91   *Par. 2
———— Round About, p.6–18, 104–
  21   *Basic 1
Ousley, Open the Gate, p.35–40
                                  *Pre–2
Quinlan, To and Fro, p.165–72   *1
Russell, D. H., Friends Far and Near,
  p.129–42 (Drakestail)   *3–2
———— Little White House, p.136–41
                                      *P
———— We Are Neighbors, p.123–27
                                    *2–1
Sewell, Blue Barns   *RA (K–2)
Sheldon, Our Town, p.166–71   *1
Unwin, Poquito, the Little Mexican
  Duck   *RA; In (3)

EAR
Bauer, Seven or So, p.73–77   2
Brownell, All Day, Every Day, p.58–
  59   1
———— Come Rain, Come Shine,
  p.132–38   3
Charters, Health Secrets, p.77–79 3

Hallock, Health and Happy Days,
  p.79–81   1
Irwin, Keeping Fit for Fun, p.40–43
                                   3
Jones, E., Easy Steps to Health, p.78–
  81   3
O'Keefe, How We Grow, p.145–60
                                   3
Thurber, Exploring Science Three,
  p.36–41   3
Wilcox, Step Lively, p.40–42   3

EARNING MONEY
Bond, G. L., Down Our Way, p.2–
  10, 44–52   *2–1
Burton, W. H., Our Good Neighbors,
  p.26–33   *3
Gray, New More Friends and Neigh-
  bors, p.183–88   *2–2
Gruenberg, Favorite Stories Old and
  New, p.65–70 (from P-Penny)
                                   *RA
Haywood, Here's a Penny, p.94–111
                                  *In (3)
Leavell, Open Doors, p.112–18   *2
———— Open Roads, p.198–204   *3
McKee, Come Along, p.219–43
                                    *2–1
———— Looking Ahead, p.47–67
                                    *3–1
O'Donnell, Down the River Road,
  p.120–59   *Read. 2
———— Five-and-a-Half Club, p.27–
  32   *Par. 3
———— Neighbors on the Hill, p.18–
  71   *Par. 2
———— Round About, p.29–40
                                  *Basic 1
———— Wishing Well, p.13–19
                                  *Par. P
Quinlan, Faces and Places, p.133–
  39   *2
Russell, D. H., We Are Neighbors,
  p.133–41 (The Red Shoes from
  Snipp, Snapp, Snurr)   *2–1

Thomas, Your Town and Mine, p.134, 152–53   3

EARTH: *see also* Ocean
Barnard, Macmillan Science-Life Series, Bk.3, p.158–95   3
Bond, A. D., Knowing about Science, p.79–88   3
——— Thinking about Science, p.94–97   2
Craig, Science around You, p.40–51   2
——— Science Everywhere, p.99–114   3
——— Science near You, p.60–69   1
Frasier, Science—Adventures, p.7–59   3
——— Science—All the Year, p.8–16   2
——— Science—For You, p.16–27   1
Knox, Wonderworld of Science, Bk.2, p.95–106   2
——— Wonderworld of Science, Bk.3, p.32–55 (changes), 109–24   3
Schneider, H., Science for Here and Now, p.3–9   2
Smith, V. C., Science under the Sun, p.93–112   2
Whipple, Our Earth, p.199–214   3

EARTHWORMS
Huntington, Let's Go Outdoors, p.18–23   In (3)
Johnson, E. M., Treat Shop, p.237–41   *3

EASTER
Burton, W. H., Meet Our Friends, p.203–8   *2
Child Study Association of America, Holiday Storybook   *RA
Heyward, Country Bunny and the Little Gold Shoes   *RA; In (2)

Hildreth, Along the Way, p.192–203   *2–1
——— Good Stories, p.108–21   *Pre–2
——— I Know a Secret, p.143–51   *1–1
Jones, M. A., Tell Me about Jesus, p.67–72   *RA
Milhous, Egg Tree   *In (3)
Sheldon, Story Caravan, p.106–20 (from Country Bunny and the Little Gold Shoes)   *3–2
Tudor, Tale for Easter   *RA
Urell, Big City Neighbors, p.53–59 (Russian)   3+

EDISON, THOMAS ALVA
Betts, ABC Along Friendly Roads, p.146–52   3–2

EGGS: *see also* Birds—Eggs and Nests; Chickens; Reproduction
Mitchell, Farm and City, p.24–25 *1
Ousley, Open the Gate, p.17–22   *Pre–2
Partch, Basic Social Studies, p.52–53   3
Schloat, Wonderful Egg   In (3)
Selsam, All about Eggs   RA (K–1); In (2)
Smith, J. R., Our Neighbors at Home, p.19–20   3

EGYPT
Gates, Good Times Today and Tomorrow, p.304–11   Alt. 3
——— Good Times Tomorrow, p.204–11   3–2

ELECTION DAY
Leaf, Fair Play, p.44–45   In (3)

ELECTRICIANS
Partch, Basic Social Studies, p.184 3

ELECTRICITY: *see also* Dams; Magnetism; Radio; Telegraph; Telephone

Baker, A. O., In Your Neighborhood,
p.96 3
Barnard, Macmillan Science-Life Se-
ries, Bk.3, p.212–17, 230–33 3
Blough, Doing Work, p.10–16 3
Bond, A. D., Knowing about Science,
p.135–47 3
——— Thinking about Science,
p.138–41 2
Craig, Science Everywhere, p.77–84
  3
Cutright, Living Together Today and
Yesterday, p.100–105 *3
Frasier, Science—Adventures, p.153–
57 3
——— Science—All the Year, p.122–
26 2
——— Science—For You, p.28–33
  1
——— We Wonder, p.26 PP
Schneider, H., Science Far and Near,
p.264–77 3
Thomas, Your Town and Mine,
p.119–21 3
Thorn, Let's Look Around, p.147–
51 2
Thurber, Exploring Science Two,
p.92–102 2
Urell, Big City Homes, p.61–65 3+

ELEPHANTS
Betts, ABC Beyond Treasure Valley,
p.185–92 *3–1
Bond, G. L., Happy Times, p.2–32
  *1
——— Stories from Everywhere,
p.2–19, 26–37 *3–1
Goudey, Here Come the Elephants!
In (3)
Gray, New Streets and Roads, p.131–
39 *3–1
Gruenberg, Favorite Stories Old and
New, p.324–31 (Elephant's Child)
  *RA

Hildreth, Fun in Story, p.48–58, 123–
38 *P–2
——— Story Road, p.64–90 *2–2
McKee, Climbing Higher, p.309–15
  *3–2
——— On We Go, p.165–86 *2–2
Mitchell, Another Here and Now
Story Book, p.286–91 *RA
——— Here and Now Story Book,
p.185–88 *RA
Nolen, Fun and Frolic, p.268–72
  *3–1
Ousley, Ranches and Rainbows,
p.135–40 *Pre–3
Petersham, Circus Baby *RA (K–2)
Russell, D. H., Around the Corner,
p.55–61 *2–2
——— We Are Neighbors, p.77–82
  *2–1
Sheldon, Fields and Fences, p.140–
50 *2–1
——— Story Caravan, p.144–66
  *3–2
Tarry, Runaway Elephant *In (3)
Will, Chaga *RA (K–2)
Yoakam, Children Everywhere,
p.193–206 3
Zim, Elephants In (3)

ELEVATORS: *see also* Apartment
Houses; Skyscrapers
Association for Childhood Education,
Told under the Magic Umbrella,
p.64–67 *RA
Ousley, Come with Us, p.13–14
  *Pre–P

ELVES: *see* Fairies

ENERGY
Baker, A. O., In Your Neighborhood,
p.92–96 (wind, water, electric
power) 3
Barnard, Macmillan Science-Life Series, Bk.2, p.96–97 (air), 98–100
(water), 101 (electricity) 2

———— Macmillan Science-Life Series, Bk.3, p.196–205   3

Bond, A. D., Knowing about Science, p.8–11, 13–21 (wind), 22–25 (water), 26–31 (oil)   3

Craig, Science around You, p.118–31   2

Thorn, Let's Look Around, p.141–45   2

Thurber, Exploring Science Three, p.114–28   2

ENGLAND

Bulla, Sword in the Tree   *In (2)

Haywood, Primrose Day, p.30–41   *In (3)

O'Donnell, If I Were Going, p.90–93, *94–144   Basic 3

ENGLAND—FOLKLORE

Association for Childhood Education, Told under the Green Umbrella (Old Woman and Her Pig; Scrapefoot)   *RA

Baker, A. B., Talking Tree   *RA

ERRANDS: see Helpfulness

ESKIMOS

Beim, L. L., Little Igloo   *In (3)

Carpenter, Our Little Neighbors at Work and Play: Here, There, Then, and Now, p.202–11   3+

Creekmore, Lokoshi Learns To Hunt Seals   *In (2)

Gates, Good Times Today and Tomorrow, p.295–303   Alt. 3

———— Good Times Tomorrow, p.195–203, 221–29   *3–2

Hildreth, Faraway Ports, p.74–75   *3–1

Johnson, E. M., Treat Shop, p.129–36   *3

Nolen, Do and Dare, p.96–102   *3–2

Quinlan, Busy World, p.288–300   *3

True, Their First Igloo on Baffin Island   RA

ETHICAL STORIES: see Character Building

ETIQUETTE: see Manners

EVENING: see Night

EVERGREEN TREES

Bond, A. D., Knowing about Science, p.49–51 (pine)   3

EXCURSIONS: see Field Trips

EXERCISE: see also Ball; Games; Racing; Skating

Bauer, From Eight to Nine, p.33–37   3

Hallock, Health and Safety for You, p.69–71 (foot)   3

Leaf, Health Can Be Fun, p.16–20   In (3)

O'Keefe, How We Grow, p.78–85   3

EXHIBITIONS: see also Art Museums; Fairs; Pet Shows

Urell, Big City Homes, p.82–89   3+

EXPERIMENTS

Barnard, Macmillan Science-Life Series, Bk.1   1

———— Macmillan Science-Life Series, Bk.2   2

———— Macmillan Science-Life Series, Bk.3   3

Blough, Water Appears and Disappears, p.11–13   3

Bond, A. D., Looking at Science, p.10, 18, 30–31, 53, 83, 87   1

———— Thinking about Science, p.13, 19, 24, 53, 104, 108–9, 115, 120   2

Bradley, Cappy and the Jet Engine   *In (3)

Craig, Science around You, p.39, 49, 80–81, 83, 85   2

———— Science Everywhere, p.51, 53, 67–69, 75–77, 97   3

———— Science near You, p.27–31, 41, 44–47, 77–79   1

Frasier, Science—Adventures, p.13, 23, 25, 27, 52–55, 158–61, 210–16   3

——— Science—All the Year, p.39, 43–44, 57–60, 63, 69–70, 82–84, 132–33   2

Knox, Wonderworld of Science, Bk.3, p.66–67, 73   3

Pine, Sounds All Around   RA

Schneider, H., Let's Find Out   In (3)

——— Now Try This   In (3)

Schwartz, J., Now I Know   In (2)

Thorn, Let's See Why, p.88–93 (chemical change)   3

Thurber, Exploring Science Three, p.48–50   3

——— Exploring Science Two, p.70–71, 136–37, 164–69   2

EXPLORERS: *see also* Lewis and Clark Expedition; also names of explorers, as Columbus, Christopher

Cavanah, Our Country's Story, p.10–15   In (3)

EYE: *see also* Light

Baker, A. O., In Your Neighborhood, p.101–6   3

Barnard, Macmillan Science-Life Series, Bk.3, p.120–28   3

Bauer, Being Six, p.56–57   1

——— From Eight to Nine, p.166–67   3

Brownell, Blue Skies, p.97–100   2

——— Come Rain, Come Shine, p.163–67   3

Charters, Health Secrets, p.80–83   3

Hallock, Health and Happy Days, p.101–3 (glasses)   1

Irwin, Keeping Fit for Fun, p.48–53   3

Jones, E., Easy Steps to Health, p.84–88   3

O'Keefe, How We Grow, p.65–77   3

Wilcox, Here We Go, p.79–81   2

——— Step Lively, p.36–39   3

FACTORIES AND MILLS

Burkhardt, Our Neighborhood, p.68–71 (shoe factory)   2

Hanna, In City, Town, and Country, p.28–29, 88–89   3

——— In the Neighborhood, p.89–96   2

Hunnicutt, I Know People, p.208–28 (automobile)   3

McIntire, Working Together, p.111–13 (clothing)   3

Mitchell, Animals, Plants, and Machines, p.38–41, 46–49 (paper)   2

——— Our Country, p.138–41 (canning)   3

Partch, Basic Social Studies, p.148–49 (shoe)   3

Smith, J. R., Our Neighbors at Home, p.173–84, 198–207   3

Smith, M. E., Bob's Story of the Retail Food Market, p.20–21 (flour mills), p.26–27 (canning)   2+

Thomas, Your Town and Mine, p.109 (cement), 73 (woolen mills), 78–80 (cotton mill), 40–43 (flour mills), 48–49 (cannery)   3

Urell, Big City Workers, p.54–64 (clothing), 74–76 (food), 81–85 (toys)   3+

Whipple, Our Earth, p.150–53 (lumber)   3

FAIRIES

Adshead, Brownies—It's Christmas   *RA (K–1)

Johnson, C., Harold's Fairy Tale   *RA (K–1)

FAIRNESS

Leavell, Open Doors, p.16–22   *2

——— Open Roads, p.73–78, 108–14, 239–44   *3

FAIRS

Betts, ABC Around Green Hills, 110–28, 135–40   *1

Burton, W. H., Our Good Neighbors, p.93–100   *3
Françoise, Jeanne-Marie at the Fair   *RA
Gates, Good Times Today and To-
morrow, p.273–82   *Alt. 3
——— Good Times Tomorrow, p.161–68   *3–2
Hallock, Health and Safety for You, p.11–15   *3
Lattimore, Little Pear, p.105–19   *In (3)
Leavell, Open Roads, p.73–78 (Mexi-
can festival)   *3
McKee, Looking Ahead, p.99–129   *3–1
Ousley, Open the Gate, p.23–28   *Pre–2
Quinlan, To and Fro, p.122–36   *1
Sheldon, Town and Country, p.181–88   *2–2
Smith, J. R., Our Neighbors at Home, p.54–56   1
Urell, Big City Neighbors, p.80–89 (Festival of All Nations)   3+

FAIRS—CHINA
Johnson, E. M., Treat Shop, p.202–9   *3

FAITH
Jones, M. A., Tell Me about Jesus, p.48–49   *RA

FALL: *see* Autumn

FAMILY: *see* Home Life

FARM ANIMALS
Betts, ABC Down Singing River, p.92–98   *2–1
Bond, G. L., Down Our Way, p.128–66   *2–1
Boutwell, Red Rooster   *RA (K–2)
Brown, M. W., Big Red Barn   *RA (K–1)

Carpenter, Our Little Neighbors at Work and Play: Here, There, Then, and Now, p.121–26   3+
Gates, Ted and Sally, p.90–94, 99–111   *P
Gray, New Our New Friends, p.80–84   *1–2
Irwin, Growing Day by Day, p.143–47   2
Johnson, M. S., Story of Rickey   *In (3)
Lewellen, True Book of Farm Ani-
mals   In (2)
McIntire, Billy's Neighbors, p.141–45   2
Monroe, New We Three, p.56–60 *1
O'Donnell, Day In and Day Out, p.98–104, 113–19   *Basic P
——— Round About, p.104–21   *Basic 1
O'Keefe, How We Grow, p.1–10   3
Sheldon, Our School, p.110–36   *P
——— Town and Country, p.9–14   *2–2
Slobodkina, Wonderful Feast   RA (K–1)
Smith, V. C., Science under the Sun, p.9–10   2

FARM LIFE: *see also* Farm Animals; Plantation Life; Ranch Life
Association for Childhood Education, Told under the Blue Umbrella, p.76–79, 114–25   *RA
Aulaire, Don't Count Your Chicks   *In (3)
Blough, Doing Work   3
Bond, A. D., Knowing about Science, p.53–54   3
Bond, G. L., Happy Times, p.66–68, 96–100   1
Boutwell, Red Rooster   *RA (K–2)
Brown, M. W., Country Noisy Book   RA
——— Willie's Adventures *In (2)

Brownell, All Day, Every Day, p.100–14   1

———— Blue Skies, p.139–50   2

Bulla, Donkey Cart   *In (2)

Burton, W. H., Days of Fun, p.105–24   *P

———— Meet Our Friends, p.135–40   *2

———— Our Good Neighbors, p.61–65   *3

———— Our Happy Ways, p.158–82   *1

Carpenter, Our Little Neighbors at Work and Play: Here, There, Then, and Now, p.118–27   3+

Cook, Looking for Susie   *RA (K–1); In (2)

Craig, Science around You, p.132–43   2

De Regniers, Snow Party   *RA

Eberle, Secrets and Surprises, p.140–86   *2–2

Floethe, Farmer and His Cows   In (3)

Gates, Good Times Today, p.3–12, 57–63, 166–76   *3–1

———— Good Times Today and Tomorrow, p.39–45   *Alt. 3

———— Mr. and Mrs. Big   *Unit P

———— On Four Feet, p.119–57   *1

———— Ted and Sally, p.87–124   *P

———— Toby, p.15–32   *Unit 1

Goudey, Good Rain   In (3)

Gray, New Fun with Dick and Jane, p.88–114   *1–1

———— New Our New Friends, p.51–55   *1–2

———— New Streets and Roads, p.58–122   *3–1

Hader, Cock-a-Doodle Doo   *RA

———— Farmer in the Dell   *In (3)

Hallock, Health and Safety for You, p.6–9   3

Hanna, In the Neighborhood, p.8–39   2

Haywood, Two and Two Are Four   *In (3)

Hildreth, At Play, p.29–65   *P–1

Hugley, Around the Home, p.18–22   3

Hunnicutt, I Have Friends, p.13–18, 27–65   2

———— I Live with Others, p.6–21   1

Ipcar, One Horse Farm   *RA (K–2)

Irwin, Growing Day by Day, p.139–52   2

Johnson, M. S., Carlo, the Hound Who Thought He Was a Calf   *In (3)

———— Derry the Wolfhound   *In (3)

———— Story of Rickey   *In (3)

Jones, E., My First Health Book, p.78–89   1

———— My Second Health Book, p.98–102, 113–16   2

Koch, When the Cows Got Out   *In (2)

Lattimore, Holly in the Snow   *In (3)

Lenski, Little Farm   *RA (K–2)

Lewellen, Tommy Learns To Drive a Tractor   *In (3)

McIntire, Billy's Neighbors, p.132–45   2

Mason, Happy Jack   *In (3)

Mitchell, Another Here and Now Story Book, p.277–82, 327–36, 357–58   *RA

———— Farm and City   1

———— Our Country, p.112–25   *3

Monroe, New We Three, p.56–65   *1

———— New What Next, p.61–67   *2–1

O'Donnell, Down the River Road, p.32–76, 91–100   *Read. 2

———— Five-and-a-Half Club, p.148–88, 199–212   *Par. 3

———— Neighbors on the Hill   Par. 2

———— Round About, p.6–9, 68–71, 82–88, 104–21   *Basic 1

Orton, Queenie   *RA

Otto, Little Brown Horse *RA; In (2)
Ousley, Open the Gate, p.82–86
　　　　　　　　　　　　　　*Pre–2
———— Under the Apple Tree, p.52–
78　　　　　　　　　　　　　*Pre–1
Paull, Pancakes for Breakfast
　　　　　　　　　　　　　*RA; In (3)
Potter, Tale of Peter Rabbit　　*RA
Quinlan, Day by Day, p.131–38　*P
———— To and Fro　　　　　　*1
Russell, D. H., Finding New Neigh-
bors, p.8–17, 242–51　　　　*3–1
———— Friends Far and Near, p.32–
42, 226–33　　　　　　　　　*3–2
———— Little White House, p.97–114
　　　　　　　　　　　　　　*P
———— On Cherry Street, p.146–74
　　　　　　　　　　　　　　*1
———— We Are Neighbors, p.196–
200　　　　　　　　　　　　*2–1
Schlein, Something for Now, Some-
thing for Later　　　　　　*In (3)
Sewell, Blue Barns　　*RA (K–2)
Sheldon, Here and Away, p.63–66
　　　　　　　　　　　　　*PP3
———— Our School, p.110–41　*P
———— Town and Country, p.6–38
　　　　　　　　　　　　　*2–2
Smith, J. R., Our Neighbors at Home,
p.8–97　　　　　　　　　　　3
Smith, M. E., Bob's Story of the Re-
tail Food Market, p.8–9 (truck),
10–11 (orchards), 12–13 (cattle
ranch), 14–15 (dairy), 16–17
(chickens), 18–19 (wheat)　2+
———— Mother's Story of Dairying,
p.8–23 (dairy)　　　　　　2+
Smith, V. C., Science along the Way,
p.14–17　　　　　　　　　　1
Sorensen, Ways of Our Land, p.39–
41 (school)　　　　　　　　3
Stolz, Emmett's Pig　　　*In (1)
Tensen, Come to the Farm　In (2)
Thomas, Stories about Linda and
Lee, p.76–90　　　　　　　　1

———— Your Town and Mine, p.46–
49 (truck farm)　　　　　　3
Tresselt, Sun Up　　　*RA (K–2)
———— Wake Up, Farm! *RA (K–1)
Whipple, Our Earth, p.59–71 (dairy),
75–97 (grains and cattle)　3
Wilcox, Here We Go, p.141–45　2

FARM LIFE—RUSSIA
Beim, L. L., Sasha and the Samovar
　　　　　　　　　　　　　*In (3)
Reyher, My Mother Is the Most
Beautiful Woman in the World
　　　　　　　　　　　　*RA; In (3)

FARM LIFE—(THE) SOUTH
Sharpe, Tobe　　　　　　*In (3)

FARM MACHINERY: *see also* Trac-
tors
Lewellen, Tommy Learns To Drive a
Tractor　　　　　　　　*In (3)
Mitchell, Another Here and Now
Story Book, p.363–68　　*RA
———— Farm and City, p.48–49　1
Russell, D. H., On Cherry Street,
p.161–66 (tractor)　　　　　*1
———— We Are Neighbors, p.196–
200 (tractor)　　　　　　2–1

FEARS
Barnard, Macmillan Science-Life Se-
ries, Bk.2, p.69–78　　　　　2
Brownell, Come Rain, Come Shine,
p.62–63, 67　　　　　　　　3
Dalgliesh, Bears on Hemlock Moun-
tain　　　　　　　　*RA; In (3)
Gruenberg, Favorite Stories Old and
New, p.220–22 (Foolish, Timid
Little Hare)　　　　　　　*RA
Haywood, Back to School with Betsy,
p.12–22　　　　　　　　*In (3)
Jones, M. A., Tell Me about God,
p.27–40　　　　　　　　　*RA
O'Donnell, Through the Green Gate,
p.29–70　　　　　　　*Read. 3
Olds, H. D., Silver Button　*In (2)

Schneider, N., While Susie Sleeps
RA (K–2)
FEET: *see* Foot; Shoes
FENCES
 Russell, D. H., On Cherry Street,
  p.171–74   *1
FERRIES: *see* Boats
FESTIVALS: *see* Fairs; Holidays; Mar-
 kets; also names of special days, as
 Thanksgiving Day
FIBERS: *see* Cotton; Flax; Linen;
 Rayon; Wool
FIELD TRIPS
 Bond, A. D., Knowing about Science,
  p.161 (brook)   3
 Burkhardt, Our Community, p.94–
  101 (town hall)   3
 ———— Our Neighborhood, p.14–20
                                                      2
 Burton, W. H., Meet Our Friends,
  p.109–16 (water front)   *2
 ———— Our Good Neighbors, p.19–
  25 (circus animals)   *3
 Dowling, New Seeing Why, p.11–28
                                                      2
 Hanna, At School, p.76–90 (country
  school)   P
 Hunnicutt, I Have Friends, p.119–31
  (train)   2
 ———— I Know People, p.45–50
  (office)   3
 ———— I Live with Others, p.69–81
  (fire department)   1
 Monroe, New What Next, p.61–67
  (farm)   *2–1
 Sheldon, Our School, p.100–41
  (farm)   *P
 Thomas, Stories about Linda and
  Lee, p.76–93   1
 Urell, Big City Fun, p.60–92 (meat
  factory, museums, parks, buildings,
  boat rides, airports, parades, department stores)   3+

FILLING STATIONS
 Barr, Ben's Busy Service Station
                                                   *In (2)
 Gruenberg, Favorite Stories Old and
  New, p.25–27   *RA
 Mitchell, Animals, Plants, and Ma-
  chines, p.132–39   2
FINGERNAILS
 Irwin, Keeping Fit for Fun, p.86–89
                                                      3
FINLAND—FOLKLORE
 Gruenberg, Favorite Stories Old and
  New, p.260–67 (Terrible Olli)
                                                   *RA
FIRE: *see also* Bonfires; Fire Depart-
 ments; Forest Fires; Heating
 Baker, A. O., Around the Corner,
  p.42–44   2
 Bond, G. L., Down Our Way, p.80–
  86   *2–1
 Deming, Indians in Winter Camp,
  p.60–72   In (3)
 Emerson, Pioneer Children of Amer-
  ica, p.142–43   3
 Gray, New More Streets and Roads,
  p.74–81   *3–2
 Gruenberg, Favorite Stories Old and
  New, p.282–83 (Prometheus) *RA
 Hanna, In City, Town, and Country,
  p.98–102 (country)   3
 ———— In the Neighborhood, p.80–
  87   2
 Hildreth, Along the Way, p.102–15
                                                   *2–1
 Knox, Wonderworld of Science,
  Bk.3, p.59–64   3
 O'Donnell, Five-and-a-Half Club,
  p.123–32   *Par. 3
 Sheldon, Our Town, p.81–86   *1
 Smith, V. C., Science along the Way,
  p.92–102   1
 Thurber, Exploring Science Three,
  p.48–60   3

Urell, Big City Water Supply, p.57–
60, 66–68 (pioneer life)   3+
Wilcox, Step Lively, p.23–26   3

FIRE DEPARTMENTS: *see also* Play-
ing Fireman
Beim, J., Country Fireman *RA (K–2)
Bond, G. L., Down Our Way, p.77–
86   *2–1
Brownell, Come Rain, Come Shine,
p.158–60   3
Burkhardt, Our Neighborhood, p.21–
25   2
Burton, W. H., Meet Our Friends,
p.8–14   *2
Gates, Friends and Fun, p.95–106
(from Smoky and the Red Fire
Engine), 169–90   *Alt. 2
———— New Friends and New
Places, p.79–100   *2–2
Hanna, In City, Town, and Country,
p.103   3
Haywood, Eddie and the Fire En-
gine   *In (3)
Hefflefinger, Firemen   In (2)
Hugley, Around the Home, p.15–17
(volunteer)   3
Jones, E., My Second Health Book,
p.76–77   2
Leaf, Fair Play   In (3)
McIntire, Billy's Neighbors, p.20–37
                                    2
Miner, True Book of Policemen and
Firemen   In (2)
O'Donnell, Anything Can Happen,
p.132–55   *Par. 1
O'Keefe, Side by Side, p.85–95   2
Reese, Basic Social Studies, p.70–84
(firemen)   2
Thomas, Stories about Sally, p.38–
42   2
Zaffo, Big Book of Real Fire Engines
                              RA; In (3)

FIRE DEPARTMENTS—HISTORY
Olds, E., Big Fire   RA

FIRE DRILLS
Hanna, At School, p.24–27   1
FIREFLIES
O'Donnell, Neighbors on the Hill,
p.142–48   *Par. 2
Sears, Firefly   In (3)

FIRES: *see also* Forest Fires
Anderson, Blaze and the Forest Fire
                                *In (3)
Association for Childhood Education,
Told under the Blue Umbrella,
p.114–19   *RA
Gruenberg, Favorite Stories Old and
New, p.37–43 (Tabby and the Boat
Fire, Twins and Tabiffa)   *RA

FIREWORKS
Lattimore, Little Pear, p.52–67
                                *In (3)
FIRST AID
Bauer, From Eight to Nine, p.152–
53 (dog bites)   3
Brownell, Come Rain, Come Shine,
p.50–54   3
Hallock, Health in Work and Play,
p.68–71   2
Irwin, Growing Day by Day, p.135–
38   2
———— Keeping Fit for Fun, p.161–
67   3

FISH: *see also* Aquariums; Goldfish;
Sea Horses
Barnard, Macmillan Science-Life Se-
ries, Bk.3, p.44–52   3
Betts, ABC Down Singing River,
p.48–53   *2–1
Bond, A. D., Looking at Science,
p.67–68, 70 (aquarium)   1
Hugley, Around the Home, p.87–89
(salmon), 90–91 (sardines)   3
McIntire, Working Together, p.79–80
(as food)   3
Mitchell, Our Country, p.206–10
(salmon)   3

Partch, Basic Social Studies, p.54–57
  3

Schneider, H., Science Far and Near,
  p.163–67 3

Sheldon, At Home and Away, p.78–
  81 *SPP

——— Here and Away, p.28–30
  (goldfish) *PP3

Smith, J. R., Our Neighbors at
  Home, p.140–44 (marketing) 3

Thorn, Let's See Why, p.176–80 3

——— Let's Try, p.56–59 (goldfish) P

Whipple, Our Earth, p.190–95 3

FISH AS FOOD
Blough, Useful Plants and Animals,
  p.13–14 3

FISHERMEN
Association for Childhood Education,
  Told under the Green Umbrella
  (Fisherman and His Wife) *RA
Beim, L. L., Lucky Pierre *In (3)
Brown, M. W., Little Fisherman *RA
Gates, Friends and Fun, p.122–34
  *Alt. 2

——— New Friends and New
  Places, p.32–44 *2–2
Mitchell, Animals, Plants, and Ma-
  chines, p.164–67 2
Norling, Pogo's Fishing Trip *In (3)
Smith, J. R., Our Neighbors at
  Home, p.144–46 3
Sorensen, Ways of Our Land, p.7–11
  *3

Whipple, Our Earth, p.173–89 3

FISHERMEN—NORWAY
Aulaire, Ola *In (3)

FISHING: see also Fish; Fishermen
Allison, Fishing for Tuna In (3)
Betts, ABC Around Green Hills,
  p.103–8 1

——— ABC Down Singing River,
  p.24–30, 36–40 *2–1

Bond, G. L., Down Our Way, p.33–
  35 *2–1
Burkhardt, Our Neighborhood,
  p.118–27 *2
Burton, W. H., Our Good Neigh-
  bors, p.271–78 *3
Carpenter, Our Little Neighbors at
  Work and Play: Here, There, Then,
  and Now, p.36–37 3+
Deming, Indians in Winter Camp,
  p.30–31, 86–87 In (3)
——— Little Eagle, p.84 *In (2)
Eberle, Secrets and Surprises, p.220–
  42 *2–2
Gray, New More Streets and Roads,
  p.226–34 *3–2
Haywood, Primrose Day, p.164–80
  *In (3)
Leavell, Open Doors, p.68–74 *2
Lenski, Little Sail Boat *RA (K–2)
Monroe, New We Three, p.66–71 *1
Myers, Fishing Cat *RA; In (2)
Nolen, Do and Dare, p.76–85 *3–2
O'Donnell, Down the River Road,
  p.85–90, 101–18 *Read. 2
——— If I Were Going, p.193–200
  *Basic 3
——— Wishing Well, p.81–89
  *Par. P
Russell, D. H., Friends Far and
  Near, p.8–21 (whaling) *3–2
——— On Cherry Street, p.149–54
  *1
Smith, J. R., Our Neighbors at
  Home, p.137–40 3
Sorensen, Ways of Our Land, p.5–11
  3

FLAG DAY
Burkhardt, Our Home and School,
  p.116–21 1
Child Study Association of America,
  Holiday Storybook *RA

FLAX: see also Linen
Partch, Basic Social Studies, p.114–
  15 3

FLOODS: *see also* Dams; Rivers
Betts, ABC Along Friendly Roads,
p.129–35   *3–2
——— ABC Beyond Treasure Val-
ley, p.46–53   *3–1
Hanna, In City, Town, and Country,
p.66–79   3
Mason, Happy Jack, p.45–61 *In (3)
Sorensen, Ways of Our Land, p.53–
55   3
Urell, Big City Book of Conserva-
tion, p.84–91   3+

FLORIDA
Nolen, Do and Dare, p.103–14
                                   *3–2
Sorensen, Ways of Our Land, p.18–
19, 29–30   3

FLORISTS: *see* Stores (flower)

FLOUR: *see* Bread; Corn; Grain;
Wheat

FLOWERS: *see also* Gardens; Plants;
Seeds
Brownell, All Day, Every Day,
p.114, 118–23 (black-eyed Susan)
                                   *1
Dowling, New Seeing Why, p.60–66
                                   2
Jones, M. A., Tell Me about God,
p.23–24   *RA
Podendorf, True Book of Weeds and
Wildflowers   In (2)
Sheldon, At Home and Away, p.65–
68   *SPP
Smith, V. C., Science along the Way,
p.31–38   1
Thorn, Let's Find Out, p.33–35   1
——— Let's Look Around, p.13–16
                                   2

FLUTES: *see* Musical Instruments

FLYING: *see* Airplanes; Balloons;
Birds

FLYING FIELDS: *see* Airports

FOG: *see also* Water; Weather
Blough, Water Appears and Disap-
pears, p.26–27   3
Palmer, Lost and Found, p.33–37
                                   *2–1
Schneider, H., Science for Here and
Now, p.137–38   2

FOOD: *see also* Bakery; Cooking;
Fruit; Grain; Markets; Nuts and
Nutting; Stores (bakery, grocery,
butcher); Vegetables; also names
of foods, as Bread, Butter, Milk
Barnard, Macmillan Science-Life Se-
ries, Bk.2, p.44–45   2
——— Macmillan Science-Life Se-
ries, Bk.3, p.55–79   3
Bauer, From Eight to Nine, p.72–
75 (cooking)   3
——— Just Like Me, p.25–27, 40,
57   P
Betts, ABC Up the Street and Down,
p.60–64   *P
Blough, Useful Plants and Animals,
p.13–15, 31–35   3
Brownell, All Day, Every Day, p.16,
31–36   1
——— Blue Skies, p.25–27, 44–53
                                   *2
——— Come Rain, Come Shine,
p.15, 84–97   *3
Buchheimer, Let's Go to a Candy
Factory   In (3)
Burkhardt, Our Community, p.41–
60   3
——— Our Neighborhood, p.39–57
                                   2
Carpenter, Our Little Neighbors at
Work and Play: Here, There,
Then, and Now, p.33–37, 75–86,
123–27   3+
Charters, Health Secrets, p.129–39
                                   3
Clark, A. N., In My Mother's House
                            RA; In (2)

Emerson, Pioneer Children of America, p.282–83 (corn and wheat)   3

Frasier, Science—All the Year, p.93–95   2

Gruenberg, Favorite Stories Old and New, p.257–59 (Vegetable Tree)   *RA

Hallock, Health and Safety for You, p.6–9, 22–26, 40–44, 50–54, 58–60   3

———— Health in Work and Play, p.19–21, 90–93, 102–3   2

Hanna, In City, Town, and Country, p.154–55   3

Hugley, Around the Home, p.41–100   3

Irwin, Awake and Away, p.18–24   1

————Growing Day by Day, p.16–18, 39–40, 50–53   2

———— Keeping Fit for Fun, p.123–43   3

Jones, E., Easy Steps to Health, p.29–45   3

———— My Second Health Book, p.11–14   2

Jones, M. A., Tell Me about God, p.28–31   *RA

Jupo, Nothing To Eat—But Food   In (3)

Knox, Wonderworld of Science, Bk.1, p.104–7 (animal), p.108–15 (plants)   1

———— Wonderworld of Science, Bk.3, p.8–13   3

Leaf, Health Can Be Fun   In (3)

McIntire, Working Together, p.42–90, 246–47 (map)   3

Mitchell, Another Here and Now Story Book, p.13–14, 50–54, 117–20   *RA

O'Keefe, How We Grow, p.89–117   3

———— Side by Side, p.57, 134–35   2

Partch, Basic Social Studies, p.6–100   3

Paull, Pancakes for Breakfast   *RA; In (3)

Reese, Basic Social Studies, p.149–59 (school lunch)   2

Russell, D. H., We Are Neighbors, p.259–64 (Stone Soup)   *2–1

Schneider, H., Science Far and Near, p.149–59   3

———— Science for Here and Now, p.89–98   2

Smith, J. R., Our Neighbors at Home, p.17–103, 137–48, 213–17   3

Smith, M. E., Bill's Story of the Wholesale Produce Market   2+

———— Bob's Story of the Retail Food Market   2+

Thomas, Your Town and Mine, p.30–65   3

Whipple, Our Earth, p.223–27   3

Wilcox, Come On, p.57–62   1

———— Here We Go, p.93–108   2

———— Step Lively, p.81–94   3

FOOD SUPPLY: *see also* Farm Life; Markets; also names of food industries, as Dairy

Mitchell, Here and Now Story Book, p.131–40   *RA

FOOT: *see also* Shoes

Brownell, Blue Skies, p.62   2

Gray, New Friends and Neighbors, p.21–25   *2–1

Irwin, Keeping Fit for Fun, p.145–59   3

FOOTBALL: *see also* Ball; Baseball; Basketball; Playing Ball

Fishel, Terry and Bunky Play Football   *In (3)

Haywood, Betsy and the Boys, p.20–112   *In (3)

Russell, D. H., We Are Neighbors, p.110–16   *2–1

FOREST FIRES
Anderson, Blaze and the Forest Fire
                              *In (3)
Betts, ABC Along Friendly Roads,
  p.315–22   *3–2
Russell, D. H., Friends Far and
  Near, p.64–75   *3–2
Whipple, Our Earth, p.27–35   3

FORESTS AND FORESTRY: see also
  Arbor Day; Conservation; Lum-
  bering; Trees; Wood
Hanna, In City, Town, and Country,
  p.90–93   3
Mitchell, Our Country, p.215–24
                                 3
Thomas, Your Town and Mine,
  p.100–3   3
Whipple, Our Earth, p.23–27 (rang-
  ers), p.138–43   3

FORGETFULNESS
Leavell, Open Windows, p.38–50 *1

FOSSILS: see also Animals, Prehistoric;
  Dinosaurs
Bond, A. D., Knowing about Science,
  p.57–70   3

FOURTH OF JULY
Betts, ABC Over a City Bridge,
  p.248–53   *2–2
Bond, G. L., Down Our Way, p.11–
  13   *2–1
Cavanah, Our Country's Story, p.28–
  29   RA
Child Study Association of America, Holiday Storybook   *RA
Haywood, Two and Two Are Four,
  p.56–70   *In (3)

FOXES
Bond, G. L., Down Our Way, p.210–
  21   *2–1
——— Stories from Everywhere,
  p.292–98   *3–1
Goudey, Here Come the Wild Dogs!
                             In (3)

Gray, New More Streets and Roads,
  p.156–59, 193–200   *3–2
McKee, Looking Ahead, p.272–81
                                *3–1

FRANCE: see also Brittany
Diska, Andy Says Bonjour!
                         *RA (K–2)
Françoise, Jeanne-Marie at the Fair
                                 *RA
——— Jeanne-Marie in Gay Paris
                                 *RA
——— Springtime for Jeanne-Marie
                     *RA; In (2)
Marokvia, Jannot, a French Rabbit
                                 *RA
Matias, A Little Donkey—Un Petit
  Âne   *RA; In (2)
Quinlan, Busy World, p.118–28   *3

FREEZING: see Frost; Refrigeration;
  Snow; Water

FRICTION
Bond, A. D., Knowing about Science,
  p.30   3
Craig, Science around You, p.110–
  17   2
Dowling, New Learning Why, p.151–
  59   3
Schneider, H., Now Try This
                                In (3)

FRIENDLINESS
Jones, M. A., Tell Me about Jesus,
  p.52–56   *RA
Leavell, Open Doors, p.44–50   *2
——— Open Roads, p.18–31, 80–86
                                  *3

FRIENDSHIP
Barnard, Macmillan Science-Life Se-
  ries, Bk.3, p.140–57   3
Betts, ABC Down Singing River,
  p.19–23, 112–17, 124–29   *2–1
Brownell, Blue Skies, p.63–67   *2
——— Come Rain, Come Shine,
  p.16–18, 55–59   *3

Burton, W. H., Meet Our Friends, p.57–62   *2

Eberle, Secrets and Surprises, p.3–15, 25–29   *2–2

Gates, Friends and Fun, p.16–19   *Alt. 2

———— On Four Feet, p.13–19 *1

———— Today We Go, p.16–19 *2–1

Gray, New Friends and Neighbors, p.55–59, 183–86   *2–1

———— New Our New Friends, p.11–39   *1–2

———— New Streets and Roads, p.86–92   *3–1

Hanna, In the Neighborhood, p.156–61   2

Leavell, Open Windows, p.59–64 *1

O'Keefe, From Head to Toe, p.27–32   1

Russell, D. H., On Cherry Street, p.141–44   *1

Steiner, A Friend Is "Amie"   *RA; In (3)

Wilcox, Step Lively, p.153–56   3

FROGS: *see also* Toads

Baker, A. O., Around the Corner, p.12   2

Barnard, Macmillan Science-Life Series, Bk.2, p.129–30   2

Blough, Animals and Their Young, p.10–11   3

———— Aquarium, p.32–36   3

Burton, W. H., Our Good Neighbors, p.51–56   *3

Flack, Tim Tadpole and the Great Bullfrog   *In (3)

Frasier, Science—For You, p.138–42   1

Gall, All the Year Round, p.3–8   In (3)

Gates, Good Times Today, p.155–65   *3–1

———— Good Times Today and Tomorrow, p.103–13   *Alt. 3

Haywood, "B" Is for Betsy, p.45–59   *In (3)

Hildreth, Along the Way, p.38–46   *2–1

———— Good Stories, p.35–48, 133–53   *Pre–2

Huntington, Let's Go Outdoors, p.62–71   In (3)

Monroe, New What Next, p.10–15   *2

O'Donnell, Round About, p.122–38   *Basic 1

Palmer, Lost and Found, p.98–105   *2–1

Quinlan, Busy World, p.78–91   *3

Schneider, H., Science Far and Near, p.168–69   3

Sears, Tree Frog   In (3)

Sheldon, Our Town, p.112–17   *1

Thurber, Exploring Science Three, p.170–74   3

FRONTIER AND PIONEER LIFE: *see* Pioneer Life

FROST: *see also* Refrigeration; Snow; Water

Blough, Water Appears and Disappears, p.20   3

Burton, W. H., Our Good Neighbors, p.67–73   3

FRUIT: *see also* Berries; also names of fruit, as Apples

Carpenter, Our Little Neighbors at Work and Play: Here, There, Then, and Now, p.123–27   3+

Hunnicutt, I Know People, p.157–63 (farms)   3

Irwin, Growing Day by Day, p.66–67   2

McIntire, Working Together, p.46–57   3

Partch, Basic Social Studies, p.61–67   3

Quinlan, Before Winky, p.12–17   *Pre–PP

———— Happy Days, p.20–24
                              *Read. P
Smith, J. R., Our Neighbors at Home,
    p.51–64   3
Sorensen, Ways of Our Land, p.133–
    37   3
Thomas, Your Town and Mine, p.30–
    32   3

FUEL: see Coal; Fire; Heating

FUN
Bond, G. L., Many Surprises, p.71–
    74   *P
Burkhardt, Our Community, p.142–
    48   3
Burton, W. H., Our Happy Ways,
    p.115–19 (water)   *1
Gray, New Fun with Dick and Jane
                                       *1
———— New Our New Friends, p.61–
    64   *1–2
Hanna, In the Neighborhood, p.97–
    102 (recreation)   2
Hildreth, At Play, p.125–30   *P–1
Irwin, Growing Day by Day, p.48–
    49 (rainy day)   2
McKee, Jack and Janet, p.115–83
                                      *1–1
O'Donnell, Day In and Day Out,
    p.29–34 (rainy day)   *Basic P
Urell, Big City Fun   3+

FUR
Blough, Useful Plants and Animals,
    p.18   3
McIntire, Working Together, p.108–
    9   3
Partch, Basic Social Studies, p.150–
    52   3

FURNACES: see also Heating
Thurber, Exploring Science Three,
    p.58–59   3

FURNITURE: see also Doll Houses;
    Houses; Playing House; Wood
    Carving

Ousley, Under the Apple Tree, p.98–
    102 (chair)   *Pre–1
Quinlan, Day by Day, p.78–94   *P

GALLS (BOTANY): see Insects

GAMES: see also Ball; Kites; Play-
    grounds; Plays; Rainy Day Fun;
    Riddles; Soap Bubbles
Association for Childhood Education,
    Told under the Magic Umbrella,
    p.217–37 (skipping rope)   *RA
Betts, ABC Up the Street and Down,
    p.6–9   P
Bond, G. L., Many Surprises, p.32–
    37, 49–51, 55–58   *P
Brownell, Blue Skies, p.133–37   *2
———— Come Rain, Come Shine,
    p.32–34   *3
Carlson, Junior Party Book   T
Charters, Health Secrets, p.91–93,
    177–79   3
Deming, Indians in Winter Camp
                                    In (3)
Durlacher, Play Party Book   T
Evans, Something Different, p.80–
    96   *1
Frankel, 101 Best Action Games for
    Boys 6–12   T
———— 101 Best Games for Girls
    6–12   T
Gray, New Friends and Neighbors,
    p.16–20, 43–48   *2–1
———— New Streets and Roads,
    p.13–20   *3–1
Hallock, Health and Safety for You,
    p.45–49   3
Irwin, Keeping Fit for Fun, p.27–
    28   3
Jones, E., Easy Steps to Health,
    p.24–26, 144–46   3
———— My First Health Book, p.11,
    19, 25, 33, 43, 51, 61, 77, 91   1
———— My Second Health Book,
    p.15, 34–35, 40–41, 55–56, 63,
    68–69, 96–97, 106–7, 122–23   2

Kohl, Games for Children   T
Monroe, New We Three, p.46–49, 77–82   *1
———— New What Next, p.44–47 (boxing)   *2
O'Keefe, How We Grow, p.139–41, 177–81   3
———— Side by Side, p.50–52, 111–13   2
Quinlan, Day by Day, p.50, 62–76   P
———— To and Fro, p.156–59   *1
Russell, B., Run Sheep, Run *In (2)
Russell, D. H., Little White House, p.179–82   *P
———— On Cherry Street, p.118–22   *1
Sheldon, Fields and Fences, p.16–25 (wishing)   *2–1
Webb, M. A., Games for Younger Children   T
Yoakam, Children Everywhere, p.145–56   *3
———— Making Storybook Friends, p.46–47 (Round the Mulberry Bush)   1

GAMES—INDIANS OF NORTH AMERICA
Deming, Indians in Winter Camp   In (3)

GARAGES: *see also* Filling Stations
Beim, J., Country Garage   *In (3)
Goodspeed, Let's Go to a Garage   In (3)

GARBAGE
McIntire, Billy's Neighbors, p.127   2
Sheldon, Our Town, p.68–73   *1
Zion, Dear Garbage Man *RA (K–1)

GARDENS: *see also* Flowers; Plants; Soils; Vegetables; Weeds
Baker, A. O., Around the Corner, p.89–91   2
Betts, ABC Beyond Treasure Valley, p.39–45   *3–1

———— ABC Down Singing River, p.175–81   *2–1
Bond, A. D., Looking at Science, p.79–91   1
Brownell, All Day, Every Day, p.112–14   *1
———— Come Rain, Come Shine, p.168–70   *3
Burton, W. H., Meet Our Friends, p.146–59   *2
Cooke, Fun-Time Window Garden   In (2)
Credle, Down, down the Mountain   *In (3)
Dowling, New I Wonder Why, p.48–60   1
Fiedler, Green Thumb Story *In (3)
Frasier, Science—Adventures, p.205–21   3
Gray, New Friends and Neighbors, p.209–13   *2–1
Knox, Wonderworld of Science, Bk.1, p.99–102   1
———— Wonderworld of Science, Bk.2, p.137–43   2
———— Wonderworld of Science, Bk.3, p.155–60, 169–72   3
Mitchell, Animals, Plants, and Machines, p.100–9   2
———— Farm and City, p.145–47, 174–77   1
O'Donnell, Day In and Day Out, p.50–55   *Basic P
———— Wishing Well, p.60–71   *Par. P
Palmer, Lost and Found, p.17–28, 41–45   *2–1
Russell, D. H., Around the Corner, p.89–100   *2–2
———— On Cherry Street, p.181–87   *1
Selsam, Seeds and More Seeds   In (2)
Sheldon, Magic Windows, p.227–36   *3–1

―――― Our Town, p.118–23   *1
Smith, J. R., Our Neighbors at Home, p.17–19   3
Thomas, Stories about Sally, p.64   2
Thorn, Let's See Why, p.64–67 (indoor)   3
Yoakam, Stories We Like, p.184–91
                                    *2

GAS
Blough, How the Sun Helps Us, p.5–7   3
Thomas, Your Town and Mine, p.116–18 (pumping station)   3

GAS STATIONS: *see* Filling Stations

GATES
Hanna, In the Neighborhood, p.19–24   2
Ousley, Open the Gate, p.13–16
                                    *Pre–2
Russell, D. H., We Are Neighbors, p.8–13   *2–1

GEESE
Association for Childhood Education, Told under the Blue Umbrella, p.58–62 (from Poppy Seed Cakes)
                                    *RA
Child Study Association of America, Read-to-Me Storybook, p.14–18
                                    *RA
Clark, M., Poppy Seed Cakes *In (3)
Gray, New Friends and Neighbors, p.170–76   *2–1
―――― New More Friends and Neighbors, p.109–14   *2–2
―――― New More Streets and Roads, p.135–43   *3–2
Gruenberg, Favorite Stories Old and New, p.9–11 (from Poppy Seed Cakes)   *RA
Koch, Gone Is My Goose
                                    *RA (K–2)
Russell, D. H., Around the Corner, p.208–14   *2–2

Sewell, Blue Barns   *RA (K–2)
Thomas, Your Town and Mine, p.63–64, 204–6   3
Yoakam, Stories We Like, p.114–25 (from Poppy Seed Cakes)   *2

GENEROSITY
Burton, W. H., Our Good Neighbors, p.26–33   *3
Credle, Down, down the Mountain
                                    *In (3)
Hill, Down-along Apple Market Street   *In (3)
Sheldon, Magic Windows, p.6–18
                                    *3–1

GENTLENESS
Gruenberg, Favorite Stories Old and New, p.228–29 (White Hare of Inabi)   *RA

GEOGRAPHY: *see* Earth; Industries; Maps; Traveling; also names of countries, as Netherlands

GERMANS IN THE UNITED STATES
Urell, Big City Neighbors, p.40–46
                                    3+

GERMANY
Association for Childhood Education, Told under the Blue Umbrella, p.55–57   *RA

GERMS
Barnard, Macmillan Science-Life Series, Bk.2, p.27–28   2
Charters, Health Secrets, p.109–11
                                    3
Hallock, Health and Safety for You, p.118–25   3

GHOSTS
Bright, Georgie   *RA; In (3)
Brock, Spooks and Spirits and Shadowy Shapes   *In (3)
Gruenberg, Favorite Stories Old and New, p.351–54 (Elizabeth the Cow Ghost)   *RA

Leavell, Open Roads, p.158–64 *3
Nolen, Fun and Frolic, p.230–40
       *3–1

GIRAFFES
Nolen, Fun and Frolic, p.213–25
       *3–1
Rey, Cecily G. and the Nine Mon-
 keys   *RA; In (2)

GLASS: *see also* Mirrors
Partch, Basic Social Studies, p.200–1
         3
Schneider, H., Science for Here and
 Now, p.75–80   2

GLASSES: *see also* Eye
Barnard, Macmillan Science-Life Series, Bk.3, p.126–27 3
Brownell, Come Rain, Come Shine,
 p.163–66   *3

GOATS
Asbjørnsen, Three Billy Goats Gruff
        *RA
Association for Childhood Education,
 Told under the Green Umbrella
 (Three Billy Goats Gruff) *RA
Betts, ABC Along Friendly Roads,
 p.121–28   *3–2
 —— ABC Down Singing River,
 p.78–84, 130–34 *2–1
 —— ABC Over a City Bridge,
 p.80–84   *2–2
Bond, G. L., Happy Times, p.150–
 57   *1
 —— Many Surprises, p.79–83,
 88–90   *P
Clark, M., Poppy Seed Cakes
       *In (3)
Françoise, Biquette, the White Goat
     *RA (K–1)
Gates, Good Times Today and To-
 morrow, p.197–205 *Alt. 3
 —— Good Times Tomorrow,
 p.53–61   *3–2
 —— New Friends and New Places,
 p.19–30   *2–2

Gray, New Friends and Neighbors,
 p.142–48, 232–36 *2–1
 —— New More Friends and
 Neighbors, p.115–20, 218–22 *2–2
Haywood, Eddie and Gardenia
       *In (3)
Hildreth, Faraway Ports, p.243–57
       *3–1
Hutchinson, Chimney Corner Stories
 (Three Billy Goats Gruff) *RA
Le Grand, Matilda *In (3)
McKee, Jack and Janet, p.68–78
       *1–1
O'Donnell, Day In and Day Out,
 p.78–83   *Basic P
 —— Friendly Village, p.46–72
      *Basic 2
Ousley, Open the Gate, p.8–28
       *Pre–2
Sheldon, Story Caravan, p.192–232
       *3–2

GOD: *see also* Religion
Fitch, Book about God RA; In (2)
Jones, M. A., Tell Me about God
       *RA

GOLDFISH
Association for Childhood Education,
 Told under the Magic Umbrella,
 p.154–64   *RA
Blough, Aquarium, p.20–25 3
Zim, Goldfish   In (3)

GORILLA
Hoff, Julius   *In (1–2)

GOVERNMENT: *see also* Citizenship;
 Election Day; Law; United Na-
 tions; also names of government
 services, as Police
Burkhardt, Our Community, p.88–
 101   3
 —— Our Neighborhood, p.137–
 45   2
Cutright, Living Together Today and
 Yesterday, p.81–91 3

Hanna, In City, Town, and Country
3
Leaf, Fair Play   In (3)
────── Let's Do Better, p.40–49
In (3)
McIntire, Billy's Neighbors, p.129 3
Thomas, Your Town and Mine,
p.191–92 (sanitation department),
p.193 (health), 196 (fire department), 206 (humane society),
198–99 (election)   2

GRAIN: *see also* Corn; Rice; Wheat
Charters, Health Secrets, p.28–29 3
Hugley, Around the Home, p.57–69
3
Partch, Basic Social Studies, p.25–
31, 36–41   3
Thomas, Your Town and Mine,
p.40–44   3

GRAIN ELEVATORS
Hunnicutt, I Know People, p.180–
83   3

GRASSES
Mitchell, Our Country, p.42–43 3
Thurber, Exploring Science Three,
p.176–88   3

GRASSHOPPERS
Blough, Animals and Their Young,
p.8–9   3
────── Insect Parade, p.27   3
Huntington, Let's Go Outdoors,
p.54–57   In (3)
Thurber, Exploring Science Two,
p.6–18   2
Yoakam, Children Everywhere,
p.227–34   3

GRAVITATION
Thurber, Exploring Science Two,
p.50–64   2

GREAT PLAINS
Emerson, Pioneer Children of America, p.264–81   *3

Hunnicutt, I Know People, p.171–
200   3
Mitchell, Our Country, p.41–46,
*47–64, 66–91   2

GREEDINESS
Gruenberg, Favorite Stories Old and
New, p.280–81 (King Midas),
289–92 (Why the Sea Is Salt)
*RA

GROUND HOGS: *see* Woodchucks

GROUP PLANNING
Bauer, From Eight to Nine, p.106–
7   3

GROWTH
Bauer, From Eight to Nine, p.174–
79   3
────── Seven or So, p.16–25   2
Charters, Health Secrets, p.65–67
(child), 70–71 (child), 68 (plant),
69 (animal)   3
Dowling, New Seeing Why, p.76–82
2
Hallock, Health and Happy Days,
p.90–93, 108–10, 118–19   1
────── Health in Work and Play,
p.116–18   2
Irwin, Growing Day by Day, p.73–
82   2
Jones, E., Easy Steps to Health,
p.51–57   3
O'Keefe, From Head to Toe, p.56–
61   *1
────── How We Grow, p.163–66 3
────── Side by Side, p.18–21   2
Schneider, H., Science for Here and
Now, p.176–78   2
Wilcox, Step Lively, p.75–80   3

GUINEA PIGS
Blough, Pet Show, p.27–29   3

GULF OF MEXICO
Hunnicutt, I Know People, p.129–70
3

GULLS
  Bond, Guy L., Once upon a Story-
    time, p.146–60   *3–2
  Huntington, Let's Go to the Sea-
    shore, p.84–87   In (3)
  Mitchell, Here and Now Story Book,
    p.193–96   *RA
  Robinson, W. W., At the Seashore
                             In (3)

GYPSIES
  Anderson, Blaze and the Gypsies
                             *In (3)

HABITS
  Brownell, All Day, Every Day, p.11–
    12 (health)   1
  Wilcox, Step Lively, p.167–70
    (health), 128–30 (neatness)   3

HAIR: *see also* Cleanliness
  Barnard, Macmillan Science-Life Se-
    ries, Bk.3, p.98–100   3
  Charters, Health Secrets, p.200–2   3

HALLOWEEN: *see also* Dressing Up;
    Pumpkins
  Averill, Jenny's Moonlight Adventure
                             *In (2)
  Bond, Guy L., Once upon a Story-
    time, p.206–12   *3–2
  Brock, Spooks and Spirits and Shad-
    owy Shapes   *In (3)
  Burton, W. H., Meet Our Friends,
    p.209–14   *2
  ———— Our Good Neighbors, p.34–
    40   *3
  Child Study Association of America,
    Holiday Storybook   *RA
  Gates, Two Boys and a Tree, p.41–
    46, 123–26   *Sup. 1
  Gray, New Friends and Neighbors,
    p.109–14   *2–1
  Hallock, Health and Safety for You,
    p.40–49   3
  Hanna, In the Neighborhood, p.50–
    54   2

Haywood, Betsy and Billy, p.30–44
                             *In (3)
———— Here's a Penny, p.64–93
                             *In (3)
Hildreth, At Play, p.112–16   *P–1
———— Fun in Story, p.92–104 *P–2
Hill, Jack o'Lantern for Judy Jo
                             *In (3)
McIntire, Billy's Neighbors, p.39–48
                               2
Massey, Littlest Witch   *RA
O'Keefe, How We Grow, p.21–32   3
Russell, D. H., Finding New Neigh-
    bors, p.242–51   *3–1
Sheldon, Magic Windows, p.107–14
                             *3–1
Tudor, Pumpkin Moonshine   *RA

HALLOWEEN—PARTIES
  Betts, ABC Along Friendly Roads,
    p.54–60   *3–2
  ———— ABC Around Green Hills,
    p.144–49   *1
  ———— ABC Down Singing River,
    p.85–90   *2–1
  Gray, New Streets and Roads, p.35–
    41   *3–1

HANDICRAFT: *see also* names of
    handicrafts, as Clay Modeling;
    Wood Carving
  Haywood, Primrose Day, p.42–60
                             *In (3)
  Jordan, Mother Goose Handicraft T

HANUKKAH
  Child Study Association of America,
    Holiday Storybook   *RA

HAPPINESS
  Association for Childhood Education,
    Told under the Magic Umbrella,
    p.145–53   *RA
  Hildreth, Along the Way, p.144–50
                             *2–1
  Leavell, Open Windows, p.174–79
                               *1

O'Donnell, Day In and Day Out, p.148–49 *Basic P

HARBORS
Agle, Three Boys and a Tugboat *In (3)
Betts, ABC Over a City Bridge, p.30–35 *2–2
Mitchell, Farm and City, p.103–11 1
——— Our Country, p.205 3

HARMONICAS
McCloskey, Lentil *In (3)

HATS
Brownell, All Day, Every Day, p.106–9 *1
——— Blue Skies, p.47–52 *2
Gates, New Friends and New Places, p.8–17 *2–2
Gray, New More Friends and Neighbors, p.121–26 *2–2
Leavell, Open Doors, p.52–58 (Mexican) *2
Ousley, Under the Apple Tree, p.94–97 *Pre–1
Russell, D. H., Around the Corner, p.190–95 *2–2
Seuss, 500 Hats of Bartholomew Cubbins *RA
Ward, N. W., Black Sombrero *RA (K–1)

HAWAIIAN ISLANDS
Bare, Maui's Summer *In (3)

HAY: see also Grasses
Mitchell, Farm and City, p.37–47 1
Smith, J. R., Our Neighbors at Home, p.40–41 3

HEALTH: see also Air; Cleanliness; Clothing; Diseases; Germs; Lighting; Mental Health; Physiology; Posture; Skin; Sleep
Barnard, Macmillan Science-Life Series, Bk.1, p.58–62 1

——— Macmillan Science-Life Series, Bk.2, p.26–31 2
Irwin, Keeping Fit for Fun, p.90–95 3
Jones, E., Easy Steps to Health, p.113–34 (protection) 3
Leaf, Health Can Be Fun In (3)
Quinlan, Busy World, p.161–204 *3
Wilcox, Come On, p.114–19 (play) 1
——— Here We Go, p.46–56 2
——— Step Lively, p.163–65 (fresh air) 3

HEAT: see also Fire; Sun; Thermometers
Barnard, Macmillan Science-Life Series, Bk.3, p.221–30 3
Dowling, New Learning Why, p.90–96 3
Frasier, Science—Adventures, p.149–52 3
——— Science—All the Year, p.131–36 2
——— We Wonder, p.17 PP
Knox, Wonderworld of Science, Bk.3, p.65–75 3
Schneider, H., Let's Find Out, p.6–20 In (3)
——— Science Far and Near, p.211–26 3
Smith, V. C., Science around the Clock, p.77–98 3
Thorn, Let's See Why, p.101–5 3

HEATING: see also Coal; Furnaces; Wood
Hugley, Around the Home, p.169–75 3

HEBREWS: see Bible Stories; Shepherds

HELICOPTERS
Agle, Three Boys and a Helicopter *In (3)

Russell, D. H., Around the Corner, p.126–31　　　　　　　　　*2–2

HELPERS: *see also* types of community helpers, as Bakery; Garbage
Burton, W. H., Meet Our Friends, p.2–7 (ice-cream man)　　　*2
Hanna, At School, p.17–23, 33–35　　　　　　　　　　　　1
────── In City, Town, and Country, p.14–17 (community)　　　3
Hunnicutt, I Know People, p.33–44 (community)　　　　　　　3
McIntire, Billy's Friends, p.70–86　1
────── Billy's Neighbors　　　　　2
────── Working Together, p.20–22 (contractors)　　　　　　3
Mitchell, Animals, Plants, and Machines, p.213–25　　　　　　*2
Ousley, Ranches and Rainbows, p.68–73 (shoe repairman) *Pre–3
Reese, Basic Social Studies, p.116–17 (railroad), 122–25 (airport) 2
Russell, D. H., We Are Neighbors, p.173–78 (expressman)　　　*2–1
Sheldon, Here and Near, p.47–50 (ice-cream man)　　　　　*PP2
Smith, M. E., Bill's Story of the Wholesale Produce Market, p.14–15 (sweeper), 16–17 (swamper), 18–19 (weigher), 20–21 (inspector), 22–23 (packer)　　　2+
────── Bob's Story of the Retail Food Market, p.30–31 (checker), 32–33 (stock clerk), 42–45 (check stand)　　　　　　　　　2+
────── Joe's Story of the Airport　2+
────── Mother's Story of Dairying, p.30–31, 32–33 (inspector)　2+
Urell, Big City Book of Conservation, p.39–41, 52–57 (protective)　　　　　　　　　　　3+
────── Big City Homes, p.38–52 (school remodeling)　　　　　3+
────── Big City Workers　　　　　3+

Wilcox, Here We Go, p.59–62　　2

HELPFULNESS
Betts, ABC Beyond Treasure Valley, p.27–32　　　　　　　　*3–1
────── ABC Up the Street and Down, p.41–45, 70–73, 106–10, 144–49　　　　　　　　　　　*P
Brownell, Blue Skies, p.*20–24, 80–81　　　　　　　　　　2
Burkhardt, Our Home and School, p.23–46, 86–88　　　　　　1
────── Our Way, p.8–11, 16–19 PP
Gray, New Friends and Neighbors, p.49–54　　　　　　　　*2–1
────── New More Friends and Neighbors, p.160–71　　　*2–2
────── New Our New Friends, p.56–60　　　　　　　　　*1–2
Hallock, Health in Work and Play, p.141–44　　　　　　　　2
Hanna, At Home, p.54–57　　　P
────── In the Neighborhood　2
Hunnicutt, I Live with Others, p.16–18, 45–47　　　　　　　1
Jones, M. A., Tell Me about Jesus, p.33–35　　　　　　　*RA
Leavell, Open Doors, p.172–77　*2
Monroe, New We Three, p.29–32 *1
O'Donnell, Five-and-a-Half Club, p.216–55　　　　　　　*Par. 3
Palmer, Lost and Found, p.135–39　　　　　　　　　　　*2–1
Russell, D. H., Finding New Neighbors, p.92–102　　　　　　*3–1
────── Little White House, p.183–87　　　　　　　　　　*P
Sheldon, Here and Near, p.52–54　　　　　　　　　　*PP2

HENS: *see* Chickens

HEROES: *see* Bravery; Fire Departments

HERONS
Blough, Birds in the Big Woods, p.11　　　　　　　　　　3

HIBERNATION: *see also* Animals in Winter; Bears; Woodchucks

Betts, ABC Over a City Bridge, p.218–23   2–2

Blough, Animals round the Year, p.14–16, 20–22   3

Bond, A. D., Knowing about Science, p.41–44   3

Craig, Science around You, p.68   2

Frasier, Science—Adventures, p.72–74   3

O'Donnell, Neighbors on the Hill, p.93–108   *Par. 2

—— Round About, p.134–38   *Basic 1

Quinlan, To and Fro, p.179–81   *1

Thorn, Let's Look Around, p.39–43   2

Yoakam, Stories We Like, p.178–83   2

HIGHWAYS: *see* Streets and Roads; Transportation

HIPPOPOTAMUS

Gruenberg, Favorite Stories Old and New, p.96–97 (from Puddle) *RA

HISTORY: *see* United States—History

HOBBIES: *see also* Carpentry; Experiments; Gardens; Handicraft

Hallock, Health and Safety for You, p.175–80 (hobby shows)   3

HOLIDAYS: *see also* Birthdays; Fairs; also names of holidays, as Christmas

Carlson, Junior Party Book   T

Child Study Association of America, Holiday Storybook   *RA

Hastings, All Kinds of Days In (1)

HOLLAND: *see* Netherlands

HOME LIFE: *see also* Character Building

Barnard, Macmillan Science-Life Series, Bk.1   1

Brown, M. W., Indoor Noisy Book   RA

Brownell, All Day, Every Day, p.8–50   1

Buckley, Grandfather and I   *RA

Burkhardt, Our Family   P

—— Our Home and School, p.23–46, 78–82, 89–101   1

—— Our Way, p.6–11, 42–43 PP

Carpenter, Our Little Neighbors at Work and Play: Here, There, Then, and Now   3+

Cook, Looking for Susie
                          *RA (K–1); In (2)

De Angeli, Ted and Nina Go to the Grocery Store   *In (2)

Evans, Something Different   *1

Frank, Daddies   RA (K–2)

Gates, Friends and Fun, p.20–23
                                         *Alt. 2

—— Splash   *PP1

—— Ted and Sally   *P

—— Today We Go, p.20–23 *2–1

—— Tommy Little, p.37–44
                                       *Sup. P

Gray, New Fun with Dick and Jane
                                         *1–1

—— New Our New Friends *1–2

Hanna, At Home   P

Hawkins, Who Wants an Apple?
                                        *In (3)

Haywood, Here's a Penny   *In (3)

—— Primrose Day   *In (3)

Hildreth, At Play   *P–1

—— I Know a Secret, p.56–64
                                         *1–1

Hunnicutt, I Play, p.43–61   P

Jones, E., My First Health Book, p.62–75   1

Jones, M. A., Tell Me about God, p.14–16   *RA

—— Tell Me about Jesus, p.11–32   *RA

Krauss, Backward Day *RA (K–2)

Leavell, Open Windows, p.68–93 *1

Lenski, Davy's Day *RA
—— Papa Small
  *RA (K–2); In (2)
—— Surprise for Mother *RA
McIntire, Billy's Friends, p.45–63 1
—— Working Together, p.38–40
  3
McKee, Jack and Janet, p.47–112
  *1–1
—— Looking Ahead, p.5–46 *3–1
Mitchell, Another Here and Now
  Story Book *RA
O'Donnell, Day In and Day Out
  *Basic P
—— Five-and-a-Half Club, p.48–
  55 *Par. 3
—— Round About, p.160–84
  *Basic 1
—— Wishing Well, p.20–33
  *Par. P
O'Keefe, From Head to Toe, p.98–
  119 1
Russell, D. H., Friends Far and Near,
  p.76–84 *3–2
—— Little White House, p.6–30
  *P
—— My Little Green Story Book
  *PP2
—— My Little Red Story Book
  *PP1
Shackelford, My Happy Days, p.1–
  65 *In (3)
Sheldon, At Home *PP1
—— At Home and Away *SPP
—— Here and Near *PP2
Thomas, Stories about Linda and
  Lee, p.28–64 1
Urell, Big City Fun, p.26–29 3+

HOME LIFE—CHINA
Lattimore, Little Pear *In (3)
—— Story of Lee Ling *In (3)

HOME LIFE—SWEDEN
Beskow, Pelle's New Suit
  *RA; In (3)

HONESTY
Jones, M. A., Tell Me about Jesus,
  p.40–44 *RA
Leavell, Open Doors, p.32–38, 87–
  93, 120–26, 184–90 *2
—— Open Roads, p.50–56, 166–
  72, 206–12, 223–29 *3
—— Open Windows, p.98–103,
  112–17, 120–25, 167–73 *1
McKee, Climbing Higher, p.75–92
  *3–2
O'Donnell, Five-and-a-Half Club,
  p.87–104 *Par. 3
HONEY: *see also* Bees
Mason, Little Jonathan, p.94–108
  *In (3)

HORNED TOADS: *see* Lizards
HORSES
Anderson, Billy and Blaze *In (2)
—— Blaze and the Forest Fire
  *In (3)
—— Blaze and the Gypsies *In (3)
—— Blaze Finds the Trail *In (3)
Association for Childhood Education,
  Told under the Blue Umbrella,
  p.97–100 *RA
—— Told under the Magic Um-
  brella, p.180–88 *RA
Beatty, Little Wild Horse *RA (K–1)
Betts, ABC Along Friendly Roads,
  p.236–43 (wild) *3–2
—— ABC Beyond Treasure Val-
  ley, p.130–37 *3–1
—— ABC Down Singing River,
  p.66–70 *2–1
—— ABC Over a City Bridge,
  p.*12–17, 85–90 *2–2
Blough, Useful Plants and Animals,
  p.3–6 3
Bond, G. L., Down Our Way, p.69–
  73 *2–1
—— Happy Times, p.66–76 *1
Brown, Paul, Sparkie and Puff Ball
  *In (3)
Bulla, Old Charlie *In (3)

Burton, V. L., Calico, the Wonder Horse   *RA (K–2)

Child Study Association of America, Read-to-Me Storybook, p.111–16   *RA

Clark, A. N., In My Mother's House, p.35–37   RA; In (2)

Crowell, What Can a Horse Do That You Can't Do?   RA; In (3)

Dennis, W., Flip   *RA

———— Flip and the Cows   *RA

Gates, Friends and Fun, p.68–80 (from Billy and Blaze)   *Alt. 2

———— Good Times Today, p.135–43   *3–1

———— Good Times Today and Tomorrow, p.257–72   *Alt. 3

———— Good Times Tomorrow, p.143–58   *3–2

———— Toby   *Unit 1

———— Today We Go, p.73–85 (from Billy and Blaze), 86–97 (from Blaze and the Forest Fire)   *2–1

Gray, New More Friends and Neighbors, p.70–80   *2–2

———— New Our New Friends, p.172–77   *1–2

———— New Streets and Roads, p.155–64   *3–1

Gruenberg, Favorite Stories Old and New, p.115–20 (Shire Colt)   *RA

Hader, Little Appaloosa   *In (3)

Haywood, Two and Two Are Four, p.88–102   *In (3)

Hogner, Daisy, a Farm Fable   *RA (K–2)

Ipcar, One Horse Farm   *RA (K–2)

Johnson, E. M., Treat Shop, p.8–11, 65–71   *3

Jones, E., My Second Health Book, p.117–18   2

Leavell, Open Road, p.58–63   *3

McGinley, Horse Who Had His Picture in the Paper   *RA (K–2)

———— Horse Who Lived Upstairs   *RA

McIntire, Working Together, p.147–48   3

Mitchell, Animals, Plants, and Machines, p.123–29   *2

———— Another Here and Now Story Book, p.221–23, 277–82   *RA

———— Farm and City, p.33–35   1

Monroe, New We Three, p.9–13   *1

Nolen, Fun and Frolic, p.67–98   *3–1

O'Donnell, Day In and Day Out, p.70–76   *Basic P

———— Friendly Village, p.25–44   *Basic 2

———— Through the Green Gate, p.15–70   *Read. 3

Orton, Prancing Pat   *RA

Otto, Little Brown Horse   *RA; In (2)

Ousley, Open the Gate, p.94–101   *Pre–2

———— Ranches and Rainbows, p.8–21, 52–59, 96–124, 152–57   *Pre–3

Quinlan, To and Fro, p.104–8   *1

Russell, D. H., Around the Corner, p.70–74   *2–2

———— Finding New Neighbors, p.8–16, 200–7, 217–23 (burro)   *3–1

———— My Little Blue Story Book, p.25–28   *PP3

———— On Cherry Street, p.146–48, 193–98   *1

———— We Are Neighbors, p.128–32   *2–1

Sheldon, Magic Windows, p.6–18   *3–1

———— Our School, p.122–26   *P

———— Town and Country, p.76–101, 160–73   *2–2

Slobodkin, Horse with the High-heeled Shoes   *RA (K–1)

Thorn, Let's See Why, p.14–19   3
Will, Even Steven   *RA
Yoakam, Stories We Like, p.165–
75   *2

HOSPITALS: *see also* Doctors; Health;
Nurses and Nursing
Bauer, Seven or So, p.126–32   2
Bemelmans, Madeline   *RA
Sheldon, Our Town, p.74–80   *1

HOUSEKEEPING
Gág, Gone Is Gone   *RA; In (3)
Gray, New More Friends and Neigh-
bors, p.210–17   *2–2
Hutchinson, Candle-Light Stories
(Husband Who Was Left To Mind
the House)   *RA
Watts, Cow in the House
*RA (K–2)

HOUSES: *see also* Animals—Houses;
Apartment Houses; Automobiles
—Trailers; Bird Houses; Doll
Houses; Log Cabins
Barnard, Macmillan Science-Life Se-
ries, Bk.1, p.101–3   1
——— Macmillan Science-Life Se-
ries, Bk.3, p.219–20   3
Beim, L. L., Little Igloo   *In (3)
Betts, ABC Down Singing River,
p.6–11   *2–1
Burkhardt, Our Community, p.17–
40   3
Burton, V. L., Little House   *RA
Burton, W. H., Our Good Neighbors,
p.111–19   *3
Carpenter, Our Little Neighbors at
Work and Play: Here, There,
Then and Now, p.8–12, 17–23, 66–
69, 119, 139, 144–46, 204   3+
Child Study Association of America,
Read-to-Me Storybook, p.4–5 *RA
Emerson, Pioneer Children of Ameri-
ca, p.54–73, 264–70   *3
Evans, Something Different, p.2–17
*1

Hader, Little Stone House   *RA
Hanna, At Home, p.42–45 (dog) P
——— In City, Town, and Country,
p.26   3
Hildreth, Faraway Ports, p.62–96
*3–1
Hugley, Around the Home, p.136–68
3
Hunnicutt, I Have Friends, p.70–79,
89–91   2
McIntire, Working Together, p.9–37
3
McKee, Up and Away, p.168–80
*1–2
Mitchell, Animals, Plants, and Ma-
chines, p.202–10 (play)   2
——— Another Here and Now Story
Book, p.193–98, 318–20   *RA
Partch, Basic Social Studies, p.176–
213 (building; carpentry; masonry;
plumbing)   3
Quinlan, Happy Days, p.42–46 (toy)
*Read. P
Russell, D. H., Around the Corner,
p.76–82   *2–2
Sheldon, Our Town, p.50–55   *1
Urell, Big City Homes   3+
Wilcox, Here We Go, p.35–38 (play)
2

HOUSES—OTHER LANDS
Carpenter, Our Little Neighbors at
Work and Play: Here, There, Then,
and Now, p.11–12   3+

HOUSES—PLANS
Burkhardt, Our Community, p.29–34
3
Cutright, Living Together Today and
Yesterday, p.233–39   3
McIntire, Working Together, p.14–
15   3
Partch, Basic Social Studies, p.177 3

HOUSING DEVELOPMENTS
Urell, Big City Homes, p.23–26   3+

HUMOR

Association for Childhood Education, Told under the Blue Umbrella, p.125–33   *RA

———— Told under the Magic Umbrella, p.55–58, 101–18   *RA

Beattie, In Came Horace *RA(K–2)

Bishop, Five Chinese Brothers
                    *RA; In (3)

———— Man Who Lost His Head
                        *RA

Bright, Georgie   *RA; In (3)

Chalmers, Hundreds and Hundreds of Pancakes   *In (3)

Charles, Roundabout Turn   *RA

Child Study Association of America, Read Me Another Story   *RA

Dalgliesh, Bears on Hemlock Mountain   *RA; In (3)

Daugherty, Andy and the Lion
                   *RA; In (3)

Dennis, W., Flip   *RA

Dobbs, No Room   *In (3)

———— Once upon a Time *In (3)

Elkin, Gillespie and the Guards *RA

———— Loudest Noise in the World
                        *RA

Ets, Mister Penny   *RA

Gág, Gone Is Gone   *RA; In (3)

———— Millions of Cats   *RA

———— Nothing at All   *RA

Gates, Good Times Today, p.199–204 (Hole in the Wall), 205–11 (Mrs. Goose's Rubbers), 212–15 (Nothing at All), 216–24 (Waggable Tail), 226–29 (Muddy Mouse), 230–40 (Tuffy Bear's Sugar Party)   *3–1

———— Good Times Today and Tomorrow, p.135–60 (Hole in the Wall, Mrs. Goose's Rubbers, Nothing at All, Waggable Tail) *Alt. 3

Gramatky, Hercules   *RA

———— Little Toot   *RA (K–2)

———— Loopy   *RA

Gray, New More Streets and Roads, p.98–154   *3–2

Gruenberg, Favorite Stories Old and New, p.71–76 (from Jane's Father), 319–63   *RA

Guilfoile, Nobody Listens to Andrew
                       *In (2)

Kahl, Duchess Bakes a Cake *RA

Leaf, Story of Ferdinand   *In (3)

McCloskey, Lentil   *In (3)

———— Make Way for Ducklings
                    *RA; In (2)

McKee, Come Along, p.69–89 2–1

———— Looking Ahead, p.188–89
                        *3–1

———— On We Go, p.189–227 *2–2

Milne, House at Pooh Corner *RA

———— Winnie-the-Pooh   *RA

Monroe, New Tall Tales, p.50–55 (Peter, the Parking Meter), 56–64 (No Time To Stop), 65–74 (Mr. Scrunch)   *3–1

Nolen, Fun and Frolic, p.202–12 (Ebenezer Nevercouldsneezer), 213–25 (Tame Giraffe), 274–80 (Good Flea and Wicked King)
                        *3–1

Ousley, Ranches and Rainbows, p.32–37 (Mrs. Turtle and the New Hat), 39–44 (At the Animal Show), 45–51 (Aunt Daisy and Her Things), 52–59 (Horse in the House), 60–66 (Fisherman Fred)
                      *Pre–3

———— Under the Apple Tree, p.86–93 (Boppet, Please Stop It!)
                      *Pre–1

Rickert, Bojabi Tree   *RA; In (3)

Robison, Fun and Fancy, p.138–42 (My Father Meets a Lion), 144–48 (Georgie), 149–57 (Hospital Mouse), 160–75 (Henry Huggins)
                      *Pre–4

Russell, D. H., Finding New Neighbors, p.92–131   *3–1

———— Friends Far and Near, p.248–
59   *3–2
Seuss, And To Think That I Saw It
on Mulberry Street   *RA
———— Cat in the Hat Comes Back
*In (1)
———— 500 Hats of Bartholomew
Cubbins   *RA
Sheldon, Story Caravan, p.122–90
*3–2
Yoakam,   Children   Everywhere,
p.169–74, 180–89   *3

HUNGARY—FOLKLORE
Baker, A. B., Talking Tree   *RA
Gruenberg, Favorite Stories Old and
New, p.249–52 (Little Rooster and
the Turkish Sultan)   *RA

HUNTING
Deming, Indians in Winter Camp
In (3)
———— Little Eagle   *In (2)
Russell, D. H., Friends Far and Near,
p.302–9   *3–2

HYGIENE: *see* Health

ICE CREAM
Gruenberg, Favorite Stories Old and
New, p.132–34   *RA
McKee, Climbing Higher, p.142–52
(cones)   *3–2
Nolen, Do and Dare, p.126–31 (in-
vention of cones)   *3–2
Sheldon, Here and Away, p.8–10
*PP3

ICE SKATING: *see* Winter Sports

ICELAND
Russell, D. H., Friends Far and Near,
p.204–11   *3–2

IMAGINATION
Daugherty, Andy and the Lion
*RA; In (3)
Ets, In the Forest   *RA

Gruenberg, Favorite Stories Old and
New, p.129–71   *RA
Johnson, C., Harold's Fairy Tale
*RA (K–1)
———— Harold's Trip to the Sky
*RA (K–2)
Milne, House at Pooh Corner *RA
———— Winnie-the-Pooh   *RA
Seuss, And To Think That I Saw It
on Mulberry Street   *RA
Slobodkin, Clear the Track for Mi-
chael's Magic Train   *RA
———— Magic Michael *RA (K–2)
Vreeken, Boy Who Would Not Say
His Name   *In (2)

IMMIGRANTS: *see also* names of national groups in the United States,
as Germans in the United States
Cavanah, Our Country's Story, p.60–
61   In (3)

INCLINED PLANES
Blough, Doing Work, p.26–28   3
Craig, Science near You, p.33–37   1

INDEPENDENCE DAY: *see* Fourth
of July

INDIA
Bannerman, Story of Little Black
Sambo   *RA; In (2)
Russell, D. H., Around the Corner,
p.134–37   *2–2
———— Friends Far and Near, p.234–
45   *3–2

INDIA—FOLKLORE
Baker, A. B., Talking Tree   *RA
Gruenberg, Favorite Stories Old and
New, p.220–22 (Foolish, Timid
Little Hare)   *RA

INDIANS OF NORTH AMERICA:
see also Eskimos
Betts, ABC Along Friendly Roads,
p.153–60 (Winnebago), 244–57
(Navahos)   *3–2

—— ABC Beyond Treasure Valley, p.194–200, 226–33, 274–81
*3–1

Bond, G. L., Stories from Everywhere, p.62–114 *3–1

Brock, One Little Indian Boy (Pueblo) *RA; In (3)

Bulla, Squanto, Friend of the White Men (Patuxet) *In (3)

Burton, W. H., Our Good Neighbors, p.194–227 *3

Carpenter, Our Little Neighbors at Work and Play: Here, There, Then, and Now, p.14–64 3+

Clark, A. N., In My Mother's House (Pueblo) RA; In (2)

—— Little Indian Basket Maker (Papago) *RA; In (2)

—— Little Indian Pottery Maker (Pueblo) *RA; In (2)

Cutright, Living Together Today and Yesterday, p.133–54 (Navaho), 155–86 (Pueblo), 188–95 (Woodland), 209–17 (Plains), 218–24 (Northwest), 225–28 3

Deming, Indians in Winter Camp In (3)

—— Little Eagle *In (2)

Fletcher, Big Book of Indians (Plains) RA

Gray, New More Streets and Roads, p.60–66 *3–2

Gruenberg, Favorite Stories Old and New, p.12–13 *RA

Hildreth, Along the Way, p.48–62 *2–1

—— Faraway Ports, 69–71 *3–1

Leavell, Open Doors, p.148–77 *2

—— Open Roads, p.92–106 *3

McGaw, How Medicine Man Cured Paleface Woman *RA; In (3)

McIntire, Working Together, p.198–228 3

Mitchell, Our Country, p.148–52 (Woodland), *153–75 (Delaware), 176–80 (Seneca), 181–89 (Iroquois), 234–51 (Navaho), 253–64 (Hopi) 3

Moon, One Little Indian *In (2)

Nolen, Do and Dare, p.222–31 (New Mexico), 272–82 (Shawnee), 283–92 (Sioux), 293–303 (Karankawas) *3–2

O'Donnell, Friendly Village, p.149–76 *Basic 2

Quinlan, Busy World, p.180–92 *3

—— Faces and Places, p.175–81 *2

Russell, D. H., Finding New Neighbors, p.134–88 *3–1

Sheldon, Magic Windows, p.157–210 *3–1

—— Town and Country, p.174–88, 189–97 *2–2

Smiley, Little Boy Navaho *RA; In (3)

Sorensen, Ways of Our Land, p.76–77, 118–30 (Navaho) 3

Yoakam, Stories We Like, p.61–66 *2

Zolotow, Indian Indian *RA (K–1)

INDIANS OF NORTH AMERICA —FOLKLORE

Association for Childhood Education, Told under the Green Umbrella, p.156–61 (Little Scar Face) *RA

Gruenberg, Favorite Stories Old and New, p.217–19 (Why the Baby Says "Goo") *RA

INDUSTRIES: *see also* Factories and Mills; also names of industries, as Lumbering

Beim, J., Twelve o'Clock Whistle *RA

Buchheimer, Let's Go to a Candy Factory In (3)

INFECTION: *see* Germs

INJURIES: *see* First Aid

INNS
  Leavell, Open Roads, p.108–14   *3

INSECTS: *see also* names of insects, as
    Ants; Bees; Butterflies
  Baker, A. O., Around the Corner,
    p.10   2
  Barnard, Macmillan Science-Life Se-
    ries, Bk.3, p.36–41   3
  Blough, Animals round the Year,
    p.17–18, 29–30, 34–35   3
  ———— Insect Parade   3
  Dowling, New Seeing Why, p.1–10
                                        2
  Frasier, Science—All the Year, p.36,
    48–54   2
  Knox, Wonderworld of Science, Bk.2,
    p.10–16   2
  Parker, Six-legged Neighbors   2
  Schneider, H., Science Far and Near,
    p.170–71   3
  Smith, V. C., Science around the
    Clock, p.41–62   3
  Thorn, Let's See Why, p.50–53, 132–
    36, 169–75   3
  ———— Let's Try, p.15–19   P

INTERDEPENDENCE: *see also* Com-
    munity Life; Cooperation
  Goudey, Good Rain   In (3)
  Mitchell, Here and Now Story Book,
    p.325–38   *RA
  Schlein, Something for Now, Some-
    thing for Later   *In (3)

INVENTIONS: *see also* names of in-
    ventions, as Radio
  Cavanah, Our Country's Story, p.44–
    45, 62–65   In (3)
  Dowling, New Learning Why, p.146–
    49   3
  Monroe, New Tall Tales, p.65–74
                                      *3–1

IRELAND
  Hildreth, Faraway Ports, p.82–83
                                      *3–1

IRELAND—FOLKLORE
  Baker, A. B., Talking Tree   *RA
  Gruenberg, Favorite Stories Old and
    New, p.239–42 (Week of Sun-
    days)   *RA

IRON: *see also* Steel
  Schneider, H., Science for Here and
    Now, p.70–72   2
  Thomas, Your Town and Mine,
    p.113–15   3

IRRIGATION: *see also* Dams; Rice
  Clark, A. N., In My Mother's House,
    p.26–29   RA; In (2)

ISLANDS
  Betts, ABC Beyond Treasure Valley,
    p.284–91   *3–1
  Bond, G. L., Stories from Every-
    where, p.224–37 (South Seas)
                                     *3–1
  Palmer, Lost and Found, p.3–50
                                     *2–1
  Sorensen, Ways of Our Land, p.14–
    15   3

ITALIANS IN THE UNITED STATES
  Silverman, Ciri-biri-bin   *In (2)
  Urell, Big City Neighbors, p.11–16
                                      3+

ITALY
  Baker, A. B., Talking Tree   *RA
  Bettina, Pantaloni   *RA (K–2)
  ———— Piccolo   *RA (K–2)
  Politi, Little Leo   *In (3)
  Schreiber, Bambino Goes Home
                              *RA; In (3)
  Yoakam, Children Everywhere, p.46–
    53   *3

JACK FROST: *see also* Winter
  Betts, ABC Over a City Bridge,
    p.119–22   *2–2

JACK-O'-LANTERNS: *see* Halloween;
    Pumpkins

JAPAN
  Brown, J. P., Surprise for Robin
                              *RA (K–1)

Gruenberg, Favorite Stories Old and New, p.228–29, 253–56 (White Hare of Inabi; Boy Who Drew Cats)   *RA
Lifton, Joji and the Dragon
                              *RA(K–2)

JESUS CHRIST: *see also* Bible Stories; Christmas; Easter
Fitch, Child Jesus   RA
Glover, First Christmas   RA
Gruenberg, Favorite Stories Old and New, p.307–17 (Nativity; Jesus in the Temple; Jesus Healing the Blind; Loaves and the Fishes; Three Parables)   RA
Jones, M. A., Tell Me about God, p.53–57   *RA
—— Tell Me about Jesus   *RA
—— Tell Me about the Bible   *RA

JET PROPULSION
Bradley, Cappy and the Jet Engine
                              *In (3)

JEWS—FOLKLORE
Baker, A. B., Talking Tree   *RA

JOBS: *see* Earning Money; Occupations

JOKES
Chrystie, First Book of Jokes and Funny Things   RA
O'Donnell, Five-and-a-Half Club, p.133–47   *Par. 3

JOSEPH: *see* Bible Stories

JUNGLE LIFE
Gates, Good Times Today, p.114–22   *3–1
—— Good Times Today and To-morrow, p.80–88   *Alt. 3
—— Three Little Elephants, p.1–14   *Unit 1
Hildreth, Story Road, p.160–69 *2–2

KANGAROOS
Bond, G. L., Stories from Everywhere, p.20–25   *3–1

Gruenberg, Favorite Stories Old and New, p.121–27 (Karoo, the Kangaroo)   *RA
McKee, Come Along, p.40–58   *2–1

KANSAS
Nolen, Do and Dare, p.187–94 (Cats for Kansas)   *3–2

KILDEER
Blough, Animals and Their Young, p.14–16   3

KINDNESS
Jones, M. A., Tell Me about the Bible, p.87–92   *RA
Leavell, Open Doors, p.8–14   *2
—— Open Roads, p.246–53   *3
Nolen, Do and Dare, p.161–67 *3–2
Sheldon, Story Caravan, p.25–31
                              *3–2

KINDNESS TO ANIMALS: *see also* Animals—Care; Animals—Protection
Gruenberg, Favorite Stories Old and New, p.285–86 (Androcles and the Lion)   *RA

KINGFISHERS
Blough, Birds in the Big Woods, p.10, 20   3
Gall, All the Year Round   In (3)

KITES
Ayer, Nu Dang and His Kite
                    *RA (K–2); In (3)
Lattimore, Little Pear, p.68–77
                              *In (3)
McKee, Jack and Janet, p.147–62
                              *1–1
Quinlan, Day by Day, p.118–28 *P
Wiese, Fish in the Air   *In (3)

KITTENS: *see* Cats

KNITTING
Haywood, Primrose Day, p.181–200
                              *In (3)

LABOR DAY
Child Study Association of America, Holiday Storybook   *RA

LADYBIRDS: *see* Beetles

LAKES
Clark, A. N., In My Mother's House, p.24   RA; In (2)
Gates, At the Lake   *Sup. PP
Hunnicutt, I Know People, p.129–35   3
Mitchell, Here and Now Story Book, p.211–18   *RA
Ousley, Under the Apple Tree, p.104–35   *Pre-1
Sorensen, Ways of Our Land, p.72–77   3
Thomas, Stories about Sally, p.113–15   2
Whipple, Our Earth, p.108–10   3

LAMBS: *see* Sheep

LAMPS: *see also* Pioneer Life
Burton, W. H., Our Good Neighbors, p.121–28   *3

LANDSCAPING
Hanna, In the Neighborhood, p.164–69   2

LANGUAGE: *see also* Dictionaries; Words
Liang, Tommy and Dee-Dee   RA (K–1); In (2)
McGaw, How Medicine Man Cured Paleface Woman   *RA; In (3)

LANGUAGE—CHINESE
Wiese, You Can Write Chinese   In (3)

LAPLAND
Aulaire, Ola   *In (3)
Gates, Good Times Today and Tomorrow, p.284–94   Alt. 3
———— Good Times Tomorrow, p.184–94   3–2
O'Donnell, If I Were Going, p.64–88   *Basic 3

LAUNDROMAT
Burkhardt, Our Neighborhood, p.66–67   *2
Russell, D. H., Around the Corner, p.196–99   *2–2
Sheldon, Here and Near, p.44–46   *PP2

LAUNDRY
Betts, ABC Along Friendly Roads, p.291–98   *3–2
Burkhardt, Our Community, p.76–78   3
Dean, At the Laundry   In (3)

LAW: *see also* Government; Police
Leaf, Fair Play   In (3)

LAWN MOWER
Ousley, Under the Apple Tree, p.42–46   *Pre-P

LAZINESS
Gruenberg, Favorite Stories Old and New, p.239–42 (Week of Sundays)   *RA

LEATHER: *see also* Shoes
Blough, Useful Plants and Animals, p.18–19   3
Burkhardt, Our Community, p.72   3
McIntire, Working Together, p.105–6   3
Partch, Basic Social Studies, p.146–49   3

LEAVES
Mitchell, Another Here and Now Story Book, p.216–19   *RA
———— Here and Now Story Book, p.315–39   *RA
Ousley, Open the Gate, p.63–70   *Pre-2
Parker, Leaves   2
Thorn, Let's Look Around, p.35–38   2
———— Let's Try, p.10–14   P

LETTERS: *see also* Post Office; Postman

Betts, ABC Up the Street and Down, p.74–79   *P

Bond, G. L., Just for Fun, p.30–40   *2–2

Burton, W. H., Our Happy Ways, p.153–56   *1

Carpenter, Our Little Neighbors at Work and Play: Here, There, Then, and Now, p.50–52 (Indian picture writing)   3+

Gates, Friends and Fun, p.24–28 (picture post cards)   *Alt. 2

———— On Four Feet, p.125–28 *1

———— Today We Go, p.24–28 (picture post cards)   *2–1

Hanna, In the Neighborhood, p.124–35   2

Hill, Jack o'Lantern for Judy Jo   *In (3)

Hunnicutt, I Have Friends, p.154–59   2

———— I Live with Others, p.100–103   1

Jones, M. A., Tell Me about the Bible, p.74–80   *RA

McIntire, Billy's Neighbors, p.115–16   2

———— Working Together, p.175–77   3

Mitchell, Farm and City, p.148–49 1

Norling, Pogo's Letter   *In (3)

Quinlan, Busy World, p.213–17 *3

———— Faces and Places, p.1–7   *2

Sheldon, Our School, p.14–17   *P

———— Town and Country, p.40–42   *2–2

LEVERS

Barnard, Macmillan Science-Life Series, Bk.3, p.197–98   3

Beauchamp, How Do We Know? p.86–93   3

Dowling, New Seeing Why, p.148–49   2

Schneider, H., Now Try This   In (3)

———— Science Far and Near, p.234–39   3

LEWIS AND CLARK EXPEDITION

Cavanah, Our Country's Story, p.36–37   In (3)

LIBERTY

Leavell, Open Roads, p.134–40 *3

LIBRARIANS: *see* Books; Libraries

LIBRARIES: *see also* Books; Reading

Colonius, At the Library   In (2)

Felt, Rosa-Too-Little   *RA (K–2)

Hanna, In the Neighborhood, p.117–23   2

Hunnicutt, I Have Friends, p.136–40   2

Jones, E., My Second Health Book, p.70–75   2

Jones, M. A., Tell Me about the Bible, p.81–86   *RA

McIntire, Billy's Friends, p.105–7 1

———— Billy's Neighbors, p.50–62 2

———— Working Together, p.180 3

Quinlan, Faces and Places, p.130–43   *2

Reese, Basic Social Studies, p.10–28   2

Sheldon, Our Town, p.100–101, 158–59   *1

Thomas, Stories about Sally, p.28–30   2

Urell, Big City Book of Conservation, p.25–29   3+

LIGHT: *see also* Color; Eye; Lighting; Photography; Rainbow; Sun

Barnard, Macmillan Science-Life Series, Bk.3, p.116–20, 138   3

Bond, A. D., Knowing about Science, p.111–19   3

Dowling, New Seeing Why, p.171–82   2

Frasier, We Wonder, p.16–17   PP

Hallock, Health and Happy Days, p.75–78   1

Schwartz, J., Now I Know   In (2)
Thorn, Let's Look Around, p.55–59
                                        2

LIGHTHOUSES
Agle, Three Boys and a Lighthouse
                                   *In (3)
Betts, ABC Over a City Bridge, p.36–
41   *2–2
McKee, Looking Ahead, p.190–95,
*196–210   3–1
Palmer, Lost and Found,   p.9–12
                                  *2–1
Russell, D. H., Friends Far and Near,
p.86–94   *3–2
Smith, V. C., Science under the Sun,
p.98–103   2
Sorensen, Ways of Our Land, p.12–
13   3
Swift, Little Red Lighthouse *In (2)

LIGHTING: *see also* Candles; Electricity
Hugley, Around the Home,   p.175–
76   3

LIGHTNING: *see* Weather

LIGHTNING BUGS: *see* Fireflies

LIMESTONE
Schneider, H., Science Far and Near,
p.115–18   3

LIMPETS
Huntington, Let's Go to the Seashore,
p.80–83   In (3)

LINCOLN, ABRAHAM
Aulaire, Abraham Lincoln   In (3)
Cavanah, Our Country's Story, p.50–
53   In (3)
Child Study Association of America,
Holiday Storybook   *RA
Coblentz, Martin and Abraham Lin-
coln   *In (3)
Emerson, Pioneer Children of Ameri-
ca, p.288–91   3

LINEN: *see also* Flax
Blough, Useful Plants and Animals,
p.30   3
Burkhardt, Our Community, p.71   3
McIntire, Working Together, p.99–
100   3
Thomas, Your Town and Mine, p.81
                                     3

LIONS
Bond, G. L., Once upon a Storytime,
p.258–61   *3–2
——— Stories from Everywhere,
p.38–43 (sea)   *3–1
Brown, M. W., Sleepy Little Lion
                            RA (K–2)
Daugherty, Andy and the Lion
                          *RA; In (3)
Du Bois, Lion   *RA
Goudey, Here Come the Lions!
                                In (3)
Gray, New More Streets and Roads,
p.107–14   *3–2
Johnson, E. M., Treat Shop, p.166–
75   *3
McKee, Climbing Higher, p.75–92
                                  *3–2
Robison, Fun and Fancy, p.138–42
                                *Pre–4
Russell, D. H., Finding New Neigh-
bors, p.70–75   *3–1
——— Friends Far and Near,
p.248–59   *3–2

LIZARDS
Frasier, Science—Adventures, p.75–
78 (horned toad)   3

LOBSTER FISHERIES
O'Donnell, If I Were Going, p.158–
76   *Basic 3
Sorensen, Ways of Our Land, p.5–6
                                     3

LOCOMOTIVES: *see* Trains

LOCUSTS: *see* Grasshoppers

LOG CABINS
Carpenter, Our Little Neighbors at Work and Play: Here, There, Then, and Now, p.66–74   3+
Emerson, Pioneer Children of America, p.187–88   3
Gray, New More Streets and Roads, p.89–96   *3–2
Hugley, Around the Home, p.140–49   3

LOGGING: *see* Lumbering

LOST AND FOUND: *see also* Stores
Gray, New Streets and Roads, p.42–49   *3–1

LOVE
Jones, M. A., Tell Me about Jesus, p.62–66   *RA

LUMBERING: *see also* Wood
Norling, Pogo's House   *In (3)
Partch, Basic Social Studies, p.192–95   3
Smith, J. R., Our Neighbors at Home, p.99–121   3
Thomas, Your Town and Mine, p.100–103   3
Whipple, Our Earth, p.144–49 (logging)   3

LUNCH: *see also* Breakfast
Bauer, Seven or So, p.137–39   2
Bond, G. L., Just for Fun, p.62–68   *2–2
Burkhardt, Our Community, p.57–60 (school)   3
Evans, Something Different, p.126–30   *1
Irwin, Keeping Fit for Fun, p.12–13, 32–35 (picnic)   3
Jones, E., My First Health Book, p.44–49 (school)   1
Reese, Basic Social Studies, p.150–53 (school)   2
Sheldon, Our School, p.89–93   *P

Thomas, Stories about Linda and Lee, p.57 (picnic)   1

LUNCH ROOMS: *see* Restaurants, Lunch Rooms, etc.

MACHINES: *see also* Farm Machinery; Inclined Planes; Inventions; Levers; Pulleys
Barnard, Macmillan Science-Life Series, Bk.2, p.82–91   2
Beauchamp, All around Us, p.30–40   2
——— How Do We Know? p.76–85   3
——— Look and Learn, p.26–37   1
Blough, Doing Work   3
Bond, A. D., Getting Ready, p.50–57   P
——— Thinking about Science, p.6–25   2
Child Study Association of America, Read-to-Me Storybook, p.69–80   *RA
Craig, Science near You, p.33–37   1
Dowling, New Seeing Why, p.147–70   2
Frasier, Science—Adventures, p.170–75   3
——— Science—All the Year, p.139–43   2
——— We Wonder, p.25–26   PP
Gray, New Friends and Neighbors, p.225–30 (shovels)   *2–1
——— New More Friends and Neighbors, p.152–58   *2–2
Hanna, In the Neighborhood, p.152–55   2
Knox, Wonderworld of Science, Bk.3, p.81–93   3
McKee, Come Along, p.90–107 (tractor)   *2–1
Partch, Basic Social Studies, p.211   3
Schneider, H., Science Far and Near, p.243–61   3

——— Science for Here and Now, p.15–24   2

Smith, M. E., Mother's Story of Dairying, p.34–37   P

Thorn, Let's See Why, p.117–20   3

Thurber, Exploring Science Three, p.114–27   3

——— Exploring Science Two, p.130–41   2

Zaffo, Big Book of Real Building and Wrecking Machines   In (3)

MAGIC: *see also* Tricks

Gruenberg, Favorite Stories Old and New, p.157–61   *RA

McKee, On We Go, p.133–57, 234–42   *2–2

MAGNETISM: *see also* Electricity

Barnard, Macmillan Science-Life Series, Bk.1, p.35–37   1

——— Macmillan Science-Life Series, Bk.2, p.92–95   2

——— Macmillan Science-Life Series, Bk.3, p.205–11   3

Bond, A. D., Knowing about Science, p.125–28, 134, 145–47   3

——— Looking at Science, p.25–31   1

——— Thinking about Science, p.123–29   2

Branley, Mickey's Magnet   *In (2)

Craig, Science Everywhere, p.65–75   3

——— Science near You, p.24–31   1

Frasier, Science—Adventures, p.158–61   3

——— Science—All the Year, p.118–21   2

——— Science—For You, p.34–39   1

Knox, Wonderworld of Science, Bk.2, p.82–90   2

Leavell, Open Doors, p.44–50   *2

Parker, Toys, p.27–29   2

Schneider, H., Science for Here and Now, p.149–62   2

Smith, V. C., Science under the Sun, p.117–29   2

Thorn, Let's See Why, p.72–76   3

MAGPIES

Russell, D. H., Finding New Neighbors, p.36–41   *3–1

MAIL SERVICE: *see* Communication; Letters; Post Office; Postman

MALAYA

Carpenter, Our Little Neighbors at Work and Play: Here, There, Then, and Now, p.185–92   3+

MAMMALS: *see also* names of mammals, as Cows

Dowling, New Learning Why, p.197–217   3

Schneider, H., Science Far and Near, p.185–86   3

MANN, HORACE

Leavell, Open Roads, p.150–56   *3

MANNERS: *see also* Character Building; Letters; School Life

Averill, School for Cats   *In (2)

Bauer, From Eight to Nine, p.126–27   3

——— Seven or So, p.91–98   2

Brownell, All Day, Every Day, p.90   1

Gray, New Streets and Roads, p.124–30   *3–1

Hallock, Health in Work and Play, p.104–6   2

Irwin, Keeping Fit for Fun, p.58–61, 72–76 (table)   3

Johnson, E. M., Treat Shop, p.8–11   *3

Joslin, What Do You Say, Dear?   RA (K–1)

Leaf, Manners Can Be Fun   In (3)

Leavell, Open Roads, p.183–87   *3

McKee, Climbing Higher, p.185–99
                                              *3–2
Wilcox, Step Lively, p.148–51   3

MAPLE SUGAR
O'Donnell, Neighbors on the Hill,
   p.18–64   *Par. 2
Thorn, Let's See Why, p.137–40   3
Whipple, Our Earth, p.45–58   3

MAPS
Bond, G. L., Once upon a Storytime,
   p.111–13 (picture)   *3–2
Burkhardt, Our Neighborhood, p.14–
   17, 146–47   2
Cutright, Living Together Today and
   Yesterday, p.9, 13, 48, 188, 193,
   209   3
Hanna, In City, Town, and Country,
   p.50–51, 62–65, 80–81, 104–6,
   128–29, 183   3
—— In the Neighborhood, p.39,
   69, 103, 143, 180   2
Hunnicutt, I Know People, p.16–22,
   247–48   3
—— I Live with Others, p.104–5
                                      1
Reese, Basic Social Studies, p.160–61
                                      2
Sorensen, Ways of Our Land, p.14,
   21, 73   3
Thomas, Your Town and Mine   3

MARIONETTES: see Puppet Shows

MARKETS: see also Fairs; Stores
Bond, G. L., Down Our Way, p.53–
   60   *2–1
Eberle, Secrets and Surprises, p.155–
   70 (roadside stand)   *2–2
Mitchell, Another Here and Now
   Story Book, p.277–82   *RA
Sheldon, Magic Windows, p.31–40
   (fruit stands)   *3–1
Smith, J. R., Our Neighbors at Home,
   p.213–16 (produce)   3
Smith, M. E., Bill's Story of the
   Wholesale Produce Market   2+

—— Bob's Story of the Retail
   Food Market   2+

MARKETS—MEXICO
Gay, Z., Pancho and His Burro *RA

MARKETS—NETHERLANDS
Brock, To Market! To Market!
                                *RA (K–2)

MASONRY: see Bricks; Concrete;
   Dams; Houses

MASQUERADES: see also Dressing
   Up
Betts, ABC Up the Street and Down,
   p.101–5   *P

MAY DAY
Betts, ABC Around Green Hills,
   p.24–29   *1
Bromhall, Belinda's New Shoes
                                *RA; In (3)
Haywood, Betsy and Billy, p.123–41
                                   *In (3)

MAYAS—FOLKLORE
Gruenberg, Favorite Stories Old and
   New, p.257–59 (Vegetable Tree)
                                    *RA

MAYFLOWER (SHIP): see Pilgrims

MEALS: see Food

MEASURES: see Weights and Measures

MEAT: see also Stores (butcher)
McIntire, Working Together, p.80–
   81   3
Partch, Basic Social Studies, p.42–
   51   3

MEMORIAL DAY
Child Study Association of America,
   Holiday Storybook   *RA

MENTAL HEALTH: see also Character Building; Contentment; Fears;
   Imagination
Barnard, Macmillan Science-Life Series, Bk.1, p.117–19   1

———— Macmillan Science-Life Series, Bk.2, p.68–81 2
———— Macmillan Science-Life Series, Bk.3, p.143–49, 240–42 3
Bauer, Being Six, p.68–73, 82–87 1
———— From Eight to Nine, p.50–55, 60–65, 108–9, 118–21 3
———— Seven or So, p.68–72, 133–36 2
Brownell, All Day, Every Day, p.37–42, 43–45 1
———— Blue Skies, p.33–38 (self-control) *2
———— Come Rain, Come Shine, p.10–13, 21–24 (anger), 44–47, 69–72, 78–82, 84–88, 115–18 *3
Charters, Health Secrets, p.53–54, 94–97 3
Hallock, Health in Work and Play, p.127–30 (homesickness) 2
Wilcox, Step Lively, p.131–40 3

MENUS: *see* Food

MERRY-GO-ROUNDS: *see also* Parks
Association for Childhood Education, Told under the Magic Umbrella, p.18–22 *RA
Bond, G. L., Ride with Us, p.19–24 *PP4
Brown, M. J., Little Carousel *RA (K–2)
Charles, Roundabout Turn *RA
Gray, New Our New Friends, p.185–89 *1–2
Gruenberg, Favorite Stories Old and New, p.332–35 *RA
Ousley, Come with Us, p.48–50 *Pre–P
———— Open the Gate, p.108–15 *Pre–2
Perera, Frisky *In (3)

METER
Monroe, New Tall Tales, p.50–55 (parking) *3–1

MEXICANS IN THE UNITED STATES
Politi, Juanita *RA (K–2)
———— Pedro, the Angel of Olvera Street *In (3)
Quinlan, Busy World, p.95–112 *3

MEXICO
Beim, L. L., Burro That Had a Name *In (3)
Betts, ABC Along Friendly Roads, p.228–35 *3–2
Bond, G. L., Stories from Everywhere, p.208–23 *3–1
Brenner, Hero by Mistake *RA; In (3)
Bulla, Poppy Seeds *RA; In (2)
Garrett, Angelo, the Naughty One *In (2)
Gay, Z., Pancho and His Burro *RA
Hader, Story of Pancho and the Bull with the Crooked Tail *RA
Leavell, Open Roads, p.73–78 *3
Morrow, Painted Pig *In (3)
Nolen, Do and Dare, p.161–67 *3–2
Russell, D. H., Friends Far and Near, p.213–25 *3–2

MEXICO—FOLKLORE
Bryan, C., Pito's House *In (3)

MICE
Association for Childhood Education, Told under the Green Umbrella (Town Mouse and the Country Mouse) *RA
———— Told under the Magic Umbrella, p.50–54 *RA
Bond, G. L., Once upon a Storytime, p.26–37 *3–2
———— Stories from Everywhere, p.286–91 *3–1
Brown, Palmer, Cheerful *RA (K–1)
Ets, Mr. T. W. Anthony Woo *RA (K–2)
Freeman, D., Norman the Doorman *RA

Freeman, L., Pet of the Met
*RA (K–2)
Gág, Snippy and Snappy   *RA
Gates, Good Times Today, p.226–
29, 144–52   *3–1
Gray, New Friends and Neighbors,
p.258–61   *2–1
—— New More Friends and
Neighbors, p.127–32   *2–2
—— New More Streets and Roads,
p.98–106   *3–2
—— New Streets and Roads,
p.282–86 (Bell for the Cat) *3–1
Johnson, E. M., Treat Shop, p.228–
35   *3
Mitchell, Another Here and Now
Story Book, p.322–36   *RA
—— Farm and City, p.84–87   1
Monroe, New Tall Tales, p.23–27 *3
Nolen, Fun and Frolic, p.59–66 *3–1
O'Donnell, Neighbors on the Hill,
p.109–13   *Par. 2
Ousley, Open the Gate, p.102–7
*Pre–2
Peterson, Whitefoot Mouse
RA; In (3)
Potter, Tailor of Gloucester   *RA
Robison, Fun and Fancy, p.149–
57   *Pre–4
Russell, D. H., Friends Far and Near,
p.164–72 (white-footed)   *3–2
—— Little White House, p.160–
64   *P
Sheldon, Fields and Fences, p.56–
68, 78–81   *2–1
Thorn, Let's See Why, p.94–100   3
Titus, Anatole   *RA
—— Anatole and the Cat   *RA
Yoakam, Making Storybook Friends,
p.56–65   *1

MICROBES: *see* Germs

MIGRATION OF BIRDS: *see* Birds—
Migration

MILK
Bauer, From Eight to Nine, p. 164–
65   3
Brownell, Blue Skies, p.143–46   2
Charters, Health Secrets, p.21–27 3
Hallock, Health and Happy Days,
p.55–58, 62–66   1
—— Health and Safety for You,
p.16–26   3
—— Health in Work and Play,
p.82–88   2
Hugley, Around the Home, p.42–49
3
Jones, E., Easy Steps to Health,
p.127–29   3
Mitchell, Farm and City, p.16–23 1
O'Keefe, From Head to Toe, p.42–
44   1
Partch, Basic Social Studies, p.7–24
3
Quinlan, To and Fro, p.68–74   *1
Smith, J. R., Our Neighbors at Home,
p.46–47   3
Thomas, Stories about Sally, p.81–
85   2

MILKMAN
Barr, Mike, the Milkman   *In (2)
Hallock, Health and Safety for You,
p.16–20   3
McIntire, Billy's Neighbors, p.126 2
Quinlan, To and Fro, p.94–101 *1
Russell, D. H., We Are Neighbors,
p.164–67   *2–1
Smith, M. E., Mother's Story of
Dairying, p.42–45   2+

MILKMAN—SPAIN
O'Donnell, If I Were Going, p.238–
49   *Basic 3

MILKWEEDS
Thorn, Let's Look Around, p.27–29
2

MILLS AND FACTORIES: *see* Factories and Mills

MINERALS: *see also* Rocks; also names of minerals, as Coal; Salt
Podendorf, True Book of Rocks and Minerals   In (3)
Schneider, H., Science Far and Near, p.120–28   3
Urell, Big City Book of Conservation, p.58–62   3+

MINERS
Agle, Three Boys and a Mine *In (3)
Norling, Pogo's Mining Trip *In (3)

MINING
Smith, J. R., Our Neighbors at Home, p.122–28   3
Sorensen, Ways of Our Land, p.60–69 (coal)   3

MINK
Russell, D. H., Friends Far and Near, p.156–63   *3–2

MIRRORS
Gray, New More Streets and Roads, p.13–19   *3–2
Thurber, Exploring Science Two, p.78–89   2

MISSISSIPPI RIVER
Bulla, Down the Mississippi *In (3)

MODELING: *see* Clay Modeling

MONEY: *see also* Banks and Banking; Earning Money
Betts, ABC Up the Street and Down, p.128–33   *P
Bond, G. L., Down Our Way, p.2–6   *2–1
Gray, New Friends and Neighbors, p.65–71   *2–1
——— New Our New Friends, p.40–44   *1–2
Leavell, Open Roads, p.176–81 *3
——— Open Windows, p.22–27 *1
McIntire, Billy's Friends, p.80–83 1
O'Donnell, Anything Can Happen, p.68–100   *Par. 1

Russell, D. H., Around the Corner, p.238–52   *2–2
Yoakam, Children Everywhere, p.56–70   *3

MONKEYS: *see also* Baboons; Chimpanzees; Organ-Grinders
Betts, ABC Over a City Bridge, p.94–99   *2–2
——— ABC Up the Street and Down, p.23–28, 116–21   *P
Bond, G. L., Down Our Way, p.36–42, 222–30   *2–1
——— Just for Fun, p.101–10, *131–42   2–2
——— Stories from Everywhere, p.44–49   3–1
Hildreth, At Play, p.86–94   *P–1
——— Good Stories, p.2–14 *Pre–2
——— Story Road, p.44–52   *2–2
Kepes, Five Little Monkeys   *RA
Lathrop, Skittle-Skattle Monkey
                              *In (3)
McKee, Climbing Higher, p.95–132
                              *3–2
——— Come Along, p.108–30 (Curious George)   *2–1
O'Donnell, Friendly Village, p.205–16   *Basic 2
——— Round About, p.42–60
                              *Basic 1
Ousley, Ranches and Rainbows, p.80–87   *Pre–3
Quinlan, Busy World, p.40–48 *3
——— Day by Day   *P
——— Faces and Places, p.37–44, 184–90   *2
——— To and Fro   *1
Rey, Cecily G. and the Nine Monkeys   *RA; In (2)
——— Curious George   *In (2)
——— Curious George Gets a Medal   *RA (K–2)
——— Curious George Rides a Bike
                              *In (3)

—— Curious George Takes a Job
*In (2)

Russell, D. H., On Cherry Street,
p.104–8, 123–27   *1

—— We Are Neighbors, p.44–
50, 240–44   *2–1

Slobodkina, Caps for Sale   *RA

Yoakam, Stories We Like, p.37–51
*2

MOON: *see also* Tides

Bond, A. D., Knowing about Science,
p.95–104   3

—— Looking at Science, p.19–23
1

Craig, Science Everywhere, p.126–
30   3

Frasier, Science—Adventures, p.102–
9   3

—— Science—All the Year, p.21–
26   2

—— We Ask, p.22–23   P

Knox, Wonderworld of Science,
Bk.1, p.62–66   1

Smith, V. C., Science along the Way,
p.65–66   1

Thorn, Let's See Why, p.106–10   3

Thurber, Exploring Science Two,
p.30–31   2

Wavle, Rain and Shine, p.80–94
*P–2

MOOSE

Bond, G. L., Once upon a Storytime,
p.179–204   3–2

MORNING

Brownell, All Day, Every Day, p.8–
16   1

Quinlan, Day by Day, p.1–4   *P

—— Winky, p.22–27   *PP

Tresselt, Sun Up   *RA (K–2)

—— Wake Up, Farm! *RA (K–1)

MOSQUITOES

Thorn, Let's See Why, p.169–75   3

MOSS

Thorn, Let's See Why, p.68–71   3

MOTHER'S DAY

Hanna, At School, p.71–75   1

Hildreth, Along the Way, p.204–13
*2–1

McIntire, Billy's Friends, p.108–11
1

Monroe, New What Next, p.21–26
*2–1

MOTHS: *see also* Butterflies; Caterpillars; Cocoons; Silkworms

Barnard, Macmillan Science-Life Series, Bk.2, p.16–19   2

Blough, Animals round the Year,
p.17   3

—— Insect Parade, p.19–26   3

Parker, Six-legged Neighbors, p.26–
33   2

MOTION

Schneider, H., Now Try This   In(3)

MOTION PICTURES

Brownell, Come Rain, Come Shine,
p.150–54 (homemade)   *3

Burton, W. H., Our Good Neighbors,
p.42–50 (homemade)   *3

McIntire, Working Together, p.192–
95   3

Quinlan, Busy World, p.242–50
(homemade)   *3

MOUNTAIN LIFE

Gray, New More Streets and Roads,
p.217–25 (peddler)   *3–2

O'Donnell, Friendly Village, p.74–
120   *Basic 2

Ousley, Open the Gate, p.71–76
*Pre–2

Palmer, Lost and Found, p.124–206
*2–1

MOUNTAIN LIFE (SOUTHERN
STATES)

Credle, Down, down the Mountain
*In (3)

MOUNTAINS
Betts, ABC Beyond Treasure Valley, p.68–74, 105–11   *3–1
Clark, A. N., In My Mother's House, p.52–55   RA; In (2)
Mitchell, Our Country, p. 215–19 (Sierras)   3
Urell, Big City Water Supply, p.9–26 (Catskills)   3+
Whipple, Our Earth, p.1–42   3

MOVING DAY
Betts, ABC Over a City Bridge, p.136–42   *2–2
Burton, W. H., Meet Our Friends, p.50–56   *2
Clymer, Yard for John, p.18–23 *RA
Gates, Tommy Little, p.13–44   *Sup. P
Hanna, In the Neighborhood, p.146–51   2
Hawkins, Who Wants an Apple?   *In (3)
Nolen, Fun and Frolic, p.117–32   *3–1
O'Donnell, Down the River Road, p.4–31   *Read. 2
Partch, Basic Social Studies, p.187 3

MULES
Beatty, Droopy   *RA (K–2)
Mason, Happy Jack   *In (3)
Mitchell, Another Here and Now Story Book, p.357–68   *RA
Monroe, New Tall Tales, p.42–49   *3–1
O'Donnell, Friendly Village, p.98–104   *Basic 2
Robison, Fun and Fancy, p.76–86   *Pre–4

MUSCLES: *see* Physiology

MUSIC: *see also* Harmonicas; Organ-Grinders
Freeman, L., Pet of the Met   *RA (K–2)

Hanna, In City, Town, and Country, p.175–80 (concerts)   3
Johnson, E. M., Treat Shop, p.12–19 (bass horn)   *3
O'Donnell, Friendly Village, p.108–20   *Basic 2
——— If I Were Going, p.210–36   *Basic 3
Steiner, Kiki Loves Music   *In (2)

MUSICAL INSTRUMENTS: *see also* Violins
Nolen, Do and Dare, p.86–94 (flute)   *3–2

MUSKRATS
Gall, All the Year Round, p.43–48   In (3)

NANTUCKET (ISLAND)
Nolen, Do and Dare, p.261–70 *3–2

NATIONAL SONGS
Cavanah, Our Country's Story, p.38–39 (Star-Spangled Banner) In (3)

NATURE: *see also* Aquariums
Association for Childhood Education, Told under the Blue Umbrella, p.10–11   *RA
Bendick, All around You   In (3)
Blough, Who Lives in This House?   In (3)
Deming, Indians in Winter Camp   In (3)
Gall, Here and There and Everywhere   In (2)
Goudey, Good Rain   In (3)
Huntington, Let's Go Outdoors   In (3)
Krauss, Growing Story *RA; In (2)
Peterson, Whitefoot Mouse   RA; In (3)
Selsam, Nature Detective   In (3)
Zion, All Falling Down   RA (K–1)

NATURE—PHOTOGRAPHY
Huntington, Let's Go Outdoors   In (3)

———— Let's Go to the Seashore
In (3)

NAVAHO INDIANS: *see* Indians of North America

NEGROES
Beim, L. L., Two Is a Team
*RA; In (3)
Brown, J. P., Ronnie's Wish
*RA (K–1)
Evans, Araminta   *In (3)
Lattimore, Bayou Boy   *In (3)
Shackelford, My Happy Days
*In (3)
Sharpe, Tobe   *In (3)
Urell, Big City Neighbors, p.30–39
3+

NEGROES—FOLKLORE
Gruenberg, Favorite Stories Old and New, p.223–24 (Wonderful Tar-Baby Story)   *RA

NEIGHBORHOODS: *see* Community Life

NEIGHBORS
Brown, M. J., Stone Soup   *RA
Evans, Something Different, p.18–24
*1
Hunnicutt, I Have Friends, p.80–84
2
Jones, M. A., Tell Me about the Bible, p.67–73   *RA
McIntire, Billy's Friends, p.64–67   1
O'Donnell, Neighbors on the Hill
*Par. 2
Russell, D. H., We Are Neighbors, p.8–42   *2–1

NERVES: *see* Senses

NESTS: *see* Birds—Eggs and Nests

NETHERLANDS
Brock, To Market! To Market!
*RA (K–2)
Hildreth, Enchanting Stories, p.160–79   *3–2

Quinlan, Busy World, p.130–34, *135–36   3

NETHERLANDS—FOLKLORE
Gruenberg, Favorite Stories Old and New, p.243–45 (Dutch Boy and the Dike)   *RA

NEW ENGLAND: *see also* Colonial Period, U.S.; Pilgrims
Bright, Georgie   *RA; In (3)
Hill, Along Comes Judy Jo *In (3)
———— Down-along Apple Market Street   *In (3)
———— Jack o'Lantern for Judy Jo
*In (3)
———— Summer Comes to Apple Market Street   *In (3)
———— Surprise for Judy Jo *In (3)

NEW YEAR'S DAY
Child Study Association of America, Holiday Storybook   *RA
Hildreth, Faraway Ports, p.258–73 (Chinese)   *3–1
Russell, D. H., Finding New Neighbors, p.265–72   *3–1

NEW YORK (CITY)
Beim, J., Shoeshine Boy   *In (3)
Cavanah, Our Country's Story, p.18–19   In (3)
Cutright, Living Together Today and Yesterday, p.27–35   3
Emerson, Pioneer Children of America, p.93–95   3
Mitchell, Here and Now Story Book, p.253–79   *RA
Paull, Come to the City   RA
Quinlan, Busy World, p.138–49 *3
Silverman, Ciri-biri-bin   *In (2)
Sorensen, Ways of Our Land, p.160–76   3
Urell, Big City Fun   3+
———— Big City Neighbors   3+
———— Big City Water Supply   3+
———— Big City Workers   3+

NEW YORK (CITY)—HARBOR
Agle, Three Boys and a Tugboat
*In (3)
Swift, Little Red Lighthouse and the
Great Gray Bridge   In (2)

NEWSBOYS
Betts, ABC Down Singing River,
p.201–7   *2–1
Burkhardt, Our Neighborhood, p.7–
13   2

NEWSPAPERS
Betts, ABC Along Friendly Roads,
p.323–29   *3–2
Hanna, In the Neighborhood, p.42–
49   2
McIntire, Working Together, p.178–
79   3
Thomas, Your Town and Mine,
p.46–47, 149   3

NIGHT
Frasier, Science—For You, p.10–11,
13, 15, 124–25   1
Jones, M. A., Tell Me about God,
p.44–49   *RA
Mitchell, Farm and City, p.118–22
1
Schneider, N., While Susie Sleeps
RA (K–2)
Schwartz, J., Now I Know   In (2)

NOISE
Russell, D. H., Around the Corner,
p.228–37   *2–2

NORTH CAROLINA
Sharpe, Tobe   *In (3)

NORWAY
Aulaire, Ola   *In (3)
O'Donnell, If I Were Going, p.22–
25, *26–62   Basic 3

NORWAY—FOLKLORE
Association for Childhood Education,
Told under the Green Umbrella
(Boots and His Brothers; Three

Billy Goats Gruff; Lad Who Went
to the North Wind; The Pancake)
*RA
Baker, A. B., Talking Tree   *RA

NOSE
Gates, On Four Feet, p.97–105   *1
Irwin, Keeping Fit for Fun, p.44–47
3
Johnson, E. M., Treat Shop, p.222–
27   *3
Jones, E., Easy Steps to Health,
p.81–84   3
Wilcox, Here We Go, p.82–85   2

NUMBERS: *see also* Arithmetic
Osswald, Golden Picture Book of
Numbers   In (2)

NURSES AND NURSING: *see also*
First Aid; Hospitals
Bauer, Being Six, p.51–53   1
Brownell, All Day, Every Day, p.91–
93 (school)   1
———— Come Rain, Come Shine,
p.126–28 (school)   3
Frasier, We Ask, p.62–63   P
Hallock, Health and Happy Days,
p.90–93   1
Jones, E., My Second Health Book,
p.91–95   2
Wilcox, Come On, p.35–38   1

NUTRITION: *see* Food

NUTS AND NUTTING
Gray, New Our New Friends, p.109–
13   *1–2
McIntire, Working Together, p.73–
78   3
Partch, Basic Social Studies, p.89–
94   3

NYLON: *see also* Dacron and Orlon
McIntire, Working Together, p.104
3
Mitchell, Animals, Plants, and Machines, p.88–89   2

OAK TREES

Bond, A. D., Knowing about Science, p.169–72   3

McKee, Climbing Higher, p.238–48
*3–2

Mitchell, Another Here and Now Story Book, p.270–73   *RA

OBEDIENCE

Brownell, Blue Skies, p.147–55   *2

Haywood, Two and Two Are Four, p.103–17, 136–55   *In (3)

Jones, M. A., Tell Me about the Bible, p.25–31   *RA

Leavell, Open Doors, p.68–74   *2

OBSERVATION

Betts, ABC Beyond Treasure Valley, p.250–57   *3–1

Seuss, And To Think That I Saw It on Mulberry Street   *RA

OCCUPATIONS: *see also* names of occupations, as Dentists

Frank, Daddies   RA (K–2)

Jones, E., My Second Health Book, p.48–49   2

Smith, J. R., Our Neighbors at Home, p.116–20   3

OCEAN: *see also* Tides

Evans, Something Different, p.98–133   *1

Frasier, Science—Adventures, p.12–16   3

Nolen, Do and Dare, p.241–50 *3–2

Norling, Pogo's Sea Trip   *In (2)

Schneider, H., Science Far and Near, p.100–12, 131–36   3

Sheldon, Town and Country, p.210–16   *2–2

Whipple, Our Earth, p.157–96   3

OCEAN LIFE: *see* Crabs; Crayfish; Fish; Seashore; Shellfish

OCTOPUS

Robinson, W. W., At the Seashore   In (3)

Sheldon, Fields and Fences, p.69–77   *2–1

OHIO

McCloskey, Lentil   *In (3)

OPOSSUMS

Gray, New More Streets and Roads, p.186–92   *3–2

Mitchell, Another Here and Now Story Book, p.293–99   *RA

ORANGES: *see also* Fruit

Burton, W. H., Our Good Neighbors, p.163–68   *3

Hugley, Around the Home, p.70–73   3

Hunnicutt, I Know People, p.149–56   3

Sorensen, Ways of Our Land, p.35–36   3

Thomas, Stories about Sally, p.65–66   2

ORCHARDS: *see* Fruit

ORGAN-GRINDERS

Haywood, "B" Is for Betsy, p.138–41   *In (3)

McKee, On We Go, p.87–112 (hurdy-gurdy man)   *2–2

O'Donnell, Round About, p.42–60   *Basic 1

Russell, D. H., On Cherry Street, p.118–27   *1

ORIOLES

Blough, Birds in the Big Woods, p.14, 23   3

OSTRICHES

McKee, On We Go, p.65   2–2

OTTER

Gray, New More Streets and Roads, p.174–77   *3–2

OUTDOOR LIFE: *see also* Camping; Fishing; Hunting; Nature; Picnics

Urell, Big City Fun, p.36–45   3+

OWLS
  Blough, Birds in the Big Woods, p.17
                                          3
  ———— Useful Plants and Animals,
    p.23   3
  Buff, Elf Owl   RA; In (3)
  Hildreth, Story Road, p.54–62 *2–2
  McKee, Come Along, p.135   2–1

PAINT
  Haywood, Two and Two Are Four,
    p.26–34   *In (3)
  McKee, Up and Away, p.72–92, 98–
    107, 168–80   *1–2

PAINTING: *see also* Artists; Color;
    Drawing
  Betts, ABC Beyond Treasure Valley,
    p.90–96   *3–1
  Leavell, Open Roads, p.18–24   *3
  O'Donnell, Anything Can Happen,
    p.37–94   *Par. 1
  ———— Five-and-a-Half Club, p.56–
    60   *Par. 3
  Ousley, Under the Apple Tree, p.47–
    50   *Pre–1
  Phillips, Molly, Pete, and Ginger,
    p.62–66   *PP4
  Quinlan, Day by Day, p.92–94   *P
  ———— Happy Days, p.60–63
                                *Read. P
  Russell, D. H., We Are Neighbors,
    p.14–19, 105–9   *2–1
  Sheldon, Our School, p.78–83, 94–
    98   *P

PANDAS
  Gates, On Four Feet, p.36–38, 83–91
                                     *1

PANTOMIMES: *see* Puppet Shows

PAPER
  Mitchell, Animals, Plants, and Ma-
    chines, p.46–52   2

PAPER FOLDING
  Massoglia, Fun-Time Paper Folding
                                    RA

PAPER HANGERS
  O'Donnell, Five-and-a-Half Club,
    p.61–68   *Par. 3
  Russell, D. H., We Are Neighbors,
    p.168–72   *2–1

PARACHUTES: *see also* Airplanes
  Betts, ABC All in a Day, p.62–65
                                    PP3
  Palmer, Lost and Found, p.229–33
                                   *2–1

PARADES: *see also* Circus
  Burton, W. H., Our Happy Ways,
    p.77–82 (hat)   *1
  Eberle, Secrets and Surprises, p.71–
    75   *2–2
  Leavell, Open Doors, p.8–14   *2
  McKee, Up and Away, p.118–26
                                  *1–2
  Russell, D. H., Around the Corner,
    p.8–12   *2–2
  ———— We Are Neighbors, p.99–104
    (pets)   *2–1
  Thomas, Stories about Linda and
    Lee, p.63–64   1
  Urell, Big City Neighbors, p.62–63
                                    3+

PARKS: *see also* Playgrounds; Yellow-
    stone National Park; Zoos
  Bond, G. L., Many Surprises, p.60–
    90   *P
  ———— Once upon a Storytime,
    p.115–43 (National Parks) *3–2
  Gates, Two Boys and a Tree, p.114–
    16   *Sup. 1
  Hanna, In City, Town, and Country,
    p.36–41   3
  ———— In the Neighborhood, p.136–
    41   2
  Haywood, Two and Two Are Four,
    p.8–13   *In (3)
  Reese, Basic Social Studies, p.42–49
                                     2
  Russell, D. H., Around the Corner,
    p.70–74   *2–2

Sheldon, Here and Away, p.40–42
(amusement)   *PP3
Thomas, Stories about Sally, p.31   2
Thorn, Let's Find Out, p.107–10   1
Zolotow, Park Book   RA (K–1)

PARROTS
Gates, New Friends and New Places,
p.121–33   *2–2
Gay, R., Home for Sandy, p.76–84
P–1
Gruenberg, Favorite Stories Old and
New, p.65–70 (from P-Penny)
*RA
Quinlan, To and Fro, p.30–34   *1
Sheldon, Our School, p.50–54   *P

PARTIES: *see also* Birthdays; Dances;
Games; Picnics
Betts, ABC Down Singing River,
p.215–21, 54–59   *2–1
Bond, G. L., Down Our Way, p.193–
204   *2–1
——— Many Surprises, p.32–58 *P
Burkhardt, Our Family, p.36–40   P
Carlson, Junior Party Book   T
Charters, Health Secrets, p.63–64 3
Durlacher, Play Party Book   T
Gardner, Let's Celebrate Christmas T
Gray, New Friends and Neighbors,
p.72–76   *2–1
——— New Our New Friends, p.
150–54   *1–2
——— New Streets and Roads,
p.50–56   *3–1
Hildreth, Twins   *Pre–PP
Hunnicutt, I Live with Others, p.92–
99   1
Leavell, Open Windows, p.130–56
*1
McKee, Come Along, p.196–214
*2–1
——— Up and Away, p.79–92 *1–2
Ousley, Under the Apple Tree, p.80–
85   *Pre–1

Russell, D. H., On Cherry Street,
p.167–70   *1
Sheldon, Fields and Fences, p.26–36,
56–68   *2–1
——— Our School, p.75–77, 84–88
*P
——— Our Town, p.43–48   *1
Wilcox, Here We Go, p.42–45   2

PARTRIDGES AND QUAILS
Blough, Animals and Their Young,
p.23–26   3
Burton, W. H., Our Good Neighbors,
p.246–53   *3
Gray, New More Friends and Neigh-
bors, p.64–69   *2–2
Thorn, Let's See Why, p.39–43   3

PASSOVER
Child Study Association of America,
Holiday Storybook   *RA

PATRIOTISM: *see* Citizenship; Flag
Day; Fourth of July; also names of
patriots, as Lincoln, Abraham;
Washington, George

PEARS
O'Donnell, Round About, p.32–40
*Basic 1

PEDDLERS AND PEDDLING
Mason, Little Jonathan, p.52–61
*In(3)
PELICANS
Huntington, Let's Go to the Seashore,
p.88–89   In (3)
Robinson, W. W., At the Seashore
In (3)
PENGUINS
Bryan, D., Johnny Penguin *In (3)
Darling, Penguins   In (3)

PENN, WILLIAM
Cavanah, Our Country's Story, p.20–
21   In (3)

PEOPLES OF OTHER LANDS: *see also* Eskimos; also names of countries, as Netherlands
Carpenter, Our Little Neighbors at Work and Play: Here, There, Then, and Now, p.166–229   3–4
Quinlan, Busy World, p.118–36   *3
Russell, D. H., Friends Far and Near, p.196–245   *3–2
Urell, Big City Neighbors   3+

PERIWINKLES
Huntington, Let's Go to the Seashore, p.78–79   In (3)

PERSEVERANCE
Leavell, Open Roads, p.124–30   *3
Piper, Little Engine That Could *RA

PET SHOWS
Blough, Pet Show   3
Brann, Patrick Was His Name   *RA
Gates, New Friends and New Places, p.114–20   *2–2
Gray, New Streets and Roads, p.98–105   *3–1
O'Donnell, Round About, p.12–18   *Basic 1
Palmer, Lost and Found, p.106–16   *2–1
Sheldon, Our School, p.45–60   *P

PET STORE: *see* Stores

PETROLEUM
Bond, A. D., Knowing about Science, p.72–76 (oil)   3
Hunnicutt, I Know People, p.164–70 (oil wells)   3

PETS: *see also* Kindness to Animals; also names of pets, as Cats; Dogs; Goldfish; Parrots; Rabbits
Association for Childhood Education, Told under the Blue Umbrella, p.8–9, 43–48   *RA
Barnard, Macmillan Science-Life Series, Bk.3, p.36–41 (insects), 42–43 (hamster), 44–52 (fish)   3

Bond, A. D., Thinking about Science, p.159–60   2
Bond, G. L., Down Our Way, p.61–65, 117–26, 128–66, 168–86   *2–1
―――― Many Surprises, p.118–52   *P
Brownell, Blue Skies, p.8–12   2
Flack, New Pet   *RA
Françoise, Springtime for Jeanne-Marie   *RA; In (2)
Frasier, Finding Answers, p.45–53   3
Gates, Ted and Sally, p.99–100   *P
Gray, New Friends and Neighbors, p.82–108   *2–1
―――― New Fun with Dick and Jane, p.46–64, 152–57   *1–1
―――― New More Friends and Neighbors, p.58–63   *2–2
―――― New Our New Friends, p.85–108   *1–2
―――― New Streets and Roads, p.93–97   *3–1
―――― New We Come and Go   *PP3
―――― New We Look and See   *PP1
―――― New We Work and Play   *PP2
Hallock, Health and Happy Days, p.79–81   1
Hildreth, Along the Way, p.1–4 *2–1
Irwin, Keeping Fit for Fun, p.23–25   3
McKee, Looking Ahead, p.102–29 (lamb)   *3–1
―――― On We Go, p.66–83 (cats)   *2–2
Nolen, Do and Dare, p.46–53 (marmoset), 54–58 (badger), 59–66 (antelope), 67–74 (horse)   *3–2
O'Donnell, Round About, p.160–70 (Paddy and His Pets)   *Basic 1
O'Keefe, Side by Side, p.8–15   2

Podendorf, True Book of Pets
In (3)
Russell, D. H., Finding New Neighbors, p.8–16, 18–54 *3–1
―――― Little White House, p.32–58 *P
―――― We Are Neighbors, p.44–82 *2–1
Sheldon, Our School, p.27–60 *P
Thomas, Stories about Linda and Lee, p.66–74 1
Thorn, Let's Go, p.8–10 PP

PETS—CARE: *see also* Cats—Care; Dogs—Care and Training
Barnard, Macmillan Science-Life Series, Bk.3, p.24–30, 31–34 3
Bond, G. L., Down Our Way, p.181–86 *2–1
Brownell, Come Rain, Come Shine, p.20 3
Frasier, Science—For You, p.144–45 2
Gray, New Friends and Neighbors, p.219–24 *2–1
―――― New More Friends and Neighbors, p.58–63 *2–2
McKee, Climbing Higher, p.157–58 3–2
Quinlan, Busy World, p.68–76 3
Urell, Big City Book of Conservation, p.18–19 3+

PHOEBE BIRDS
O'Donnell, Neighbors on the Hill, p.65–92 *Par. 2

PHOTOGRAPHY
Hill, Surprise for Judy Jo (tintypes) *In (3)

PHYSIOLOGY: *see also* Growth; Health; Senses; and parts of the body, as Bones, Ear
Barnard, Macmillan Science-Life Series, Bk.2., p.42–43 (muscles) 2
Frasier, Science—Adventures, p.119–39 3

PICNICS: *see also* Camping
Association for Childhood Education, Told under the Blue Umbrella, p.62–65 (from Poppy Seed Cakes) *RA
Bond, G. L., Happy Times, p.101–6 *1
Burkhardt, Our Home and School, p.89–101 1
Charters, Health Secrets, p.180–81 3
Clark, M., Poppy Seed Cakes *In (3)
Gates, Friends and Fun, p.136–48 *Alt. 2
―――― New Friends and New Places, p.46–58 *2–2
Gray, New Streets and Roads, p.21–28 *3–1
Haywood, Primrose Day, p.146–63 *In (3)
―――― Two and Two Are Four, p.56–70 *In (3)
Hill, Summer Comes to Apple Market Street *In (3)
Irwin, Growing Day by Day, p.114–19, 135–38 2
McIntire, Billy's Friends, p.122–24 1
―――― Working Together, p.43–44, 85–90 3
Mason, Happy Jack, p.121–25 *In (3)
Monroe, New What Next, p.68–75 *2–1
O'Donnell, Friendly Village, p.196–200 (clambake) *Basic 2
Russell, D. H., Around the Corner, p.222–27 *2–2
―――― On Cherry Street, p.188–92 *1
Sheldon, Here and Away, p.51–54 *PP3
―――― Our Town, p.150–56 *1
Smith, J. R., Our Neighbors at Home, p.27–28 3
Wavle, Rain and Shine, p.54–78 *P–2

PICTURE WRITING
McGaw, How Medicine Man Cured
Paleface Woman   *RA; In (3)

PICTURES: *see* Animals—Pictures;
Art; Drawing; Painting

PIGEONS
Haywood, Primrose Day, p.125–45
    *In (3)
Quinlan, Busy World, p.228–32   3
Thorn, Let's Look Around, p.17–19
    2

PIGEONS—FEEDING
Merrill, Travels of Marco   *RA

PIGS
Association for Childhood Educa-
tion, Told under the Green Um-
brella (Three Little Pigs; Old
Woman and Her Pig)   *RA
Betts, ABC Around Green Hills,
p.124–28   *1
——— ABC Beyond Treasure Val-
ley, p.138–44   *3–1
——— ABC Down Singing River,
p.99–104   *2–1
Bond, G. L., Once upon a Storytime,
p.173–78   *3–2
Brownell, All Day, Every Day,
p.115–17   *1
Gates, Good Times Today, p.216–24
    *3–1
Gray, New Our New Friends, p.168–
71   *1–2
——— New Streets and Roads, p.98–
105   *3–1
Gruenberg, Favorite Stories Old and
New, p.33–36   *RA
Hildreth, Story Road, p.14–24 *2–2
Hutchinson, Chimney Corner Sto-
ries (Old Woman and Her Pig;
Three Pigs)   *RA
Lattimore, Story of Lee Ling, p.31–
48   *In (3)

O'Donnell, Day In and Day Out,
p.98–104   *Basic P
Orton, Little Lost Pigs   *RA
Palmer, Lost and Found, p.124–206
    *2–1
Stolz, Emmett's Pig   *In (1)
Ungerer, Mellops Go Diving for
Treasure   *RA (K–1)

PILGRIMS: *see also* Colonial Period,
U.S.; Thanksgiving Day
Bulla, John Billington, Friend of
Squanto   In (3)
——— Squanto, Friend of the White
Men   In (3)
Dalgliesh, Thanksgiving Story
    *In (3)
Emerson, Pioneer Children of Ameri-
ca, p.54–73   *3
Gates, Good Times Today and To-
morrow, p.162–94   *Alt. 3
——— Good Times Tomorrow,
p.1–48   *3–2

PINE TREES: *see* Evergreen Trees

PINWHEELS: *see* Toys

PIONEER LIFE: *see also* Colonial Pe-
riod, U.S.; Log Cabins
Aulaire, Abraham Lincoln   In (3)
——— George Washington   In (3)
Betts, ABC Along Friendly Roads,
p.40–45, 82–88   *3–2
Bond, G. L., Stories from Every-
where, p.116–68   *3–1
Burton, W. H., Our Good Neigh-
bors, p.111–36   *3
Carpenter, Our Little Neighbors at
Work and Play: Here, There,
Then, and Now, p.66–114   3+
Cavanah, Our Country's Story, p.32–
35, 46–49   In (3)
Cutright, Living Together Today and
Yesterday, p.196–216   3
Emerson, Pioneer Children of Amer-
ica   3

Gates, Good Times Today and To-morrow, p.162–94 *Alt. 3

Gray, New More Streets and Roads, p.52–96 *3–2

Hugley, Around the Home, p.122–26 (clothing), 140–62 (houses) 3

Le Grand, Cats for Kansas *RA (K–2)

McIntire, Working Together, p.232–38 3

McKee, Climbing Higher, p.54–67, 294–308 *3–2

—— Looking Ahead, p.140–81 *3–1

Mason, Little Jonathan In (3)

Nolen, Do and Dare, p.272–82 *3–2

Russell, D. H., Friends Far and Near, p.302–33 *3–2

Sheldon, Story Caravan, p.6–42 *3–2

Sorensen, Ways of Our Land, p.1–4, 46–50, 78–83 *3

Urell, Big City Water Supply, p.52–74 3+

Yoakam, Children Everywhere, p.75–126 *3

PIPES

Schneider, H., Science for Here and Now, p.123–28 2

PIRATES: see Playing Pirate

PLANETS: see also Earth

Blough, How the Sun Helps Us, p.34–35 3

PLANTATION LIFE

Aulaire, George Washington In (3)

Sorensen, Ways of Our Land, p.46–50 3

PLANTS: see also Bulbs; Flowers; Gardens; also types of plants, as Cotton; Trees; Weeds

Baker, A. O., Around the Corner, p.22–25 2

—— In Your Neighborhood, p.39–50 3

Barnard, Macmillan Science-Life Series, Bk.1, p.40–44 1

—— Macmillan Science-Life Series, Bk.2, 106–9, 111–26 2

Beauchamp, All around Us, p.62–77 2

—— How Do We Know? p.54–72 3

—— Look and Learn, p.54–69 1

Blough, Plants round the Year 3

Bond, A. D., Thinking about Science, p.143–54 2

Burkhardt, Our Home and School, p.78–82 *1

Clark, A. N., In My Mother's House, p.42–49 RA; In (2)

Cooke, Fun-Time Window Garden In (2)

Craig, Science near You, p.70–81, 92–95 1

Dowling, New Learning Why, p.53–64 3

—— New Seeing Why, p.53–66, 96–99 2

Frasier, Science—Adventures, p.60–66, 205–21 3

—— Science—All the Year, p.41–44, 186–89 2

—— We Ask, p.34–35 P

—— We Wonder, p.30–31 PP

Knox, Wonderworld of Science, Bk.1, p.92–94 1

—— Wonderworld of Science, Bk.3, p.10–24, 131–77 (poison ivy) 3

Mitchell, Animals, Plants, and Machines, p.13–20 *2

Monroe, New What Next, p.21–26 *2

Schneider, H., Science Far and Near, 32–36 (desert), p.206–8 (forest) 3

—— Science for Here and Now, p.181–92 2

Smith, V. C., Science around the Clock, p.9–37 (poison ivy), 114–26   3

———— Science under the Sun, p.28–35   2

Thorn, Let's Find Out, p.73–82   1

———— Let's See Why, p.10–13, 164–68 (poison ivy)   3

Thurber, Exploring Science Two, p.104–16 (buds)   2

Urell, Big City Book of Conservation, p.67–72   3+

———— Big City Water Supply, p.44–46   3+

Webber, Bits That Grow Big   In (2)

———— Travelers All   In (3)

———— Up Above and Down Below   In (3)

Zion, Plant Sitter   *In (2)

PLANTS IN WINTER
Bond, A. D., Knowing about Science, p.46–48   3

PLAY: *see also* Games; Picnics; Rainy Day Fun
Barnard, Macmillan Science-Life Series, Bk.1, p.82–90   1

Bauer, Just Like Me, p.58–59   P

Betts, ABC All in a Day, p.52–57   PP3

———— ABC Up the Street and Down, p.36–40   *P

Bond, G. L., Fun with Us   PP3

———— Play with Us   PP2

———— See Us Come   Comp. PP1

———— See Us Have Fun   Comp. PP3

———— See Us Play   Comp. PP2

———— See Us Ride   Comp. PP4

———— Three of Us   PP1

Brownell, Blue Skies, p.15–19   *2

Burkhardt, Our Home and School, p.83–85   1

———— Our Way, p.36–40   PP

Burton, W. H., Come and See   PP2

———— Days of Fun, p.6–10, 30–46, 70–98   P

———— Don and Peggy   PP1

———— Here We Play   PP3

Carpenter, Our Little Neighbors at Work and Play: Here, There, Then, and Now, p.53–56 (Indian)   3+

Clymer, Yard for John   *RA

Eberle, Secrets and Surprises, p.172–86   *2–2

Gates, Splash   *PP1

———— Tuffy and Boots   *PP2

Gray, New Fun with Dick and Jane, p.121–25   *1–1

———— New We Come and Go   *PP2

———— New We Look and See   *PP1

———— New We Work and Play   *PP2

Hallock, Health in Work and Play, p.119–21, 137–40, 154–56   2

Hanna, In the Neighborhood, p.72–79   2

Hildreth, At Play, p.1–28   *P (level 1)

———— I Know a Secret, p.1–22   *1–1

———— Mary and Bill   *Pre–PP

Hogan, Ned and Nancy   *PP1

Hunnicutt, I Live with Others, p.30–44   1

Irwin, Awake and Away, p.26–32   1

McKee, Big Show, p.45–63   *PP3

———— Jack and Janet, p.20–29, 33–44   *1–1

———— Tip and Mitten   *PP2

Monroe, New What Next, p.48–52   *3–1

O'Donnell, High on a Hill   *PP4

———— Open the Door   *PP3

———— Skip Along   *PP1

———— Under the Sky   *PP2

———— Wishing Well, p.25–33   *Par. P

O'Keefe, From Head to Toe, p.45–47   1

———— How We Grow, p.174–81   3

———— Side by Side, p.45–52   2

Ousley, Come with Me, p.42–50, 56–58   *Pre-P

Phillips, Molly, Pete, and Ginger   *PP4

Quinlan, Before Winky, p.20–26, 30–32   *Pre–PP

———— Happy Days, p.1–18, 26–29   *Read. P

———— Winky, p.40–43   *PP

Russell, D. H., Little White House, p.166–70   *P

———— My Little Blue Story Book   *PP3

———— My Little Red Story Book   *PP1

Schloat, Playtime for You   In (2)

Sheldon, At Home and Away *SPP

Thomas, Stories about Linda and Lee   1

Whipple, Our Earth, p.115–17   3

Wilcox, Come On, p.39–44   1

Yoakam, Making Storybook Friends, p.5–11   *1

———— On the Way to Storyland, p.5–12, 48–51   *P

PLAYGROUNDS: *see also* Games; Merry-Go-Rounds; Parks; Swinging; Toys

Hallock, Health and Safety for You, p.31–34, 162–65   3

Hanna, At School, p.38–42   1

Hunnicutt, I Play, p.3–14   P

Irwin, Growing Day by Day, p.57–65   2

McIntire, Billy's Friends, p.35–43   1

Reese, Basic Social Studies, p.30–41   2

PLAYING BALL: *see* Ball; Baseball; Basketball; Football

PLAYING CIRCUS

Haywood, "B" Is for Betsy, p.126–41   *In (3)

Leavell, Open Windows, p.8–13   *1

McKee, Big Show, p.44–63   *PP3

PLAYING COWBOY

Haywood, Two and Two Are Four   *In (3)

Monroe, New We Three, p.72–75 *1

Ousley, Under the Apple Tree, p.6–24   *Pre–1

Russell, D. H., Finding New Neighbors, p.28–35   *3–1

PLAYING FIREMAN

Burton, W. H., Our Good Neighbors, p.2–9   *3

Haywood, Eddie and the Fire Engine   *In (3)

PLAYING HORSE

Burton, W. H., Meet Our Friends, p.81–85   *2

Gray, New More Friends and Neighbors, p.6–10   *2–2

Leavell, Open Windows, p.151–56 *1

Monroe, New We Three, p.34–39 *1

Ousley, Under the Apple Tree, p.26–28   Pre–1

Sheldon, Our Town, p.62–67 (sawhorse)   *1

PLAYING HOUSE

Bond, G. L., Fun with Us, p.43–48   *PP3

Burkhardt, Our Family, p.28–35 P

Carpenter, Our Little Neighbors at Work and Play: Here, There, Then, and Now, p.18–20 (Indian playhouse)   3+

Gates, Open Window (playhouse)   *Unit 1

———— Ted and Sally, p.25–44 (playhouse)   *P

Gray, New Fun with Dick and Jane, p.130–34   *1–1

———— New Our New Friends, p.46–50 *1–2

Hogan, Ned and Nancy, p.10–40 *PP1

Leavell, Open Doors, p.16–22 (doll) *2

Lenski, Let's Play House *RA (K–2)

Ousley, Come with Me, p.56–58 (playhouse) *Pre–P

———— Under the Apple Tree, p.114–17 (playhouse) *Pre–1

Quinlan, Happy Days, p.34–40 (playhouse) *Read. P

Russell, D. H., My Little Blue Story Book, p.46–50, 57–71 *PP3

Thomas, Your Town and Mine, p.130–36 (playhouse) 3

PLAYING INDIAN

Clymer, Yard for John *RA

Leavell, Open Windows, p.105–10 *1

Politi, Little Leo *In (3)

PLAYING PIRATE

Palmer, Lost and Found, p.13–16 *2–1

PLAYING POLICEMAN

Hallock, Health and Happy Days, p.40–42 1

McKee, Come Along, p.136–49 *2–1

O'Donnell, Anything Can Happen, p.80–86 *Par. 1

PLAYING SCHOOL

Burton, W. H., Our Happy Ways, p.54–60 *1

Hildreth, Going to School, p.26–30 *PP3

Hogan, Ned and Nancy, p.42–45 *PP1

Sheldon, Our School, p.10–13 *P

PLAYING SOLDIERS

Leavell, Open Doors, p.32–38 (toy) *2

PLAYING STORE

Gray, New Our New Friends, p.132–37 *1–2

O'Donnell, Under the Sky, p.51–56 *PP2

Russell, D. H., Around the Corner, p.13–18 *2–2

Sheldon, Our Town, p.37–42 *1

———— Town and Country, p.102–5 *2–2

PLAYING TELEPHONE

Gray, New Friends and Neighbors, p.60–64 *2–1

Palmer, Lost and Found, p.70–76 *2–1

PLAYING TRAIN

Bond, G. L., Fun with Us, p.58–61 *PP3

Gates, Ted and Sally, p.45–54 *P

Gray, New Friends and Neighbors, p.32–36 *2–1

Hildreth, At Play, p.71–74 *P–1

Russell, D. H., We Are Neighbors, p.84–91 *2–1

Sheldon, Our School, p.62–66 *P

Slobodkin, Clear the Track for Michael's Magic Train *RA

Woolley, David's Railroad *In (3)

PLAYING ZOO

Quinlan, Faces and Places, p.233–36 *2

PLAYMATES

Gruenberg, Favorite Stories Old and New, p.153–56 *RA

PLAYS: *see also* Puppet Shows

Betts, ABC Along Friendly Roads, p.136–43 (Sleeping Beauty) 3–2

Brownell, Come Rain, Come Shine, p.139–43 (health habits) 3

Burkhardt, Our Neighborhood, p.102–7 2

McKee, Climbing Higher, p.270–92 (radio) 3–2

────── Looking Ahead, p.284–307
                                        3–1
Russell, D. H., Finding New Neigh-
  bors, p.303–9 (Lad and the North
  Wind)   3–1
────── Friends Far and Near, p.269–
  78 (What the Old Man Does Is
  Always Right)   3–2
Sheldon, Story Caravan, p.106–20
  (Country Bunny and the Little
  Gold Shoes)   3–2

PLUMBING: *see* Houses

POCKETS
Betts, ABC Along Friendly Roads,
  p.169–75   *3–2
Brown, M. W., Willie's Adventures
                                      *In (2)

POISON IVY: *see* Plants

POLAND—FOLKLORE
Baker, A. B., Talking Tree   *RA

POLAR REGIONS: *see* Eskimos

POLICE: *see also* Playing Policeman;
  Safety
Barr, Policeman Paul   In (2)
Burton, W. H., Our Happy Ways,
  p.132–35   *1
Dillon, Policemen   In (2)
Frasier, We Ask, p.66–67   P
Hallock, Health in Work and Play,
  p.36–41   2
Hanna, In City, Town, and Country,
  p.8–13 (lost car)   3
────── In the Neighborhood, p.88 2
Haywood, "B" Is for Betsy, p.31–42
  (lost child)   *In (3)
Hildreth, Faraway Ports, p.173–83
  (lost child)   *3–1
Hunnicutt, I Know People, p.23–32
  (lost bicycle)   3
Jones, E., My Second Health Book,
  p.25–26   2

Leaf, Fair Play, p.27–29, 68   In (3)
McIntire, Billy's Friends, p.78   1
────── Billy's Neighbors, p.70–86 2
Miner, True Book of Policemen and
  Firemen   In (2)
Mitchell, Farm and City, p.102 (traf-
  fic)   1
Reese, Basic Social Studies, p.52–65
                                  2
Schlein, Amazing Mr. Pelgrew
                              *RA (K–2)
Sheldon, Here and Away, p.56–58
  (lost dog)   *PP3
Thomas, Stories about Sally, p.33–
  36   2

POLISH IN THE UNITED STATES
Nolen, Fun and Frolic, p.150–61
                                *3–1
Urell, Big City Neighbors, p.17–22
                                  3+

POLITENESS: *see* Manners

PONDS
Flack, Tim Tadpole and the Great
  Bullfrog   *In (3)
Russell, D. H., Around the Corner,
  p.177–84   *2–2

PONIES: *see* Horses

POOLS
Sheldon, Here and Near, p.60–63
  (wading)   *PP2
────── Our Town, p.144–49 (swimming)   *1

POPCORN
Frasier, Science—Adventures, p.205–
  9 (seeds)   3
McKee, Jack and Janet, p.100–4
  (balls)   *1–1

PORCUPINES
Bond, G. L., Stories from Everywhere, p.194–206   *3–1
Gray, New More Streets and Roads,
  p.178–85   *3–2

Sheldon, Magic Windows, p.135–43 *3–1

Yoakam, Children Everywhere, p.221–25 *3

POST OFFICE: *see also* Letters; Postman

Buchheimer, Let's Go to a Post Office In (3)

Colonius, At the Post Office In (3)

Hugley, Around the Home, p.10–12 3

Norling, Pogo's Letter *In (3)

Thomas, Stories about Sally, p.44–49 2

POSTMAN

Gates, Friends and Fun, p.8–15 *Alt. 2

——— Today We Go, p.8–15 *2–1

McIntire, Billy's Neighbors, p.115–19 2

——— Working Together, p.175–77 3

POSTURE

Bauer, From Eight to Nine, p.168–70 3

Brownell, Blue Skies, p.54–55 2

Hallock, Health and Safety for You, p.72–76 3

Jones, E., Easy Steps to Health, p.102–7 3

POTATO FARMS

Yoakam, Children Everywhere, p.298–313 *3

POTTERY: *see also* Clay; Clay Modeling

Clark, A. N., Little Indian Pottery Maker *RA; In (2)

POULTRY: *see* Chickens; Ducks; Eggs; Geese; Pigeons; Turkeys

PRAIRIE DOGS

Gray, New More Streets and Roads, p.167–73 *3–2

Mitchell, Another Here and Now Story Book, p.338–44 *RA

Quinlan, Faces and Places, p.78–80 *2

PRAYERS

Jones, M. A., Tell Me about Jesus, p.49–61 *RA

PREHISTORIC ANIMALS: *see* Animals, Prehistoric

PRIDE

Aulaire, Don't Count Your Chicks *In (3)

PRISMS: *see* Light; Rainbow

PROGRAMS: *see* Plays

PROMPTNESS

Hanna, At School, p.6–10 1

Hunnicutt, I Have Friends, p.98–104 2

Leavell, Open Windows, p.75–80 *1

PROTECTION: *see* Animals—Protection; Birds—Protection; Safety

PROVERBS

Jones, M. A., Tell Me about the Bible, p.52–56 *RA

PUEBLO INDIANS: *see* Indians of North America

PUERTO RICANS IN THE UNITED STATES

Urell, Big City Neighbors, p.23–29 3+

PUFFINS

Nolen, Fun and Frolic, p.230–40 *3–1

PULLEYS

Blough, Doing Work, p.23–25 3+

PUMPKINS

Association for Childhood Education, Told under the Blue Umbrella, p.69–74 *RA

Betts, ABC Around Green Hills, p.112–17 *1

Burton, W. H., Meet Our Friends, p.172–76 *2

Gray, New More Friends and Neighbors, p.194–98 *2–2

—— New More Streets and Roads, p.82–88 *3–2

Gruenberg, Favorite Stories Old and New, p.135–37 *RA

PUPPET SHOWS: _see also_ Plays

Betts, ABC Along Friendly Roads, p.136–43 (Sleeping Beauty) 3–2

—— ABC Over a City Bridge, p.74–79 *2–2

McIntire, Working Together, p.123–24 3

PUPPETS

Gruenberg, Favorite Stories Old and New, p.145–47 (from Pinocchio in America) *RA

PUPPIES: _see_ Dogs

PURIM

Child Study Association of America, Holiday Storybook *RA

QUAILS: _see_ Partridges and Quails

QUILTS

Association for Childhood Education, Told under the Blue Umbrella, p.80–82 *RA

Gates, Good Times Today, p.87–95 (patchwork) *3–1

Russell, D. H., Friends Far and Near, p.310–16 *3–2

RABBITS

Association for Childhood Education, Told under the Blue Umbrella, p.52–55, 142–47 *RA

Blough, Animals and Their Young, p.31–32 3

—— Pet Show, p.14–18 3

Bond, A. D., Getting Ready, p.65–69 P

Bond, G. L., Happy Times, p.166–78 *1

Brown, M. W., Home for a Bunny *RA; In (2)

—— Little Chicken *RA

Carroll, Where's the Bunny? *RA (K–1); In (2)

Frasier, We Ask, p.36–38 P

Gray, New Friends and Neighbors, p.131–37, 153–57, 262–67 *2–1

—— New More Friends and Neighbors, p.139–45 (Easter) *2–2

—— New Our New Friends, p.98–103 *1–2

—— New Streets and Roads, p.165–71 *3–1

Heyward, Country Bunny and the Little Gold Shoes *RA; In (2)

Hildreth, Enchanting Stories, p.12–28 *3–2

—— Fun in Story, p.2–24 *P–2

—— I Know a Secret, p.152–66 *1–1

—— Story Road, p.114–28 *2–2

Hutchinson, Chimney Corner Stories (Peter Rabbit) *RA

Irwin, Growing Day by Day, p.33–35 *2

McKee, Up and Away, p.22–38 *1–2

Marokvia, Jannot, the French Rabbit *RA

Mitchell, Animals, Plants, and Machines, p.226–35 2

—— Farm and City, p.128 1

O'Donnell, Day In and Day Out, p.6–9, 90–97 *Basic P

—— Five-and-a-Half Club, p.69–78, 199–212 *Par. 3

—— Neighbors on the Hill, p.122–28 *Par. 2

Ousley, Open the Gate, p.30–34, 56–62 *Pre–2

———— Under the Apple Tree, p.80–85   *Pre–1

Quinlan, Busy World, p.6–11 (from Raggylug)   *3

———— To and Fro, p.36–44   *1

Russell, D. H., Around the Corner, p.147–53 (Mr. Rabbit, Rainmaker)   *2–2

———— Friends Far and Near, p.110–17   *3–2

———— On Cherry Street, p.109–16, 176–80, 199–204   *1

———— We Are Neighbors, p.37–42   *2–1

Schlein, Little Rabbit   *RA (K–1)

Schwartz, E. R., Cottontail Rabbit In (2)

Sheldon, Here and Away, p.12–14   *PP3

———— Our School, p.33–38   *P

———— Our Town, p.178–83   *1

Thorn, Let's Find Out, p.101–5   1

Yoakam, Making Storybook Friends, p.48–53   *1

RACCOONS

Betts, ABC Along Friendly Roads, p.93–99   *3–2

Gall, All the Year Round, p.20–24 In (3)

Gates, Good Times Today, p.104–13   *3–1

———— Good Times Today and To-morrow, p.70–79   *Alt. 3

Gray, New Streets and Roads, p.226–33 (from Ringtail)   *3–1

Mitchell, Another Here and Now Story Book, p.293–99   *RA

Nolen, Do and Dare, p.168–74 *3–2

Russell, D. H., We Are Neighbors, p.58–64   *2–1

Sheldon, Town and Country, p.15–38   *2–2

Smith, V. C., Science under the Sun, p.22–23   2

RACES OF MEN

Mitchell, Here and Now Story Book, p.291–98   *RA

RACING

Association for Childhood Education, Told under the Green Umbrella (Race between Hare and Hedge-hog)   *RA

Burton, W. H., Our Happy Ways, p.120–24   *1

Hutchinson, Fireside Stories (Hare and the Hedgehog)   *RA

Monroe, New What Next, p.4–9, 10–15   *2

RADIO: *see also* Television

Burton, W. H., Our Happy Ways, p.61–64   *1

McIntire, Working Together, p.186–89   3

O'Donnell, Neighbors on the Hill, p.9–17   *Par. 2

RADIO STATION

Smith, M. E., Joe's Story of the Air-port, p.16–17   2+

Thomas, Stories about Sally, p.16–17   2

RAILROAD STATIONS

Hunnicutt, I Know People, p.85–93   3

Reese, Basic Social Studies, p.112–15   2

Sorensen, Ways of Our Land, p.93–96   3

Thomas, Stories about Sally, p.52–54   2

———— Your Town and Mine, p.138–40   3

RAILROADS: *see* Trains

RAIN: *see also* Floods; Snow; Um-brellas; Weather

Barnard, Macmillan Science-Life Se-ries, Bk.2, p.63–66   2

Blough, Water Appears and Disappears, p.21–22   3
Bond, A. D., Knowing about Science, p.149–53   3
———— Looking at Science, p.49–52   1
Brownell, Come Rain, Come Shine, p.62–68   *3
Child Study Association of America, Read-to-Me Storybook, p.10–13   *RA
Gates, Open Window, p.11–16   *Unit 1
———— Splash, p.3–15   *PP1
Goudey, Good Rain   In (3)
Hildreth, I Know a Secret, p.38–41   *1–1
Mitchell, Farm and City, p.44–47   1
———— Our Country, p.227–32 (desert)   *3
O'Donnell, Day In and Day Out, p.29–34   *Basic P
———— Wishing Well, p.90–100   *Par. P
Quinlan, To and Fro, p.58–65   *1
Schwartz, J., Now I Know   In (2)
Sheldon, At Home and Away, p.73–77   *SPP
———— Our Town, p.56–61   *1
Thorn, Let's Find Out, p.37–41   1
———— Let's Go, p.20–22   PP
Wavle, Rain and Shine, p.3–32 *P–2
Yoakam, Stories We Like, p.154–63   *2

RAINBOW
Barnard, Macmillan Science-Life Series, Bk.2, p.66   2
Blough, Water Appears and Disappears, p.23–24   3
Bond, A. D., Knowing about Science, p.111–14   3
Frasier, Science—Adventures, p.164–65   3
———— Science—For You, p.118–19   1

RAINY DAY FUN
Brownell, All Day, Every Day, p.27–30   *1
Burkhardt, Our Home and School, p.68–72   1
Gates, Good Times Today, p.87–95   *3–1
Gray, New Our New Friends, p.31–35   *1–2
Kuskin, James and the Rain   *RA (K–2)
Monroe, New What Next, p.34–37   *2–1

RANCH LIFE: *see also* Cattle; Cowboys; Pioneer Life; Sheep
Burton, W. H., Our Good Neighbors, p.146–54   *3
Eberle, Secrets and Surprises, p.189–218   *2–2
Gates, Good Times Tomorrow, p.159–81   *3–1
Hugley, Around the Home, p.74–93   3
Mitchell, Another Here and Now Story Book, p.341–44   *RA
Ousley, Ranches and Rainbows, p.8–30   *Pre–3
Russell, D. H., Friends Far and Near, p.318–25   *3–2
Sheldon, Town and Country, p.160–200   *2–2
Sorensen, Ways of Our Land, p.115–17   3
Thomas, Stories about Sally, p.105–17   2
———— Your Town and Mine, p.52–53 (cattle ranch)   3

RATS
Betts, ABC Along Friendly Roads, p.265–72 (pack rats)   *3–2

RAYON
McIntire, Working Together, p.102–3   3

Mitchell, Animals, Plants, and Machines, p.85–87   2

READING: *see also* Books
Gates, On Four Feet, p.80, 92   *1
Gray, New Our New Friends, p.75–78   *1–2
Jones, E., My Second Health Book, p.37–39   2
Leavell, Open Doors, p.148–54   *2

RECORDINGS
McIntire, Working Together, p.185   3

RECORDS: *see* Books

RECREATION: *see* Camping; Clubs; Games; Handicraft; Play; Vacations

REDBIRDS: *see* Cardinal Birds

REFLECTION
Buff, Dash and Dart, p.66–73 (physical)   RA; In (3)

REFRIGERATION
Dowling, New Learning Why, p.135–38   3
Smith, J. R., Our Neighbors at Home, p.216–17   3
Smith, M. E., Bob's Story of the Retail Food Market   2+

RELIGION: *see also* Bible Stories; Church; God; Jesus Christ; Prayers
Beatty, Saint Francis and the Wolf   RA
Fitch, Book about God   RA; In (2)
——— Child Jesus   RA
Jones, J. M. O., Small Rain   RA
——— This Is the Way   RA
Urell, Big City Neighbors, p.47–52   3+

REPRODUCTION
Dowling, New Learning Why, p.41–43   3

REPTILES: *see also* Snakes; Turtles
Ballard, True Book of Reptiles   In (2)

RESERVOIRS: *see* Water Supply

RESOURCEFULNESS
Bannerman, Story of Little Black Sambo   *RA; In (2)
Brownell, Come Rain, Come Shine, p.78–81   *3

RESPIRATION
Frasier, Science—Adventures, p.129–32   3

RESPONSIBILITY: *see also* Character Building; Citizenship
Brownell, Come Rain, Come Shine, p.44–47   *3
Hunnicutt, I Have Friends, p.141–51   2
——— I Live with Others, p.48–61   1
Leavell, Open Doors, p.103–6, 128–35   *2
——— Open Roads, p.33–46, 58–71, 108–14   *3
——— Open Windows, p.38–50   *1
Wilcox, Come On, p.71–82   1

REST: *see* Sleep

RESTAURANTS, LUNCH ROOMS, etc.
Brownell, Come Rain, Come Shine, p.92–96   3
Burkhardt, Our Neighborhood, p.55–57   2
Irwin, Keeping Fit for Fun, p.141–43 (cafeteria)   3
Palmer, Lost and Found, p.90–97 (automat)   *2–1
Reese, Basic Social Studies, p.150–59   2
Sheldon, Here and Away, p.48–50 (drive-in)   *PP3
Thomas, Your Town and Mine, p.173–75   3

REVERENCE
Leavell, Open Roads, p.92–99, 100–
6   *3
——— Open Windows, p.160–66,
181–86   *1

RHINOCEROS
Nolen, Do and Dare, p.210–20 *3–2

RHYMES
Russell, D. H., We Are Neighbors,
p.117–20   *2–1

RICE
Carpenter, Our Little Neighbors at
Work and Play: Here, There, Then,
and Now, p.182–84   3+

RIDDLES
Bauer, Being Six, p.88–91   1
Brown, M. W., Indoor Noisy Book
RA
Burton, W. H., Our Good Neighbors,
p.306–7   3
Chrystie, Riddle Me This   In (3)
Craig, Science Everywhere, p.132 3
Gray, New Fun with Dick and Jane,
p.126–29   1–1
Knox, Wonderworld of Science, Bk.3,
p.131–33   3
McIntire, Billy's Friends, p.100–1   1
McKee, Come Along, p.66, 245 2–1
Ousley, Open the Gate, p.73–76
Pre–2
Pistorius, What Butterfly Is It? In (3)
Quinlan, Before Winky, p.44–45
Pre–PP
Yoakam, Making Storybook Friends,
p.54–55   1

RIDES: *see also* Traveling
Bond, G. L., Ride with Us   *PP4
——— See Us Ride   *Comp. PP4
Gates, Tuffy and Boots, p.33–40
*PP2

RIVER LIFE—CHINA
Flack, Story about Ping   *RA

RIVERS: *see also* Dams; Floods; Water
Supply
Betts, ABC Down Singing River,
p.41–46, 231–37   *2–1
Bond, A. D., Knowing about Science,
p.159–60 (Missouri)   3
Clark, A. N., In My Mother's House,
p.25   RA; In (2)
Frasier, Science—Adventures, p.17–
19   3
Lenski, We Live by the River *In (3)
Mitchell, Our Country, p.4–32 (Mis-
sissippi and Tennessee), 266–79
(Colorado)   3
Sorensen, Ways of Our Land, p.46–
55 (Mississippi)   3
Whipple, Our Earth, p.144–54   3

ROADS: *see* Streets and Roads

ROADSIDE MARKETS: *see also* Markets
O'Donnell, Neighbors on the Hill,
p.155–67   *Par. 2

ROBINS
Association for Childhood Education,
Told under the Blue Umbrella,
p.30–32   *RA
Baker, A. O., In Your Neighbor-
hood, p.13–16   3
Blough, Animals and Their Young,
p.16–22   3
Bond, A. D., Thinking about Science,
p.161–65   2
Bond, G. L., Just for Fun, p.16–20
*2–2
Burton, W. H., Our Happy Ways,
p.83–86   *1
Flack, Restless Robin *RA; In (3)
Gray, New Our New Friends, p.119–
24   *1–2
Parker, Birds in Your Backyard,
p.22–23   2
Russell, D. H., We Are Neighbors,
p.265–68 (Wee Robin's Christmas
Song)   *2–1

Smith, V. C., Science under the Sun, p.133–39 2

Thorn, Let's Find Out, p.43–45, 47–53 1

Tresselt, "Hi, Mister Robin" *RA (K–2)

ROBINS—EGGS AND NESTS

Bond, G. L., Just for Fun, p.12–17 2–2

Frasier, Science—All the Year, p.174–78 2

Knox, Wonderworld of Science, Bk.2, p.123–26 2

Quinlan, Faces and Places, p.150–54 *2

Yoakam, Making Storybook Friends, p.68–74 *1

ROCKS: *see also* Stone

Bond, A. D., Knowing about Science, p.162–65 3

Craig, Science near You, p.56–59 1

Frasier, Science—Adventures, p.41–44, 57–59 3

——— Science—All the Year, p.55–60 2

Knox, Wonderworld of Science, Bk.3, p.42–43 3

Podendorf, True Book of Pebbles and Shells In (3)

——— True Book of Rocks and Minerals In (3)

Schneider, H., Science Far and Near, p.2–19, 39–45 3

Smith, V. C., Science around the Clock, p.68–73 3

Thorn, Let's See Why, p.112–16 3

RODEO

Gates, Good Times Today and Tomorrow, p.277–82 *Alt. 3

——— Good Times Tomorrow, p.163–68 *3–2

Russell, D. H., Finding New Neighbors, p.190–97 *3–1

ROLLER SKATING: *see* Skating

ROLLERS

Schneider, H., Now Try This In (3)

ROOMS: *see* Doll Houses; Houses

ROOSTERS: *see* Chickens

ROOTS

Webber, Up Above and Down Below In (3)

ROSH HASHANA

Child Study Association of America, Holiday Storybook *RA

RUBBER

Blough, Useful Plants and Animals, p.27 3

Carpenter, Our Little Neighbors at Work and Play: Here, There, Then, and Now, p.185–92 3–4

McIntire, Working Together, p.106–7 3

Mitchell, Animals, Plants, and Machines, p.90–96 2

Partch, Basic Social Studies, p.140–45 3

RUSSIA

Beim, L. L., Sasha and the Samovar *In (3)

Carrick, Picture Tales from the Russian *In (3)

Charushin, Baby Bears *In (3)

Cohn, Little People in a Big Country RA

Gruenberg, Favorite Stories Old and New, p.230–32 (Tortoise and the Elephant), 237–38 (Brave Laborer), 246–48 (Snow Maiden) *RA

Reyher, My Mother Is the Most Beautiful Woman in the World *RA; In (3)

RUSSIANS IN THE UNITED STATES

Urell, Big City Neighbors, p.53–59 3+

SABBATH
Child Study Association of America,
Holiday Storybook   *RA

SAFETY: *see also* Bicycles; Fire Departments; First Aid; Lighthouses;
Playgrounds; Police; Signals and
Signaling; Traffic
Barnard, Macmillan Science-Life Series, Bk.1, p.22–31, 84–85   1
—————— Macmillan Science-Life Series, Bk.2, p.5–6, 71–73, 144, 147–
49 (fire), 150–52 (play)   2
—————— Macmillan Science-Life Series, Bk.3, p.214–17, 232–33   3
Bauer, Being Six, p.14–17 (traffic),
58–60 (fire), 61 (school)   1
—————— From Eight to Nine, p.38–
39, 42–44 (fire), 68–69 (traffic),
142–45 (playground), 172–73
(play)   3
—————— Seven or So, p.38–41 (traffic), 102–3 (fire), 104–5 (playground), 140–41 (eye)   2
Brownell, All Day, Every Day, p.37–
42, 71–76 (traffic), 77 (play)   1
—————— Blue Skies, p.70–71 (fire),
72 (traffic), 73 (bus), 75–79,
110–13, 118–19 (play)   2
—————— Come Rain, Come Shine,
p.21–24 (toys), 60–61 (bicycle),
162 (home)   3
Burkhardt, Our Neighborhood, p.26–
30 (storm)   2
Charters, Health Secrets, p.48 (pe-
destrian), 50–52 (school bus),
166–70 (bicycle), 191–97 (home)
                                  3
Hallock, Health and Happy Days,
p.18–19, 35–37 (playground)   1
—————— Health and Safety for You,
p.142–45 (helpers), 146–48 (bicycle), 149–52, 153–55 (fire),
156–58 (bus), 167–69 (camp),
171–74 (beach)   3

—————— Health in Work and Play,
p.30–35 (home), 42–47 (tools),
48–53, 72–75 (play), 145–48
(camp)   2
Hanna, In the Neighborhood, p.56–
61 (bicycle)   2
Hunnicutt, I Live with Others, p.56–
60 (traffic)   1
—————— I Play, p.4–14 (playground),
33–34 (patrol), 38–39 (traffic) P
Irwin, Awake and Away, p.44–50
(traffic)   1
—————— Growing Day by Day, p.87–
89 (patrol), 98–102 (fire), 131–
34 (traffic), 148–52 (country)   2
—————— Keeping Fit for Fun, p.18–20
(traffic), 168–76 (school), 177–82,
188–92 (home), 184–86 (bicycle)
                                  3
Jones, E., Easy Steps to Health,
p.137–40 (street), 141–44 (home)
                                  3
—————— My Second Health Book,
p.20–22   2
Leaf, Fair Play, p.34–36   In (3)
—————— Safety Can Be Fun   In (3)
MacDonald, Red Light, Green Light
                           RA; In (2)
Quinlan, Faces and Places, p.14–24
(traffic)   *2
—————— Happy Days, p.48–52 (street)
                            *Read. P
—————— To and Fro, p.96–97 (traf-
fic)   *1
Thomas, Stories about Linda and
Lee, p.6–7, 16, 51, 56   1
Wilcox, Come On, p.10–14 (traffic),
15–20 (play), 21–26 (bicycle),
29–34 (fire)   1
—————— Here We Go, p.8–12 (fire),
13–16 (home), 21–24 (bus), 30–
32 (school), 129–32, 137–45
(play), 133–36 (work)   2
—————— Step Lively, p.8–12 (bicycle),
97–100, 101–4, 106–9, 110–14

(home), 14–17 (swimming), 19–21, 176–77 (play)   3

SAILING: *see also* Boats
Haywood, Here's a Penny, p.146–58
*In (3)

SAINT PATRICK'S DAY
Child Study Association of America, Holiday Storybook   *RA

SAINT VALENTINE'S DAY: *see* Valentine's Day

SALMON
Norling, Pogo's Fishing Trip *In (3)
Schneider, H., Science Far and Near, p.138–40   3

SALT
Carpenter, Our Little Neighbors at Work and Play: Here, There, Then, and Now, p.197–201   3+

SAN FRANCISCO
Burton, V. L., Maybelle, the Cable Car   *RA
Hurd, Cat from Telegraph Hill
*RA (K–2)

SAND
Dowling, New Learning Why, p.125–28   3
Huntington, Let's Go to the Seashore, p.2–5   In (3)
McIntire, Billy's Friends, p.35–38   1

SAND DOLLARS: *see* Sea Urchins

SANTA CLAUS: *see* Christmas—Santa Claus

SATELLITES
Branley, Book of Satellites for You
In (3)
Frasier, Science—Adventures, p.110–15   3

SAVING AND THRIFT: *see* Banks and Banking; Earning Money; Money; Thrift

SCARECROWS
Betts, ABC Down Singing River, p.182–86   *2–1
Bond, G. L., Happy Times, p.96–100
*1
Gray, New Friends and Neighbors, p.209–13   *2–1
Leavell, Open Roads, p.92–98   *3
Lifton, Joji and the Dragon
*RA (K–2)
Nolen, Fun and Frolic, p.11–17 *3–1
Sheldon, Story Caravan, p.234–67
*3–2

SCHOOL LIFE: *see also* Playing School
Barnard, Macmillan Science-Life Series, Bk.1   1
Beim, J., Andy and the School Bus
*In (2)
——— Country School   *In (3)
——— Smallest Boy in the Class
*In (3)
Brownell, All Day, Every Day, p.80–98   1
Burkhardt, Our Family, p.22–40   P
——— Our Home and School, p.10–22, 47–57, 73–77, 83–88, 109–21
1
——— Our Way, p.12–39   PP
Burton, W. H., Meet Our Friends, p.70–75   *2
Caudill, Schoolhouse in the Woods
*In (3)
Charters, Health Secrets, p.59–82 3
Clymer, Yard for John   *RA
Gates, Tommy Little, p.45–65, 84–95, 103–8   *Sup. P
Gray, New More Friends and Neighbors, p.189–93   *2–2
——— New Our New Friends, p.36–39   *1–2
Hanna, At School   1
——— In the Neighborhood, p.32–37 (country school)   2

Haywood, "B" Is for Betsy *In (3)
——— Back to School with Betsy
                              *In (3)
——— Betsy and Billy   *In (3)
——— Betsy's Little Star   *In (3)
——— Eddie Makes Music *In (3)
——— Little Eddie   *In (3)
——— Primrose Day, p.84–106
                              *In (3)
Hildreth, At Play, p.76–94   *P–1
——— Going to School   *PP3
Hoffman, School Helpers   In (2)
Hunnicutt, I Know People, p.6–20 3
——— I Play, p.15–34   P
Jones, E., My First Health Book,
    p.34–41, 52–59   1
Leavell, Open Windows, p.38–64 *1
Lenski, Dog Came to School
              *RA (K–1); In (2)
McIntire, Billy's Friends, p.88–111
                               1
Martin, Pointed Brush   *RA
Mitchell, Here and Now Story Book,
    p.89–97 (play school)   *RA
Olds, H. D., Silver Button *In (2)
Quinlan, Busy World   *3
——— Day by Day   *P
——— Faces and Places, p.126–48
                              *2
——— To and Fro, p.151–62   *1
Rothschild, Bad Trouble in Miss Al-
    corn's Class   *In (2)
Russell, D. H., On Cherry Street,
    p.6–34   *1
Shackelford, My Happy Days
                             *In (3)
Sheldon, Fields and Fences, p.6–42
                             *2–1
——— Here and Away, p.68–71
                            *PP3
——— Our School   *P
——— Town and Country, p.202–9,
    217–19   *2–2
Thomas, Stories about Linda and
    Lee, p.6–26   1

Urell, Big City Book of Conserva-
    tion, p.18–29   3+
——— Big City Fun, p.6–25   3+
Wilcox, Come On, p.29–46, 52–62,
    77–91, 108–19   1
Wynkoop, Mac Goes to School *RA
Yoakam, Children Everywhere, p.56–
    70   *3

SCHOOL LIFE—COLONIAL PERI-
    OD, U.S.
Burton, W. H., Our Good Neighbors,
    p.102–10   *3
Russell, D. H., Friends Far and Near,
    p.292–301   *3–2

SCHOOL LIFE—PIONEER
Aulaire, Abraham Lincoln   In (3)

SCIENTISTS
Barnard, Macmillan Science-Life Se-
    ries, Bk.3, p.1–7   3
Mitchell, Animals, Plants, and Ma-
    chines, p.51–54   2

SCOTLAND
Baker, A. B., Talking Tree   *RA
Leaf, Wee Gillis   *In (3)
Watts, Patchwork Kilt   *In (2)

SEA: *see* Ocean

SEA ANEMONES
Huntington, Let's Go to the Seashore,
    p.56–63   In (3)

SEA GULLS: *see* Gulls

SEA HORSES
Robinson, W. W., At the Seashore
                            In (3)

SEA URCHINS
Huntington, Let's Go to the Sea-
    shore, p.22–31   In (3)

SEALS (ANIMALS)
Gates, New Friends and New Places,
    p.106–20   *2–2
Hildreth, Enchanting Stories, p.181–
    204   *3–2

———— Faraway Ports, p.36–60 *3–1
Hoff, Sammy the Seal   *In (2)
Robinson, W. W., At the Seashore
      In (3)

SEASHORE
Association for Childhood Education,
   Told under the Blue Umbrella,
   p.140–41   *RA
———— Told under the Magic Um-
   brella, p.133–44 (Lost Merbaby)
                             *RA
Betts, ABC Along Friendly Roads,
   p.14–19   *3–2
Brown, M. W., Seashore Noisy Book
                             RA
Hill, Summer Comes to Apple Mar-
   ket Street   *In (3)
Huntington, Let's Go to the Seashore
      In (3)
Koch, I Play at the Beach
                     *RA (K–1)
Mitchell, Another Here and Now
   Story Book, p.261–65   *RA
O'Donnell, Friendly Village, p.180–
   216   *Basic 2
———— Wishing Well   *Par. P
Palmer, Lost and Found, p.17–20
                             *2–1
Robinson, W. W., At the Seashore
      In (3)
Russell, D. H., Around the Corner,
   p.222–27   *2–2
Tresselt, I Saw the Sea Come In
                     *RA (K–1)
Whipple, Our Earth, p.156–72   3

SEASONS: *see also* Autumn; Nature;
   Spring; Summer; Weather; Winter
Baker, A. O., In Your Neighborhood,
   p.147–75   3
Barnard, Macmillan Science-Life Se-
   ries, Bk.3, p.180–85   3
Betts, ABC Along Friendly Roads,
   p.184–88   3–2
Birnbaum, Green Eyes *RA (K–1)

Blough, Animals round the Year 3
———— Plants round the Year   3
Darby, What Is a Season?   In (1)
Frasier, Science—For You, p.80–83
                             1
———— We Ask, p.26–29   P
Gottlieb, Four Seasons   RA (K–2)
Hader, Farmer in the Dell   *In (3)
Thorn, Let's Find Out, p.13–27   1
———— Let's Try, p.60–64   P
Webb, A., Song of the Seasons
      In (3)

SEAWEEDS
Huntington, Let's Go to the Seashore,
   p.12–13   In (3)

SECRETS
Mitchell, Farm and City, p.72–73 1
O'Donnell, Five-and-a-Half Club,
   p.79–86   *Par. 3

SEED DISPERSAL
Knox, Wonderworld of Science,
   Bk.3, p.22–23   3
Smith, V. C., Science around the
   Clock, p.101–7   3
Thorn, Let's Look Around, p.51–53
                             2
Thurber, Exploring Science Three,
   p.21–32   3
Yoakam, Children Everywhere,
   p.210–19   3

SEEDS
Baker, A. O., In Your Neighborhood,
   p.27–38   3
Barnard, Macmillan Science-Life Series, Bk.2, p.120–24   2
Blough, Plants round the Year, p.12,
   22–26   3
Bond, A. D., Thinking about Science,
   p.151–54   2
Burkhardt, Our Home and School,
   p.73–77   *1
Dowling, New Seeing Why, p.31–51,
   60–66   2

Frasier, Science—Adventures, p.52–
56, 210–18   3
———— Science—For You, p.100–9
                                  1
Knox, Wonderworld of Science,
Bk.3, p.133–36   3
Selsam, Seeds and More Seeds
                            In (2)
Smith, V. C., Science around the
Clock, p.101–12   3
Thorn, Let's Find Out, p.61–71   1
———— Let's Go, p.40–43   PP
———— Let's Try, p.6–9 (acorns)   P
Thurber, Exploring Science One,
p.112–19   1

SEEING EYE, INC.
Blough, Useful Plants and Animals,
p.7   3

SENSES
Baker, A. O., In Your Neighborhood,
p.107–9   3
Barnard, Macmillan Science-Life Se-
ries, Bk.2, p.1–4   2
———— Macmillan Science-Life Se-
ries, Bk.3, p.111–14   3
Bauer, From Eight to Nine, p.24–32
                                  3
Frasier, Science—Adventures, p.133–
35   3
———— Science—For You, p.126–29
                                  1
Irwin, Keeping Fit for Fun, p.37–39
                                  3
Schneider, H., Science for Work and
Play, p.77–102   1
Thorn, Let's Find Out, p.7–11   1

SEWAGE DISPOSAL: *see also* Germs
Urell, Big City Water Supply, p.30–
36   3+

SHARING: *see also* Cooperation
Miller, Little Red Hen
                     *RA (K–1); In (2)

SHEEP: *see also* Wool
Association for Childhood Education,

Told under the Magic Umbrella,
p.30–32 (lamb)   *RA
Blough, Animals and Their Young,
p.32–33   3
Burton, W. H., Our Good Neighbors,
p.74–79   *3
Clark, A. N., In My Mother's House,
p.34   RA; In (2)
Françoise, Jeanne-Marie at the Fair
                                *RA
———— Jeanne-Marie Counts Her
Sheep   *RA (K–1); In (2)
———— Nöel for Jeanne-Marie
                        *RA (K–2)
Gates, Good Times Today and To-
morrow, p.217–24   *Alt. 3
———— Good Times Tomorrow,
p.73–80   *3–2
Gray, New More Streets and Roads,
p.115–22   *3–2
Gruenberg, Favorite Stories Old and
New, p.108–14 (Black Face)
                                *RA
MacDonald, Little Lost Lamb
                        *RA (K–2)
Mason, Happy Jack, p.68–73
                            *In (3)
Mitchell, Another Here and Now
Story Book, p.347–55   *RA
Norling, Pogo's Lamb   *In (3)
Robison, Fun and Fancy, p.126–36
                             Pre–4
Russell, D. H., Friends Far and Near,
p.44–51 (lambs)   *3–2
———— On Cherry Street, p.89–92
                                *1
Scott, Molly and the Tool Shed
                            *In (3)
Sheldon, Our School, p.110–15, 132–
36 (lambs)   *P
Smith, J. R., Our Neighbors at Home,
p.22–24, 65–78, 85–87   3
Thomas, Your Town and Mine,
p.69–72   3
Whipple, Our Earth, p.3–21   3

SHELLFISH: *see also* Snails
Huntington, Let's Go to the Seashore, p.72–83   In (3)
Robinson, W. W., At the Seashore In (3)

SHELLS
Goudey, Houses from the Sea   RA
Podendorf, True Book of Pebbles and Shells   In (3)

SHELTER: *see also* Houses
Clark, A. N., In My Mother's House, p.6–12 (Indians)   RA; In (2)
Partch, Basic Social Studies, p.164–74   3

SHEPHERDS
Petersham, Christ Child   RA

SHIPS: *see* Boats

SHOE STORE: *see* Stores

SHOEMAKERS
Association for Childhood Education, Told under the Green Umbrella (Elves and the Shoemaker)   *RA
Betts, ABC Over a City Bridge, p.100–5, 106–11   *2–2
Hutchinson, Chimney Corner Stories (Elves and the Shoemaker)   *RA
O'Donnell, Friendly Village, p.242–53   *Basic 2

SHOES
Association for Childhood Education, Told under the Green Umbrella (Cinderella)   *RA
——— Told under the Magic Umbrella, p.8–11, 27–29   *RA
Bauer, From Eight to Nine, p.56–59   3
Betts, ABC Down Singing River, p.163–69   *2–1
——— ABC Up the Street and Down, p.65–69   *P

Bromhall, Belinda's New Shoes *RA; In (3)
Brownell, Blue Skies, p.56–62 (cowboy)   2
Carpenter, Our Little Neighbors at Work and Play: Here, There, Then, and Now, p.88   3+
Charters, Health Secrets, p.198–99 3
Clark, M., Poppy Seed Cakes *In (3)
Gray, New More Friends and Neighbors, p.30–35   *2–2
Hallock, Health and Safety for You, p.64–68   3
Hunnicutt, I Live with Others, p.22–26   *1
Hutchinson, Chimney Corner Stories (Cinderella)   *RA
Irwin, Keeping Fit for Fun, p.153–57   3
Leavell, Open Windows, p.137–42 *1
McKee, Looking Ahead, p.213–43   *3–1
Mitchell, Animals, Plants, and Machines, p.70–74   2
O'Donnell, Anything Can Happen, p.7–36   *Par. 1
Ousley, Come with Us, p.20–22   *Pre–P
Wilcox, Step Lively, p.31–35   3

SHOPPING: *see also* Stores
Association for Childhood Education, Told under the Blue Umbrella, p.82–84   *RA
Chalmers, I Had a Penny   *RA
Haywood, Back to School with Betsy   *In (3)
La Rue, Tiny Toosey's Birthday   *In (2)

SHROVE TUESDAY
Child Study Association of America, Holiday Storybook   *RA

SIAM
Ayer, Nu Dang and His Kite   *RA (K–2); In (3)

SIGHT: *see* Eye

SIGNALS AND SIGNALING: *see also*
Lighthouses; Radio; Telegraph
Betts, ABC Beyond Treasure Valley,
p.33–38, 201–7   *3–1
Cutright, Living Together Today and
Yesterday, p.225–27 (Indian)   3

SIGNS
Eberle, Secrets and Surprises, p.33–
43   *2–2
Gates, Good Times Today, p.64–74
                                  *3–1
——— Good Times Today and To-
morrow, p.46–56   *Alt. 3
Russell, D. H., My Little Green Sto-
ry Book, p.51–54   *PP2

SILKWORMS
Blough, Insect Parade, p.30   3
——— Useful Plants and Animals,
p.16   3
Burkhardt, Our Community, p.71 3
Carpenter, Our Little Neighbors at
Work and Play: Here, There,
Then, and Now, p.179–81   3+
McIntire, Working Together, p.101–
2   3
Mitchell, Animals, Plants, and Ma-
chines, p.80–84   2
Partch, Basic Social Studies, p.118–
19   3
Thomas, Your Town and Mine, p.88–
89   3

SIZE
Berkley, Size of It   In (2)
Schneider, H., How Big Is Big?
                              In (3)

SKATING
Gray, New More Friends and Neighbors, p.11–19 (ice)   *2
Irwin, Growing Day by Day, p.108–
13 (roller skates)   2
Leavell, Open Roads, p.124–30 (roller skates)   *3

SKIING
Renick, Todd's Snow Patrol *In (3)

SKIN
Barnard, Macmillan Science-Life Series, Bk.3, p.87–100   3
Frasier, Science—All the Year, p.90–
92   2

SKIPPING ROPE: *see* Games

SKUNKS
Bond, G. L., Happy Times, p.119–22
                                   *1
Haywood, Two and Two Are Four,
p.118–35   *In (3)
Sheldon, Magic Windows, p.144–54
                                  *3–1

SKY: *see also* Air; Astronomy; Clouds;
Stars; Weather
Baker, A. O., Around the Corner,
p.46   2
Bond, A. D., Knowing about Science,
p.90–94, 105   3
——— Thinking about Science,
p.88–91 (stars)   2
Craig, Science around You, p.52–63
                                    2
——— Science Everywhere, p.117–
31   3
——— Science near You, p.50–55 1
Dowling, New Seeing Why, p.137–
41   2
Schneider, H., Science Far and Near,
p.230–40   3
Smith, V. C., Science under the Sun,
p.86–89   2

SKYSCRAPERS
Mitchell, Animals, Plants, and Ma-
chines, p.184–200   2
——— Here and Now Story Book,
p.353–60   *RA
Smith, J. R., Our Neighbors at
Home, p.219–23   3

SLEDS: *see* Winter Sports

SLEEP: *see also* Bedtime
Association for Childhood Education,
Told under the Green Umbrella
(Sleeping Beauty) *RA
Barnard, Macmillan Science-Life Series, Bk.3, p.80–81 3
Bauer, From Eight to Nine, p.76–79
3
———— Seven or So, p.66–67 2
Brownell, All Day, Every Day, p.47–
49 1
———— Blue Skies, p.39–41 2
———— Come Rain, Come Shine,
p.37–41 3
Hallock, Health and Happy Days,
p.122–24 1
———— Health and Safety for You,
p.181–84 3
———— Health in Work and Play,
p.110–15, 122–26 2
Jones, E., Easy Steps to Health, p.57–
67 3
Leaf, Health Can Be Fun In (3)
O'Keefe, From Head to Toe, p.51–
54 1
Selsam, Time for Sleep RA; In (3)
Yoakam, Making Storybook Friends,
p.14–22 *1

SMELLS
Betts, ABC Along Friendly Roads,
p.162–68 *3–2

SNAILS
Blough, Aquarium, p.26–31 3
Huntington, Let's Go Outdoors, p.2–
9 In (3)

SNAKES: *see also* Reptiles
Frasier, We Ask, p.52–53 P
Harris, L. D., Slim Green In (3)
Quinlan, Busy World, p.6–16 *3

SNOW: *see also* Winter Sports
Barnard, Macmillan Science-Life Series, Bk.2, p.67 2

Betts, ABC Over a City Bridge,
p.143–54 *2–2
Blough, Water Appears and Disappears, p.30–34 3
Bond, A. D., Looking at Science,
p.54–57 1
Brownell, All Day, Every Day, p.80–
82, 85–89 1
Burton, W. H., Our Happy Ways,
p.73–76 *1
De Regniers, Snow Party *RA
Dowling, New Seeing Why, p.24–26
2
Gates, Snow *Unit P
———— Two Boys and a Tree, p.56–
59 *Sup. 1
Gray, New More Friends and Neighbors, p.20–24 *2–2
———— New More Streets and Roads,
p.6–12 *3–2
Hader, Big Snow RA (K–2)
Hildreth, At Play, p.95–98 *P–1
———— I Know a Secret, p.24–32
*1–1
Irwin, Growing Day by Day, p.103–
7 2
Kay, Snow Birthday *In (3)
Lattimore, Holly in the Snow *In (3)
McKee, Come Along, p.90–107 *2–2
Mitchell, Farm and City, p.63–65 1
Schlein, Deer in the Snow
*RA; In (3)
Sheldon, Fields and Fences, p.106–
34 *2–1
Thorn, Let's Find Out, p.19–21 1
Tresselt, White Snow, Bright Snow
RA (K–2)
Urell, Big City Water Supply, p.43
3+
Wavle, Rain and Shine, p.96–119
*P–1

SNOW MAN
Betts, ABC Around Green Hills,
p.156–61 *1

Brownell, All Day, Every Day, p.97–98   *1
Gates, Two Boys and a Tree, p.65–74   *Sup. 1
Gray, New Friends and Neighbors, p.197–201   *2–1
Hildreth, At Play, p.99–110   *P–1
Leavell, Open Doors, p.165–70 *2
Mitchell, Another Here and Now Story Book, p.301–5   *RA
Russell, D. H., On Cherry Street, p.36–40   *1
Sheldon, Fields and Fences, p.117–21   *2–1
Zion, Summer Snowman *RA (K–1)

SOAP BUBBLES
Association for Childhood Education, Told under the Blue Umbrella, p.84–86   *RA

SOAP MAKING
Emerson, Pioneer Children of America, p.48–49 (homemade)   3
Yoakam, Children Everywhere, p.75–82   *3

SOILS: *see also* Clay; Earth; Gardens; Irrigation
Craig, Science near You, p.82–87 1
Frasier, Science—All the Year, p.185–89   2
Thorn, Let's Look Around, p.97–101   2

Urell, Big City Book of Conservation, p.42–51   3+

SOLAR SYSTEM: *see* Astronomy

SOLOMON, KING: *see* Bible Stories

SOUND: *see also* Music; Radio; Telephone
Association for Childhood Education, Told under the Blue Umbrella, p.148–50   *RA
Baker, A. O., In Your Neighborhood, p.134–46   3

Barnard, Macmillan Science-Life Series, Bk.1, p.71–73   1
——— Macmillan Science-Life Series, Bk.3, p.129–39   3
Bond, A. D., Knowing about Science, p.120–21   3
Branley, Timmy and the Tin-Can Telephone   *RA; In (3)
Brown, M. W., Country Noisy Book   RA
——— Indoor Noisy Book   RA
——— Seashore Noisy Book   RA
Craig, Science around You, p.78–89   2
Dowling, New Seeing Why, p.183–86   2
Frasier, Science—All the Year, p.127–30   2
——— Science—For You, p.120–25   1
——— We Wonder, p.22–23   PP
Gray, New More Streets and Roads, p.20–25 (ventriloquism)   *3–2
——— New Streets and Roads, p.6–12 (bird noises), 29–34 (automobile horn), 180–86 (Miss Molly Squeak)   *3–1
Pine, Sounds All Around   RA
Schwartz, J., Now I Know   In (2)
Thorn, Let's Look Around, p.61–63   2
Thurber, Exploring Science Three, p.34–46   3

(THE) SOUTH: *see also* Mountain Life (Southern States)
Burkhardt, Our Community, p.162–84   3
Burton, W. H., Our Good Neighbors, p.155–68   *3
Mitchell, Another Here and Now Story Book, p.357–68   *RA
O'Donnell, Friendly Village, p.218–40   *Basic 2

SOUTH AMERICA: *see* Brazil

SOUTH SEA ISLANDS
Gates, Good Times Today and To-
morrow, p.312–20   *Alt. 3
——— Good Times Tomorrow,
p.212–20, 230–39   *3–2
Russell, D. H., Friends Far and
Near, p.196–203   *3–2

SOW BUGS
Huntington, Let's Go Outdoors,
p.24–29   In (3)

SPACE
Ousley, Ranches and Rainbows,
p.88–94   *Pre–3
Podendorf, True Book of Space
RA; In (3)

SPACE SHIPS
Russell, D. H., Friends Far and Near,
p.279–89   *3–2

SPACE TRAVEL
Branley, Book of Satellites for You
In (3)

SPAIN
Baker, A. B., Talking Tree   *RA
Gruenberg, Favorite Stories Old and
New, p.336–38 (Story of Ferdi-
nand)   *RA
Leaf, Story of Ferdinand   *In (3)
O'Donnell, If I Were Going, p.206–
9, *210–68   Basic 3

SPIDERS
Frasier, Science—Adventures, p.199–
204   3
Huntington, Let's Go Outdoors, p.44–
49   In (3)
Mitchell, Another Here and Now
Story Book, p.127–29   *RA
Robison, Fun and Fancy, p.20–28
*Pre–4
Sheldon, Our Town, p.124–30   1
Thorn, Let's See Why, p.24–28   3

SPORTS: *see* Ball; Bicycles; Boats;
Camping; Canoes and Canoeing;
Fishing; Games; Kites; Playgrounds; Skating; Swimming; Winter Sports

SPORTSMANSHIP
Barnard, Macmillan Science-Life Se-
ries, Bk.2, p.138–42   2
Brownell, Come Rain, Come Shine,
p.115–18   *3
Charters, Health Secrets, p.164–66 3
Leavell, Open Windows, p.144–49 *1
Wilcox, Here We Go, p.69–72 (fair
play)   2
——— Step Lively, p.141–45   3

SPRING
Baker, A. O., Around the Corner,
p.83–100   2
——— In Your Neighborhood,
p.165–69   3
Betts, ABC Over a City Bridge,
p.161–66   *2–2
Blough, Animals round the Year,
p.26–31   3
Bond, A. D., Looking at Science,
p.61–68   1
Bond, G. L., Happy Times, p.114–22
*1
——— Just for Fun, p.156–85 *2–2
Buff, Dash and Dart   RA; In (3)
Craig, Science around You, p.90–
109   2
Frasier, Science—Adventures, p.182–
221   3
——— Science—All the Year,
p.162–80   2
——— We Wonder, p.20, 30–1 PP
Gall, All the Year Round   In (3)
Gates, Good Times Today, p.177–84
3–1
——— Good Times Today and To-
morrow, p.125–32   Alt. 3
Gray, New Friends and Neighbors,
p.214–18 (cleaning)   *2–1
Hildreth, I Know a Secret, p.33–47
*1–1

———— Story Road, p.102–12 *2–2
Hill, Surprise for Judy Jo *In (3)
Jones, E., My Second Health Book,
   p.50–54   2
Knox, Wonderworld of Science,
   Bk.1, p.77–91 (animals, plants) 1
Lenski, Spring Is Here RA; In (2)
O'Donnell, Neighbors on the Hill,
   p.65–71 (cleaning)   *2–3
———— Round About, p.78–80
                           *Basic 1
Parker, Spring Is Here   1
Politi, Song of the Swallows
                        *RA (K–2)
Quinlan, To and Fro, p.182–83 *1
Smith, J. R., Our Neighbors at
   Home, p.77–78   3
Smith, V. C., Science along the Way,
   p.105–20   1
Thorn, Let's Find Out, p.23–27   1
———— Let's Look Around, p.103–5
                                  2
Thurber, Exploring Science One,
   p.134–45   1
Tresselt, "Hi, Mister Robin"
                        *RA (K–2)
Urell, Big City Book of Conserva-
   tion, p.67–82   3+
Zion, Really Spring   *RA (K–1)

SQUIRRELS
Adrian, Gray Squirrel   In (3)
Betts, ABC Along Friendly Roads,
   p.206–12   *3–2
———— ABC Beyond Treasure Val-
   ley, p.170–76   *3–1
Buff, Dash and Dart, p.48–53
                          RA; In (3)
Frasier, Science—Adventures, p.194–
   98   3
Gates, Open Window   *Unit 1
Gray, New Friends and Neighbors,
   p.78–81, 149–52   *2–1
———— New More Friends and
   Neighbors, p.97–102   *2–2

———— New More Streets and Roads,
   p.201–6   *3–2
———— New Our New Friends,
   p.109–13, 156–59   *1–2
———— New Streets and Roads,
   p.193–201   *3–1
Hildreth, Fun in Story, p.14–24
                               *P–2
———— Good Stories, p.26–34
                             *Pre–2
———— Story Road, p.139–47 *2–2
Robinson, T. P., Mr. Red Squirrel
                             *In (2)
Russell, D. H., Around the Corner,
   p.83–88   *2–2
———— We Are Neighbors, p.70–75
                               *2–1
Sheldon, Fields and Fences, p.44–
   68, 82–88   *2–1
Smith, J. R., Our Neighbors at Home,
   p.105–8   3
Thorn, Let's Go, p.12–14   PP

STABLES
Mitchell, Here and Now Story Book,
   p.99–102   *RA

STAGECOACHES
Betts, ABC Beyond Treasure Valley,
   p.155–61   *3–1
Gray, New More Streets and Roads,
   p.67–73   *3–2
Hildreth, Faraway Ports, p.134–49
                               *3–1

STARFISH
Huntington, Let's Go to the Seashore,
   p.14–21   In (3)

STARS: *see also* Astronomy
Baker, A. O., In Your Neighborhood,
   p.81–86   3
Bond, A. D., Knowing about Science,
   p.90–93   3
———— Looking at Science, p.11–17,
   23   1
———— Thinking about Science, p.88–
   91   2

Frasier, Science—All the Year, p.91,
116–17　　　　　　　　　　　2
———— Science—For You, p.86–89
　　　　　　　　　　　　　　1
———— We Ask, p.24–25　　　P
Knox, Wonderworld of Science,
Bk.1, p.67–71　　　　　　　1
Schneider, H., You among the Stars
　　　　　　　　　　　　In (3)
Smith, V. C., Science under the Sun,
p.67–73　　　　　　　　　　2
Yoakam, Stories We Like, p.247–53
　　　　　　　　　　　　　*2

STATIONS: *see* Bus Stations; Railroad
Stations

STEAM: *see also* Heating; Water
Blough, Doing Work, p.17–18　　3

STEAM SHOVEL
Betts, ABC Beyond Treasure Valley,
p.177–84　　　　　　　　　*3–1
Burton, V. L., Mike Mulligan and
His Steam Shovel　　　　　*RA
Gruenberg, Favorite Stories Old and
New, p.28–32 (from Big Fellow)
　　　　　　　　　　　　　*RA
Russell, D. H., We Are Neighbors,
p.224–33 (Mike Mulligan and His
Steam Shovel)　　　　　　*2–1

STEAMSHIPS
Nolen, Do and Dare, p.144–54 *3–2

STEEL: *see also* Iron
Partch, Basic Social Studies, p.204–
7　　　　　　　　　　　　　3

STONE: *see also* Rocks
Partch, Basic Social Studies, p.196–
97　　　　　　　　　　　　3
Podendorf, True Book of Rocks and
Minerals　　　　　　　In (3)
Schneider, H., Science for Here and
Now, p.53–62　　　　　　　2

STONECUTTER
McKee, Looking Ahead, p.265–71
　　　　　　　　　　　　　*3–1

STORES: *see also* Markets
Betts, ABC Along Friendly Roads,
p.176–83　　　　　　　　　*3–2
———— ABC Down Singing River,
p.188–93 (clock), 231–37 (woodwork)　　　　　　　　　　*2–1
———— ABC Over a City Bridge,
p.42–48, 112–18, 123–28　*2–2
Bond, G. L., Once upon a Storytime,
p.5–62　　　　　　　　　　*3–2
Burkhardt, Our Neighborhood, p.45–
54 (grocery), 58–60 (clothing),
61–63 (department), 64–65 (shoe
repair)　　　　　　　　　2–1
Burton, W. H., Days of Fun, p.136–
40 (grocery)　　　　　　　*P
———— Meet Our Friends, p.15–19
(grocery)　　　　　　　　*2
———— Our Happy Ways, p.2–8,
183–86　　　　　　　　　　*1
Eberle, Secrets and Surprises, p.16–
24 (grocery)　　　　　　　*2–2
Gates, Tommy Little, p.29–36, 72–
83, 96–102, 114–16　*Sup. P
Gray, New More Friends and Neigh-
bors, p.51–56 (country)　*2–2
———— New More Streets and Roads,
p.32–40　　　　　　　　　*3–2
———— New Streets and Roads, p.42–
49 (department)　　　　　*3–1
Gruenberg, Favorite Stories Old and
New, p.359–63 (Mr. A and Mr.
P)　　　　　　　　　　　*RA
Hallock, Health and Safety for You,
p.27–29 (grocery)　　　　　3
Hanna, In the Neighborhood, p.106–
13 (grocery), 114–15　　　2
Hastings, Department Store
　　　　　　　　　　　　In (3)
Hugley, Around the Home, p.7–10
(butcher), 31–33 (department)
　　　　　　　　　　　　　3
Irwin, Keeping Fit for Fun, p.126–
32 (food), 133–36 (butcher),
137–39 (bakery)　　　　　3

Johnson, E. M., Treat Shop, p.210–13 (woodcarving), 214–20 (grocery)   *3

Leavell, Open Roads, p.50–56 (woodcarving)   *3

McIntire, Billy's Friends, p.102–4 (books)   1

—— Billy's Neighbors, p.88–90, 91–94 (grocery), 96–98 (five and ten), 99 (drug), 100 (flower), 101 (book), 102–3 (pet), 104–5 (hardware), 106–7 (department), 108 (bank), 110–11 (country)   2

—— Working Together, p.114–16 (department)   3

McKee, Climbing Higher, p.95–132 (pet shop)   *3–2

Mitchell, Farm and City, p.56–59   1

—— Here and Now Story Book, p.137–40 (grocery)   *RA

O'Donnell, Day In and Day Out, p.134–46 (animal)   *Basic P

—— Five-and-a-Half Club, p.33–47 (hardware-paint)   *Par. 3

—— High on a Hill, p.23–31
                                            *PP4

—— Open the Door, p.23–28, 65–71   *PP3

—— Round About, p.195–202 (toy)   *Basic 1

—— Under the Sky, p.33–38
                                            *PP2

Orton, Grandmother's Cookie Jar
                                            *RA

Palmer, Lost and Found, p.83–89 (department)   *2–1

Quinlan, Day by Day, p.82–86   *P

—— Faces and Places, p.26–33 (department)   *2

—— Happy Days, p.101–8 (toy)
                                    *Read. P

Reese, Basic Social Studies, p.129–46   2

Russell, B., Big Store—Funny Door
                                        *In (2)

Russell, D. H., Around the Corner, p.19–22 (department)   *2–2

—— On Cherry Street, p.60–72, 137–40 (toy)   *1

—— We Are Neighbors, p.30–36 (toy)   *2–1

Sheldon, Here and Away, p.20–22 (beauty shop), 24–26 (shoe repair)   *PP3

—— Here and Near, p.52–54
                                            *PP2

—— Our School, p.39–44 (pet)
                                            *P

—— Our Town, p.18–23 (grocery)
                                            *1

Smith, J. R., Our Neighbors at Home, p.42–43   3

Thomas, Stories about Sally, p.76–92   2

—— Your Town and Mine, p.90–96 (clothing), 55–58 (grocery), 104–8 (brick yard), 92 (wholesale clothing house), 160–63 (Indian shop), 47–48, 60–64 (wholesale food market), 170–72 (clock repair), 174–77 (dry cleaning)   3

STORKS
Brown, M. W., Wheel on the Chimney   *RA; In (3)

STORMS: *see also* Rain; Snow
Betts, ABC Over a City Bridge, p.149–54   *2–2

Thorn, Let's See Why, p.142–45   2

Zolotow, Storm Book   RA

STREET CARS
Burton, V. L., Maybelle, the Cable Car   *RA

Mitchell, Another Here and Now Story Book, p.169–72   *RA

STREET CLEANERS
McIntire, Billy's Neighbors, p.128 2

STREET REPAIR
Sheldon, Our Town, p.62–67   *1

STREET SPRINKLER
  Russell, D. H., On Cherry Street,
    p.134–36   *1

STREETS AND ROADS
  Gruenberg, Favorite Stories Old and
    New, p.44–52   *RA
  Mitchell, Our Country, p.146   3

SUBURBS
  Hunnicutt, I Know People, p.94–101
                                          3
  Smith, J. R., Our Neighbors at Home,
    p.224–28   3

SUBWAYS
  Gates, Today We Go, p.143–56 *2–1
  Mitchell, Here and Now Story Book,
    p.245–49   *RA
  Palmer, Lost and Found, p.77–81
                                        *2–1

SUGAR: *see also* Maple Sugar
  Allee, Sugar Beets to Beet Sugar
                                      In (3)
  Barnard, Macmillan Science-Life Se-
    ries, Bk.3, p.73–75   3
  Carpenter, Our Little Neighbors at
    Work and Play: Here, There, Then,
    and Now, p.169–71   3
  Hugley, Around the Home, p.92–93
                                          3
  McIntire, Working Together, p.71–
    72   3
  Partch, Basic Social Studies, p.80–
    88   3

SUMMER
  Baker, A. O., Around the Corner,
    p.105–12   2
  ——— In Your Neighborhood,
    p.171–73   3
  Blough, Animals round the Year,
    p.32–36   3
  Craig, Science around You, p.4–11
                                         2
  Frasier, We Wonder, p.21   PP
  Gates, On Four Feet, p.119–21   *1

——— Open Window, p.2–6 *Unit 1
——— Two Boys and a Tree, p.19–
  36   *Sup. 1
O'Donnell, Round About, p.68–71
                                *Basic 1
O'Keefe, Side by Side, p.1–5   2
Parker, Summer Is Here   1
Schneider, H., Science for Work and
  Play, p.138–40   1
Smith, J. R., Our Neighbors at Home,
  p.25–31, 72–76, 164–65   3
Thorn, Let's Find Out, p.111–16   1
——— Let's See Why, p.187–89   3

SUN
  Barnard, Macmillan Science-Life Se-
    ries, Bk.2, p.51–52   2
  ——— Macmillan Science-Life Se-
    ries, Bk.3, p.186–92   3
  Blough, How the Sun Helps Us   3
  Bond, A. D., Knowing about Science,
    p.85–88, 106–9   3
  ——— Looking at Science, p.3–9   1
  ——— Thinking about Science,
    p.81–87   2
  Carpenter, Our Little Neighbors at
    Work and Play: Here, There, Then,
    and Now, p.192–93   3+
  Craig, Science around You, p.52–57
                                      2
  ——— Science Everywhere, p.120–
    25   3
  Frasier, Science—All the Year, p.17–
    20   2
  ——— We Ask, p.19–21   P
  ——— We Wonder, p.14–16   PP
  Knox, Wonderworld of Science,
    Bk.1, p.57–61   1
  Smith, V. C., Science along the Way,
    p.62–64   1
  ——— Science around the Clock,
    p.94–97   3
  Thorn, Let's Go, p.16–18   PP
  Thurber, Exploring Science Three,
    p.5–18   3

———— Exploring Science Two, p.20–25   2

Wavle, Rain and Shine, p.40–52 *P–2

SUPERSTITIONS: *see also* Halloween

Brownell, Blue Skies, p.84–89   2

Dowling, New Learning Why, p.142–44   3

SWALLOWS

Gall, All the Year Round, p.25–30
                                          In (3)

Politi, Song of the Swallows
                                  *RA (K–2)

Thorn, Let's Look Around, p.127–29
                                          2

SWEDEN

Association for Childhood Education, Told under the Blue Umbrella, p.23–25 (Pelle's New Suit)   *RA

Beskow, Pelle's New Suit
                              *RA; In (3)

SWEDEN—FOLKLORE

Baker, A. B., Talking Tree   *RA

Gruenberg, Favorite Stories Old and New, p.225–27 (Three Wishes)
                                       *RA

SWIMMING

Brownell, Come Rain, Come Shine, p.172–76   3

Hallock, Health in Work and Play, p.72–76   2

Irwin, Keeping Fit for Fun, p.29–31   3

Wilcox, Step Lively, p.14–18   3

SWINGING: *see also* Playgrounds

Evans, Something Different, p.30–35
                                          *1

Irwin, Growing Day by Day, p.59–60   2

Mitchell, Another Here and Now Story Book, p.60   *RA

SWITZERLAND

Hildreth, Enchanting Stories, p.154–59   *3–2

———— Faraway Ports, p.186–99
                                        *3–1

Yoakam, Children Everywhere, p.22–31   *3

SYNTHETICS: *see also* Dacron and Orlon; Nylon; Rayon

Partch, Basic Social Studies, p.153–58   3

Thomas, Your Town and Mine, p.85–86   3

TABLE MANNERS: *see* Manners

TADPOLES: *see* Frogs; Toads

TARDINESS: *see* Promptness

TAXATION

Leaf, Fair Play, p.65–77   In (3)

TAXICABS

Burkhardt, Our Neighborhood, p.72–74   2

TEA

Betts, ABC Along Friendly Roads, p.82–88   *3–2

Gruenberg, Favorite Stories Old and New, p.268–73   *RA

TEACHER: *see also* School Life

Leavell, Open Roads, p.150–56 (Horace Mann)   *3

TEETH: *see also* Dentists

Barnard, Macmillan Science-Life Series, Bk.1, p.11–13   1

———— Macmillan Science-Life Series, Bk.2, p.32–37   2

———— Macmillan Science-Life Series, Bk.3, p.101–7   3

Bauer, Being Six, p.26–33   1

———— From Eight to Nine, p.156–59   3

———— Seven or So, p.34–37, 142–44   2

Brownell, All Day, Every Day, p.91–95   1

———— Blue Skies, p.92–96   2

———— Come Rain, Come Shine, p.98–105   3

Charters, Health Secrets, p.143–58 3
Frasier, Science—Adventures, p.133
                                        3
Hallock, Health and Happy Days,
    p.83–86   1
Haywood, Betsy and Billy, p.19–29
                                    *In (3)
Irwin, Awake and Away, p.34–40 1
——— Keeping Fit for Fun, p.103–
21   3
Jones, E., Easy Steps to Health,
    p.74–78   3
——— My Second Health Book,
    p.9–10   2
Leaf, Health Can Be Fun   In (3)
McCloskey, One Morning in Maine
                                 *RA (K–2)
O'Keefe, How We Grow, p.33–39 3
——— Side by Side, p.58, 99–108
                                        2
Ousley, Ranches and Rainbows,
    p.126–34   *Pre-3
Thurber, Exploring Science Three,
    p.62–73   3
Wilcox, Come On, p.85–98   1
——— Here We Go, p.86–90   2
——— Step Lively, p.43–48   3

TELEGRAPH: *see also* Radio; Television
McIntire, Working Together, p.181–
82   3

TELEPHONE: *see also* Radio; Tele-
vision
Branley, Timmy and the Tin-Can
    Telephone   *RA; In (3)
Burton, W. H., Meet Our Friends,
    p.130–34   *2
McIntire, Working Together, p.183–
84   3
Russell, D. H., On Cherry Street,
    p.128–33   *1

TELEVISION
Betts, ABC Beyond Treasure Valley,
    p.90–96   *3–1

Charters, Health Secrets, p.73–76
    (shadow show)   3
Irwin, Growing Day by Day, p.68–
69 (bedtime)   2
McIntire, Working Together, p.189–
91   3
Ousley, Ranches and Rainbows,
    p.88–94   *Pre-3
Russell, D. H., Around the Corner,
    p.216–21   *2–2
——— Finding New Neighbors,
    p.265–72   *3–1
——— Little White House, p.171–
78   *P
Sheldon, Town and Country, p.63–
70   *2–2
Wilcox, Step Lively, p.47–48   3

TELEVISION—REPAIRMAN
Russell, D. H., We Are Neighbors,
    p.179–82   *2–1

TELLING TIME: *see also* Clocks
Monroe, New What Next, p.38–43
                                      *2–1
Quinlan, Day by Day, p.149–51   *P

TEMPERATURE: *see also* Heat; Thermometers; Weather
Baker, A. O., In Your Neighborhood,
    p.73–79   3

TERMITES
Blough, Animals That Live Together,
    p.32–35   3
——— Insect Parade, p.31–32   3

TEXAS
LeGrand, Why Cowboys Sing, in
    Texas   *RA; In (3)
Sorensen, Ways of Our Land, p.105–
6   3

THANKSGIVING DAY
Burkhardt, Our Community, p.201–
8   *3
——— Our Family, p.52–59   P
Burton, W. H., Our Good Neighbors,
    p.137–44   *3

Cavanah, Our Country's Story, p.16–17   In (3)

Child Study Association of America, Holiday Storybook   *RA

Cutright, Living Together Today and Yesterday, p.125–27   3

Dalgliesh, Thanksgiving Story   *In (3)

Gates, Good Times Tomorrow, p.40–48   3–2

Haywood, "B" Is for Betsy, p.76–92   *In (3)

Sheldon, Magic Windows, p.193–210   *3–1

THERMOMETERS

Bond, A. D., Thinking about Science, p.116–21   2

Frasier, Science—Adventures, p.145–51   3

Schneider, H., Science for Here and Now, p.113–20   2

Smith, V. C., Science around the Clock, p.82–87   3

Thorn, Let's Look Around, p.31–34   2

Thurber, Exploring Science Two, p.34–48   2

THOUGHTFULNESS

Leavell, Open Windows, p.137–42 *1

THRIFT: *see also* Banks and Banking; Earning Money; Money

Brownell, Come Rain, Come Shine, p.120–24   3

Hunnicutt, I Know People, p.51–59   3

Monroe, New Tall Tales, p.34–41   *3–1

THUNDER: *see* Weather

TIDES: *see also* Moon

Huntington, Let's Go to the Seashore, p.6–11   In (3)

TIGERS

Bannerman, Story of Little Black Sambo   *RA; In (2)

Hutchinson, Chimney Corner Stories (Little Black Sambo)   *RA

Mitchell, Another Here and Now Story Book, p.181–86   *RA

Russell, D. H., Finding New Neighbors, p.118–21   *3–1

TIME: *see* Clocks; Telling Time

TOADS: *see also* Frogs

Bond, A. D., Knowing about Science, p.173–77   3

Charles, Roundabout Turn   *RA

O'Donnell, Neighbors on the Hill, p.93–108   *Par. 2

Thorn, Let's Look Around, p.39–43, 103–5   2

Thurber, Exploring Science Three, p.160–69   3

TOOLS: *see also* Carpentry; Machines

Beim, J., Tim and the Tool Chest   *In (2)

Deming, Little Eagle   *In (2)

Partch, Basic Social Studies, p.210 3

Thorn, Let's Try, p.41–45   P

TORTOISES: *see* Turtles

TOWN CRIER

Nolen, Do and Dare, p.261–70 *3–2

TOY MENDERS

O'Donnell, Round About, p.19–28   *Basic 1

TOYS: *see also* Ball; Bicycles; Bows and Arrows; Christmas—Toys; Doll Houses; Dolls; Games; Kites; Merry-Go-Rounds; Playgrounds; Wagons; Winter Sports (sleds)

Association for Childhood Education, Told under the Blue Umbrella, p.7–8, 20–22, 37–40, 55–57 *RA

Bell, Pawnee   *In (3)

Betts, ABC All in a Day, p.20–25, 36–41, 46–51   *PP3

——— ABC Down Singing River, p.12–18 (boat), 170–74, 224–30   *2–1

—— ABC Time To Play, p.30–33, 38–51   *PP2

—— ABC Up the Street and Down, p.92–95   *P

Bianco, Velveteen Rabbit   *In (3)

Bond, A. D., Looking at Science, p.32–41 (pinwheel)   1

Bond, G. L., Fun with Us, p.27–32, 53–57 (airplane)   *PP3

—— See Us Ride, p.48–53 (trains) *Comp. PP4

Brownell, Blue Skies, p.28–32 (sailboat)   2

Burkhardt, Our Home and School, p.47–52   1

Burton, W. H., Days of Fun, p.146–50   *P

Dowling, New Seeing Why, p.166–70   2

Gates, Open Window, p.17–20 (doll bed)   *Unit 1

—— Tommy Little, p.71–83 *Sup. P

Gray, New Friends and Neighbors, p.6–9   *2–1

—— New Fun with Dick and Jane, p.46–49, 61–82   *1–1

—— New Our New Friends, p.70–74, 126–28 (balloon), 146–49 *1–2

Gruenberg, Favorite Stories Old and New, p.148–52 (from Johnny Ping Wing)   *RA

Hildreth, At Play, p.76–84, 131–48 *P–1

—— Fun in Story, p.78–89, 140–53   *P–2

—— Good Stories, p.123–31 *Pre–2

Leavell, Open Windows, p.120–25 *1

McKee, Come Along, p.179–95 *2–1

Milne, House at Pooh Corner   *RA

—— Winnie-the-Pooh   *RA

Monroe, New We Three, p.4–7 (top) *1

Morrow, Painted Pig   *In (3)

O'Donnell, Day In and Day Out, p.10–15   *Basic P

Parker, Toys   2

Quinlan, Before Winky, p.39–41 (airplanes)   *Pre–PP

—— Day by Day, p.141–47   *P

—— Happy Days, p.80–84 (farm), 111–18 (car)   *Read. PP

Russell, D. H., Around the Corner, p.19–22   *2–2

—— Little White House, p.120–34   *P

—— My Little Red Story Book, p.35–47   *PP1

—— On Cherry Street, p.73–77 (rabbit)   *1

—— We Are Neighbors, p.92–98 (dishes)   *2–1

Sheldon, Fields and Fences, p.161–67   *2–1

—— Our Town, p.172–77   *1

Yoakam, Making Storybook Friends, p.23–29 (horse)   *1

TOYS—CARE
Leavell, Open Doors, p.80–85   *2

TRACKS OF ANIMALS: *see* Animal Tracks

TRACTORS
Burton, W. H., Meet Our Friends, p.117–22   *2

Gates, Good Times Today, p.57–63 *3–1

—— Good Times Today and Tomorrow, p.39–45   *Alt. 3

Lewellen, Tommy Learns To Drive a Tractor   *In (3)

McKee, Come Along, p.90–107 *2–1

TRADES: *see* Industries; also names of trades, as Blacksmiths

TRADING POSTS
Cutright, Living Together Today and Yesterday, p.71–79, 109–12   3

Sorensen, Ways of Our Land, p.126–
28   3

TRAFFIC: *see also* Police; Safety
Charters, Health Secrets, p.43–52   3
Hanna, In City, Town, and Country,
p.20–25   3
MacDonald, Red Light, Green Light
RA; In (2)

TRAILERS: *see* Automobiles—Trailers

TRAINS
Association for Childhood Education,
Told under the Blue Umbrella,
p.89–96   *RA
Barr, Fast Trains! Busy Trains!
In (2)
Beim, J., Country Train   *In (2)
Betts, ABC Along Friendly Roads,
p.61–67, *274–81   3–2
——— ABC Over a City Bridge,
p.56–61   *2–2
Bond, G. L., Ride with Us, p.50–54
*PP4
Burton, V. L., Choo Choo   *RA
Burton, W. H., Meet Our Friends,
p.98–102   *2
Cavanah, Our Country's Story, p.42–
43, 56–57   In (3)
Child Study Association of America,
Read-to-Me Storybook, p.26–29
*RA
Crampton, Tootle   *RA
Gates, Friends and Fun, p.136–48
*Alt. 2
——— New Friends and New Places,
p.46–58   *2–2
——— Ted and Sally, p.65–80, 133–
41   P
——— Today We Go, p.20–23
(workers)   *2–1
Gray, New More Friends and Neigh-
bors, p.133–38   *2–2
Gruenberg, Favorite Stories Old and
New, p.53–58, 108–14 (Black
Face)   *RA

Haywood, Primrose Day, p.72–78
*In (3)
Hildreth, Along the Way, p.78–100
(Little Girl Who Waved)   *2–1
Hugley, Around the Home, p.33–34
(subway and elevated)   3
Hunnicutt, I Have Friends, p.119–31
2
Hurd, Caboose   *RA
Johnson, E. M., Treat Shop, p.245–
53   *3
Leavell, Open Windows, p.89–93
(toy)   *1
Lenski, Little Train
*RA (K–2); In (2)
MacDonald, Whistle for the Train
*RA (K–2)
McIntire, Working Together, p.141–
46   3
Meigs, Wonderful Locomotive *RA
Mitchell, Animals, Plants, and Ma-
chines, p.140–43   2
——— Another Here and Now
Story Book, p.106–11   *RA
——— Farm and City, p.75–77,
112–13   1
——— Here and Now Story Book,
p.153–65, 258–65   *RA
——— Our Country, p.295–99 (rail-
roads)   3
Nolen, Do and Dare, p.115–24, 139–
43 (invention of cowcatcher) *3–2
——— Fun and Frolic, p.189–200
(from Little Black Nose)   *3–1
Norling, Pogo's Train Ride *In (3)
O'Donnell, Anything Can Happen,
p.102–30   *Par. 1
Ousley, Open the Gate, p.121–25
*Pre–2
——— Ranches and Rainbows, p.8–
12   *Pre–3
Piper, Little Engine That Could
*RA
Quinlan, Faces and Places, p.50–53,
60–61   2

Ross, Little Red Engine Gets a Name
                                     *In (3)
Russell, D. H., Friends Far and Near,
    p.54–63   3–2
——— We Are Neighbors, p.209–
    17   *2–1
Sheldon, Town and Country, p.131–
    40, 150–52   *2–2
Slobodkin, Clear the Track for Mi-
    chael's Magic Train   *RA
Sorensen, Ways of Our Land, p.96–
    106   3
Thomas, Stories about Sally, p.54–
    61   2
Woolley, David's Railroad   *In (3)
——— I Like Trains   *RA (K–2)
Yoakam, Children Everywhere,
    p.116–26   *3
——— Stories We Like, p.210–13 *2
Zaffo, Big Book of Real Trains
                               RA; In (3)
TRANSPORTATION: *see also* Air-
    planes; Automobiles; Boats; Bridges;
    Communication
Burkhardt, Our Home and School,
    p.59–67   1
——— Our Neighborhood, p.75–88
                                       2
Burton, V. L., Maybelle, the Cable
    Car   *RA
Cavanah, Our Country's Story, p.40–
    43, 56–57, 66–67   In (3)
Deming, Little Eagle   *In (2)
Hanna, In City, Town, and Country,
    p.30–35, 167–70   3
——— In the Neighborhood, p.162–
    63   2
Hildreth, Along the Way, p.75–77
                                       2–1
Mitchell, Here and Now Story Book,
    p.281–90   *RA
Partch, Basic Social Studies, p.214–
    20 (freight)   3
Quinlan, Busy World, p.221–22,
    *242–50   3

Schlein, How Do You Travel?
                               RA (K–1)
Smith, M. E., Bill's Story of the
    Wholesale Produce Market, p.26–
    27 (panel truck), 28–30 (refriger-
    ator truck), 32–35 (semitrailer
    truck), 36–37 (freight), 38–41
    (boats), 42–43 (cargo plane), 44–
    45 (huckster truck)   2+
——— Mother's Story of Dairying,
    p.24–25 (tanker), 28–29 (truck)
                                       2+
Sorensen, Ways of Our Land, p.164–
    72   3
Thomas, Stories about Sally, p.54–
    61 (train), 68–71 (airplane), 95,
    112–13 (automobile), 115–23
    (boat)   2
Wright, E. B., Saturday Walk
                               *RA (K–2)

TRAVELING: *see also* Airplanes; Au-
    tomobiles; Boats; Subways; Trains;
    Transportation; Vacations
Brown, M. W., Country Noisy Book
                                      RA
Carpenter, Our Little Neighbors at
    Work and Play: Here, There,
    Then, and Now, p.45–49, 97–105,
    128–31, 195–96   3+
Cutright, Living Together Today and
    Yesterday, p.20–50   3
Evans, Something Different, p.72–
    100   *1
Gates, Toby, p.2–6 (trains) *Unit 1
Haywood, Two and Two Are Four,
    p.155–71   *In (3)
Hunnicutt, I Have Friends, p.19–26,
    166–67 (airplane), 176–81 (bus)
                                       2
——— I Know People, p.236–48   3
McIntire, Working Together, p.125–
    64, 161–63 (other lands)   3
Mitchell, Here and Now Story Book,
    p.141–45   *RA

Nolen, Do and Dare, p.23–33 *3–2

O'Donnell, If I Were Going
Basic 3

Russell, D. H., We Are Neighbors,
p.201–17   *2–1

Sheldon, Town and Country, p.128–
40, 150–58   *2–2

Smith, V. C., Science around the
Clock, p.129–54   3

Sorensen, Ways of Our Land, p.20–
31 (automobile), 46–50 (steam-
boat), 93–106 (train), 140, 150–
58 (air)   3

Thomas, Stories about Sally, p.54–60
(train), 68–70 (airplane), 95–123
(automobile, boat)   2

TREASURE HUNTS
Ungerer, Mellops Go Diving for
Treasure   *RA (K–1)

TREE HOUSES
Betts, ABC Over a City Bridge,
p.175–80   *2–2

Gates, Good Times Today, p.75–86
                                      *3–1

———— Good Times Today and Tomorrow, p.57–68   *Alt. 3

Sheldon, Fields and Fences, p.90–
105   *2–1

———— Our Town, p.12–17   *1

TREES: *see also* Arbor Day; Christmas—Trees; Evergreen Trees; Forest Fires; Forests and Forestry;
Leaves; Lumbering; Nuts and Nutting; Wood

Association for Childhood Education,
Told under the Blue Umbrella,
p.134–39   *RA

Barnard, Macmillan Science-Life Series, Bk.2, p.117–19   2

Betts, ABC Around Green Hills,
p.150–55   *1

———— ABC Beyond Treasure Val-
ley, p.308–15   *3–1

———— ABC Down Singing River,
p.194–200   *2–1

Blough, Plants around the Year, p.6–
9   3

———— Useful Plants and Animals,
p.25–27   3

Bond, A. D., Knowing about Science,
p.46–51   3

———— Thinking about Science,
p.27–52   2

Brownell, Come Rain, Come Shine,
p.26–29   *3

Clark, A. N., In My Mother's House,
p.38–41   RA; In (2)

Frasier, Science—Adventures, p.60–
66   3

———— Science—For You, p.80–83,
92–99   1

Knox, Wonderworld of Science, Bk.3,
p.166–68   3

Leavell, Open Roads, p.246–53 (magic)   *3

Mitchell, Our Country, p.220–22
(evergreen), 223–24 (redwoods) 3

Podendorf, True Book of Trees
In (2)

Schneider, H., Science Far and Near,
p.191–203   3

Sorensen, Ways of Our Land, p.142–
48   3

Thorn, Let's Find Out, p.87–90 (evergreen)   1

———— Let's Go, p.28–30   PP

———— Let's See Why, p.122–26
(evergreen)   3

Udry, Tree Is Nice   RA (K–2)

Urell, Big City Book of Conservation, p.20–21, 30–38   3+

Whipple, Our Earth, p.138–43   3

TRICKS: *see also* Magic
Bond, G. L., Many Surprises, p.45–
48, 84–87   *P

TROLLEY CARS: *see* Street Cars

TRUCKS
Barnum, Little Old Truck   *In (2)
Burton, W. H., Meet Our Friends,
p.123–28   *2
McIntire, Working Together, p.137–
38   3
Monroe, New Tall Tales, p.16–22
                                            *3–1
Russell, D. H., Friends Far and
Near, p.95–107   *3–2
———— We Are Neighbors, p.218–
23   *2–1
Smith, M. E., Bob's Story of the Re-
tail Food Market, p.6–7   2+
———— Joe's Story of the Airport,
p.28–29 (tug)   2+

TRUSTFULNESS
Jones, M. A., Tell Me about God,
p.50–52   *RA
———— Tell Me about Jesus, p.57–
58   *RA

TULIPS: *see* Bulbs

TURKEYS
Bond, G. L., Just for Fun, p.51–61
                                            *2–2
———— Once upon a Storytime,
p.213–21   *3–2
———— Stories from Everywhere,
p.280–85   *3–1
Burton, W. H., Meet Our Friends,
p.215–19   *2
Hildreth, Along the Way, p.163–69
                                            *2–1
Quinlan, To and Fro, p.138–47 *1
Russell, D. H., Little White House,
p.147–52   *P
Thorn, Let's Try, p.29–33   P

TURTLES
Blough, Animals and Their Young,
p.3–7   3
Bond, A. D., Looking at Science,
p.69 (aquarium)   1

Bond, G. L., Stories from Every-
where, p.299–302   *3–1
Bronson, Turtles   In (3)
Clymer, Yard for John   *RA
Darby, What Is a Turtle?   In (1)
Davis, A. V., Timothy Turtle
                                        *RA (K–1)
Frasier, We Ask, p.70–74   P
Graham, Timothy Turtle   *RA
Gray, New Our New Friends, p.94–
97   *1–2
———— New Streets and Roads,
p.269–72   *3–1
Gruenberg, Favorite Stories Old and
New, p.131 (The Turtle Who
Couldn't Stop Talking)   *RA
Huntington, Let's Go Outdoors,
p.10–17   In (3)
MacGregor, Theodore Turtle
                                        *RA (K–2)
Nolen, Fun and Frolic, p.19–29
                                            *3–1
Russell, D. H., We Are Neighbors,
p.51–56   *2–1
Sheldon, Here and Away, p.36–38
                                            *PP3
Thorn, Let's See Why, p.60–63   3
Yoakam, Stories We Like, p.141–52
                                             *2

TWINS
Betts, ABC Around Green Hills,
p.18–23   *1
Burton, W. H., Our Happy Ways,
p.106–14   *1
Gay, R., Home for Sandy, p.52–62
                                            *P–1
Hanna, At School, p.19–22, 28–32 1
Hildreth, Twins   *Pre–PP
Hogan, Bigger and Bigger   *PP2
Hunnicutt, I Have Friends, p.85–88
                                             2
Leavell, Open Roads, p.40–46   *3
O'Donnell, Round About, p.62–80
                                        *Basic 1

UMBRELLAS

Association for Childhood Education, Told under the Blue Umbrella, p.1–6   *RA

Brock, Umbrella Man   *RA

Child Study Association of America, Read-to-Me Storybook, p.122–40   *RA

Gray, New Our New Friends, p.31–35, 129–31, 143–45   *1–2

Hanna, At School, p.45–49   1

McKee, Looking Ahead, p.264 3–1

Nolen, Do and Dare, p.34–44 *3–2

UNITED NATIONS

Child Study Association of America, Holiday Storybook   *RA

Mitchell, Our Country, p.308–9   3

Urell, Big City Neighbors, p.60 3+

UNITED STATES—HISTORY: *see also* Colonial Period, U.S.; National Songs; Pioneer Life

Cavanah, Our Country's Story   In (3)

Emerson, Pioneer Children of America   3

McIntire, Working Together, p.229   3

Petersham, American ABC   In (3)

Pyne, Little History of the United States   In (3)

UNIVERSE: *see* Astronomy

UNSELFISHNESS

Haywood, Betsy and Billy, p.147–52   *In (3)

Hunnicutt, I Live with Others, p.87–91   1

Jones, M. A., Tell Me about Jesus, p.45–47   *RA

Orton, Grandmother's Cooky Jar, p.56–65   *RA

Quinlan, Faces and Places, p.168–73   *2

Russell, D. H., We Are Neighbors, p.92–98   *2–1

VACATIONS: *see also* Camping

Betts, ABC Around Green Hills, p.174–79   *1

Burkhardt, Our Community, p.162–84   3

Gates, Good Times Today, p.21–30   *3–1

Hunnicutt, I Have Friends, p.6–67   2

——— I Live with Others, p.119–25   1

McIntire, Billy's Friends, p.115–31   1

——— Billy's Neighbors, p.7–17 2

Nolen, Do and Dare, p.103–14 *3–2

O'Donnell, Five-and-a-Half Club   *Par. 3

——— Friendly Village   *2–2

Thomas, Stories about Sally, p.93–124   2

Urell, Big City Book of Conservation, p.7–17   3+

VALENTINE'S DAY

Bond, G. L., Once upon a Storytime, p.234–40   *3–2

Child Study Association of America, Holiday Storybook   *RA

Gray, New More Friends and Neighbors, p.25–29   *2–2

——— New More Streets and Roads, p.208–16   *3–2

Hays, Story of Valentine   In (3)

Haywood, Betsy and Billy, p.92–107   *In (3)

——— Betsy and the Boys, p.152–75   *In (3)

Milhous, Appolonia's Valentine   *In (3)

Russell, D. H., Finding New Neighbors, p.273–82   *3–1

Sheldon, Story Caravan, p.78–88   *3–2

VEGETABLES: *see also* Food; Gardens; Health; Markets

Brownell, All Day, Every Day, p.31–35 *1

McIntire, Working Together, p.83–86 3

Partch, Basic Social Studies, p.68–75 3

VILLAGE LIFE

Clymer, Yard for John *RA

Hanna, In City, Town, and Country, p.96–138 3

———— In the Neighborhood, p.40–69 2

Hill, Along Comes Judy Jo *In (3)

———— Down-along Apple Market Street In (3)

———— Jack o'Lantern for Judy Jo *In (3)

———— Summer Comes to Apple Market Street *In (3)

Hugley, Around the Home, p.4–17 3

Hunnicutt, I Know People, p.171–74, 198–200 3

O'Donnell, Friendly Village, p.6–72 *Basic 2

VIOLINS

Ousley, Ranches and Rainbows, p.68–73 (fiddle) *Pre–3

Quinlan, Busy World, p.234–40 *3

VISION: *see* Eye

WAGONS

Evans, Something Different, p.36–41 *1

Gates, Ted and Sally, p.5–24 *P

Mitchell, Here and Now Story Book, p.73–77 *RA

O'Donnell, Anything Can Happen, p.38–66 (toy) *Par. 1

Ousley, Open the Gate, p.94–101 *Pre–2

WALES

Baker, A. B., Talking Tree *RA

WASHINGTON, D.C.

Hager, Washington, City of Destiny T

Hunnicutt, I Know People, p.74–84 3

WASHINGTON, GEORGE

Aulaire, George Washington In (3)

Burkhardt, Our Community, p.209–17 *3

Cavanah, Our Country's Story, p.30–31 In (3)

Eaton, Washington, the Nation's First Hero In (3)

Emerson, Pioneer Children of America, p.128–41 *3

Gray, New More Streets and Roads, p.52–59 *3–2

Johnson, E. M., Treat Shop, p.198–201 *3

Sheldon, Story Caravan, p.25–31 *3–2

WASHINGTON'S BIRTHDAY

Child Study Association of America, Holiday Storybook *RA

WASPS

Gray, New Streets and Roads, p.67–74 *3–1

O'Donnell, Five-and-a-Half Club, p.133–47 *Par. 3

Thorn, Let's Look Around, p.21–26 2

WATCHES: *see* Clocks

WATER: *see also* Floods; Frost; Rain

Baker, A. O., Around the Corner, p.32–41 2

———— In Your Neighborhood, p.57–71, 92–93 (power) 3

Barnard, Macmillan Science-Life Series, Bk.3, p.234–39 3

Blough, Water Appears and Disappears 3

Bond, A. D., Knowing about Science,
p.22–24, 154–67   3
——— Thinking about Science,
p.99–115   2
Charters, Health Secrets, p.119–27 3
Clark, A. N., In My Mother's House,
p.24–32   RA; In (2)
Craig, Science Everywhere, p.135–56
                                    3
——— Science near You, p.5–9   1
Dowling, New Learning Why, p.116–
24   3
Frasier, Science—All the Year, p.65–
70   2
Hanna, In City, Town, and Country,
p.42–47 (conservation), 48–49,
66–76 (floods)   3
Jones, M. A., Tell Me about God,
p.32–36   *RA
Knox, Wonderworld of Science,
Bk.2, p.65–78   2
Mitchell, Another Here and Now
Story Book, p.253–58   *RA
——— Here and Now Story Book,
p.219–27   *RA
Schneider, H., Science Far and Near,
p.58–72   3
Smith, V. C., Science under the Sun,
p.39–62   2
Sorensen, Ways of Our Land, p.135–
36   3
Thorn, Let's Look Around, p.77–81,
87–91   2
Thurber, Exploring Science Three,
p.94–107, 146–58   3
Urell, Big City Book of Conservation, p.42–51   3+

WATER BIRDS
Schneider, H., Science Near and Far,
p.180–84   3

WATER SUPPLY: *see also* Aqueducts;
Dams; Irrigation; Rivers
Gruenberg, Favorite Stories Old and
New, p.3–6   *RA

Urell, Big City Water Supply   3+

WEATHER: *see also* Air; Clouds;
Rain; Seasons; Snow; Storms;
Winds
Barnard, Macmillan Science-Life Se-
ries, Bk.1, p.14–21   1
——— Macmillan Science-Life Se-
ries, Bk.2, p.46–67   2
Bauer, Just Like Me, p.42–43   P
Beauchamp, All around Us, p.42–60
                                    2
——— Look and Learn, p.40–52
                                    1
Burkhardt, Our Home and School,
p.7–9   1
Craig, Science around You, p.32–37
                                    2
——— Science Everywhere, p.94–
95   3
Dowling, New I Wonder Why, p.62–
82   1
Frasier, Science—All the Year, p.71–
81   2
——— Science—For You, p.74–83
                                    1
Mitchell, Our Country, p.94–101
(snowstorm)   3
Nolen, Fun and Frolic, p.162–70
(tornado)   *3–1
O'Donnell, Five-and-a-Half Club,
p.216–35 (thunderstorm) *Par. 3
O'Keefe, How We Grow, p.43–61 3
Quinlan, Busy World, p.255–60,
*262–68   3
Russell, D. H., Friends Far and
Near, p.32–42 (snowstorm) *3–2
Schneider, H., Let's Find Out, p.21–
27   In (3)
——— Science for Here and Now,
p.131–44   2
Smith, M. E., Joe's Story of the Air-
port, p.22–23 (storm)   2+
Smith, V. C., Science along the Way,
p.69–85   1

Thorn, Let's See Why, p.142–45　3
Wavle, Rain and Shine　*P–2
WEAVING: *see also* Baskets and Basketry
Carpenter, Our Little Neighbors at Work and Play: Here, There, Then, and Now, p.93–96　3+
Thomas, Your Town and Mine, p.73–74, 82　3
Yoakam, Children Everywhere, p.281–94　*3
WEEDS
Podendorf, True Book of Weeds and Wildflowers　In (2)
WEIGHTS AND MEASURES: *see also* Gravitation
Barnard, Macmillan Science-Life Series, Bk.1, p.66–68　1
——— Macmillan Science-Life Series, Bk.3, p.107–8　3
Brownell, Come Rain, Come Shine, p.177–80　3
Hanna, At School, p.57–60　1
Smith, M. E., Bob's Story of the Retail Food Market, p.34–35　2+
(THE) WEST: *see also* Covered Wagons; Indians of North America; Lewis and Clark Expedition; Pioneer Life; Ranch Life; also names of states, as Texas
Betts, ABC Along Friendly Roads, p.198–205　3–2
Emerson, Pioneer Children of America, p.148–309　*3
Gates, Good Times Tomorrow, p.159–81　*3–2
Mitchell, Another Here and Now Story Book, p.338–55　*RA
——— Our Country, p.198–290　3
Yoakam, Children Everywhere, p.96–112　*3
WHALES
Duvoisin, Christmas Whale　*RA (K–2)

Goudey, Here Come the Whales!　In (3)
Russell, D. H., Friends Far and Near, p.174–85　*3–2
Schneider, H., Science Far and Near, p.141–46　3
WHEAT: *see also* Bread; Grain
Hugley, Around the Home, p.57–67　3
Hunnicutt, I Know People, p.175–87　3
McIntire, Working Together, p.65–66　3
Mitchell, Animals, Plants, and Machines, p.118–20　2
Partch, Basic Social Studies, p.26–29, 32–33　3
Quinlan, Faces and Places, p.54–58　2
Smith, J. R., Our Neighbors at Home, p.81–97　3
Sorensen, Ways of Our Land, p.102–3　3
Thomas, Stories about Sally, p.96–97　2
——— Your Town and Mine, p.40–43　3
Thorn, Let's See Why, p.34–37　3
WHISTLES
Friedman, Whistle for Tootles　*RA (K–2)
Nolen, Do and Dare, p.86–94 *3–2
WIGWAMS: *see also* Indians of North America
Hildreth, Faraway Ports, p.69–71　*3–1
WILD FLOWERS: *see* Flowers
WIND POWER
Baker, A. O., In Your Neighborhood, p.94–95　3
Blough, Doing Work, p.6–9　3
WINDMILLS
Bond, A. D., Knowing about Science, p.17–20　3

Clark, A. N., In My Mother's House, p.30   RA; In (2)

WINDS
Association for Childhood Education, Told under the Green Umbrella (Lad Who Went to the North Wind)   *RA
Betts, ABC Around Green Hills, p.12–17   *1
—— ABC Up the Street and Down, p.111–15   *P
Dowling, New Seeing Why, p.126–36   2
Mitchell, Here and Now Story Book, p.309–13   *RA
Tresselt, Follow the Wind   RA (K–2)

WINDSTORMS: *see* Weather

WINTER: *see also* Birds—Migration; Hibernation; Snow
Association for Childhood Education, Told under the Blue Umbrella, p.11–13   *RA
Baker, A. O., Around the Corner, p.119–26   2
—— In Your Neighborhood, p.157–61   3
Bond, A. D., Getting Ready, p.81–93   P
—— Looking at Science, p.43–47   1
Burton, V. L., Katy and the Big Snow   *RA
Craig, Science around You, p.64–77   2
Deming, Indians in Winter Camp   In (3)
De Regniers, Snow Party   *RA
Frasier, We Wonder, p.19   PP
Gates, Good Times Today, p.166–76   *3–1
—— Good Times Today and To-morrow, p.114–24   *Alt. 3

—— Two Boys and a Tree, p.55–91   *Sup. 1
Gruenberg, Favorite Stories Old and New, p.246–48 (Snow Maiden)   *RA
Hader, Big Snow   RA (K–2)
Kay, One Mitten Lewis *RA (K–1)
Knox, Wonderworld of Science, Bk.2, p.39–44   2
Lenski, I Like Winter   RA (K–1)
Mitchell, Another Here and Now Story Book, p.165–67   *RA
—— Farm and City, p.50–53   1
O'Donnell, Round About, p.75–77 124–38   *Basic 1
Parker, Winter Is Here   1
Quinlan, To and Fro, p.179–81   *1
Schneider, H., Science for Here and Now, p.101–10   2
—— Science for Work and Play, p.141–44   1
Sheldon, Fields and Fences, p.99–134   *2–1
Smith, J. R., Our Neighbors at Home, p.10–14, 43–50, 76–77, 89–90, 169–70   3
Thorn, Let's Look Around, p.65–69, 77–80   2
—— Let's See Why, p.44–49   3

WINTER SPORTS: *see also* Snow Man
Betts, ABC Around Green Hills, p.162–67   *1
Brownell, Come Rain, Come Shine, p.108–11   3
Deming, Little Eagle   *In (2)
Gates, Snow, p.19–32   *Unit P
—— Today We Go, p.158–61   *2–1
—— Two Boys and a Tree, p.59–64   *Sup. 1
Gray, New More Friends and Neighbors, p.199–204   *2–2
Haywood, Back to School with Betsy, p.107–39   *In (3)

Leavell, Open Windows, p.29–34 *1
Nolen, Do and Dare, p.96–102
  (sleds)   *3–2
O'Donnell, Round About, p.75–77,
  171–84   *Basic 1
Russell, D. H., On Cherry Street,
  p.41–48   *1
Sorensen, Ways of Our Land, p.90–
  91   3
Whipple, Our Earth, p.36–39 (skiing), 128–34   3

WIRES: *see also* Radio; Television
Bond, Thinking about Science, p.130–
  36   2

WOOD: *see also* Forests and Forestry;
  Lumbering; Trees
Gates, Good Times Today, p.64–74
                                      *3–1
——— Good Times Today and To-
  morrow, p.46–56   *Alt. 3
Partch, Basic Social Studies, p.192–
  95   3
Schneider, H., Science for Here and
  Now, p.65–69   2

WOOD CARVING
Hildreth, Enchanting Stories, p.154–
  59   *3–2
——— Faraway Ports, p.190–99
                                      *3–1

WOODCHUCKS
Betts, ABC Down Singing River,
  p.208–14   *2–1
——— ABC Over a City Bridge,
  p.169–74   *2–2
Bond, G. L., Once upon a Storytime,
  p.64–84   *3–2
——— Stories from Everywhere,
  p.170–75, 183–88   *3–1
Burton, W. H., Our Good Neigh-
  bors, p.230–36   *3
Gall, All the Year Round, p.31–36
                                     In (3)

Gray, New More Friends and Neighbors, p.104–8   *2–2
——— New Streets and Roads,
  p.241–48   *3–1
O'Donnell, Neighbors on the Hill,
  p.114–21   *Par. 2

WOODPECKERS
Blough, Birds in the Big Woods, p.5–
  7, 18   3
Gall, All the Year Round, p.37–42
                                     In (3)
Gray, New More Friends and Neigh-
  bors, p.223–27   *2–2
——— New Streets and Roads,
  p.148–54   *3–1

WOODS: *see* Camping; Forest Fires;
  Nature

WOODWORK: *see* Carpentry

WOOL
Beskow, Pelle's New Suit
                                  *RA; In (3)
Blough, Useful Plants and Animals,
  p.17   3
Burkhardt, Our Community, p.69   3
Carpenter, Our Little Neighbors at
  Work and Play: Here, There,
  Then, and Now, p.89–92   3+
Hugley, Around the Home, p.102–
  10   3
McIntire, Working Together, p.97–
  99   3
Mitchell, Animals, Plants, and Ma-
  chines, p.58–61   2
Norling, Pogo's Lamb   *In (3)
Partch, Basic Social Studies, p.116–
  17   3
Schneider, H., Science for Here and
  Now, p.83–86   2
Thomas, Your Town and Mine,
  p.68–74   3
Thorn, Let's See Why, p.152–57   3

WORDS: *see also* Dictionaries
Adams, ABC Picture Book   In (1)

Krauss, A Hole Is To Dig
RA; In (2)
McGaw, How Medicine Man Cured
Paleface Woman *RA; In (3)
Walpole, Golden Dictionary In (3)
Werner, Golden Picture Book of
Words In (3)

WORK
Bond, G. L., Fun with Us, p.11–16
*PP3
Brownell, Come Rain, Come Shine,
p.10–14 *3
Burkhardt, Our Home and School,
p.29–40 1
Carpenter, Our Little Neighbors at
Work and Play: Here, There, Then,
and Now, p.57–60 3+
Gray, New More Friends and Neigh-
bors, p.133–38 *2–2
Johnson, E. M., Treat Shop, p.210–
13 *3
Jones, M. A., Tell Me about God,
p.41–43 *RA
Knox, Wonderworld of Science,
Bk.3, p.95–104 3
Leavell, Open Doors, p.24–30, 87–
93 *2
——— Open Roads, p.33–38, 58–63
*3
——— Open Windows, p.105–10 *1
McKee, Come Along, p.69–89 *2–1
Mason, Happy Jack In (3)
Quinlan, Happy Days, p.48–63
*Read. P
Russell, D. H., My Little Green
Story Book, p.19–22 *PP2
Sheldon, At Home and Away, p.26–
28 *SPP

WORLD: *see also* Earth
Burkhardt, Our Community, p.185–
92 3

WORLD FRIENDSHIP
Jones, M. A., Tell Me about the
Bible *RA

Krauss, Big World and the Little
House RA (K–2)
United Nations. Department of Pub-
lic Information, Garden We Planted
Together In (3)

WORLD WAR, 1914–1918: *see also*
Armistice Day
Quinlan, Busy World, p.229–32
(Cher Ami) 3

WORLD WAR, 1939–1945
Cavanah, Our Country's Story, p.68–
69 In (3)
Haywood, Primrose Day *In (3)

WORMS: *see* Caterpillars; Earthworms;
Silkworms

WRENS
Brock, Mr. Wren's House *RA
Gray, New More Friends and Neigh-
bors, p.86–91 *2–2

YELLOWSTONE NATIONAL PARK
Quinlan, Busy World, p.28–29 3
Smith, J. R., Our Neighbors at Home,
p.149–70 3

ZEBRAS
Monroe, New Tall Tales, p.9–15
*3–1

ZOOS: *see also* Playing Zoo; also names
of zoo animals, as Bears
Bond, A. D., Knowing about Science,
p.185–88 3
Bond, G. L., Stories from Every-
where, p.1–60 *3–1
Chalmers, Hundreds and Hundreds
of Pancakes *In (3)
Eberle, Secrets and Surprises, p.89–
95 *2–2
Gates, Friends and Fun, p.44–53,
192–93 *Alt. 2
——— New Friends and New
Places, p.134–35 2–2
——— On Four Feet, p.23–41, 72–
73 *1

—— Today We Go, p.46–55 *2–1
—— Two Boys and a Tree, p.117–
22   *Sup. 1
Gray, New Fun with Dick and Jane,
    p.140–46   *1–1
Humphreys, Zoo Book   RA
Irwin, Growing Day by Day, p.9–15,
    23–25 (play)   2
McIntire, Billy's Friends, p.127–28
                                      1

Quinlan, Faces and Places, p.232–36
                                     *2
Russell, D. H., Finding New Neigh-
    bors, p.56–89   *3–1
Sheldon, Fields and Fences, p.136–
    58   *2–1
—— Our Town, p.138–43   *1
Thomas, Your Town and Mine, p.15,
    210–13   3
Wilcox, Here We Go, p.25–29   2